PUTTING GOD ON TRIAL

The Biblical Book of Job

by

Robert Sutherland

(c) 2004

Robert Sutherland can be contacted at sutherlandrobert@shaw.ca.

The tableau on the front page is the Oath of Innocence from the Egyptian Book of the Dead.

Printed in Victoria, Canada

A cataloguing record for this book that includes the U.S. Library of Congress Classification number, the Library of Congress Call number and the Dewey Decimal cataloguing code is available from the National Library of Canada. The complete cataloguing record can be obtained from the National Library's online database at: www.nlc-bnc.ca/amicus/index-e.html
ISBN: 1-4120-1847-1

This book was published *on-demand* in cooperation with Trafford Publishing. On-demand publishing is a unique process and service of making a book available for retail sale to the public taking advantage of on-demand manufacturing and Internet marketing. **On-demand publishing** includes promotions, retail sales, manufacturing, order fulfilment, accounting and collecting royalties on behalf of the author.

Suite 6E, 2333 Government St., Victoria, B.C. V8T 4P4, CANADA

Phone	250-383-6864	Toll-free	1-888-232-4444 (Canada & US)
Fax	250-383-6804	E-mail	sales@trafford.com
Web site	www.trafford.com	TRAFFORD PUBLISHING IS A DIVISION OF TRAFFORD HOLDINGS LTD.
Trafford Catalogue #03-2224	www.trafford.com/robots/03-2224.html

10   9   8   7   6

This book is dedicated to my wife

Cindy Sutherland.

TABLE OF CONTENTS

PREFACE

Every interpreter approaches a text with certain intellectual horizons. These horizons are the products of talent and training, life experience in general. They expand or narrow one's vision, as the case may be. They enable some to see farther than others.

No modern interpreter can approach the text entirely free of the limits of modern horizons. Modern culture is deeply urban, egalitarian, individualistic and scientific. Ancient Jewish culture is deeply rural, patriarchal, collectivistic and pre-scientific. Yet such limitations can be overcome. The psychological process by which any interpreter arrives at his interpretation is forever under the control of the logical process by which he justifies that interpretation. In the final analysis, what really distorts meaning is not perspective, but the deliberate ignorance and distortion of data. Intelligent and intelligible interpretations are possible, even if a full and final interpretation that satisfies all is not achieved.

To appreciate the strengths and weaknesses of an interpreter, the reader should know something of the background of the interpreter before him. It is with that thought in mind that I share something of my own background with my readers.

I hold a four year Honours Bachelor of Arts degree from the University of Toronto in history. My self-directed, multi-disciplinary program was focused on the History of Ideas from ancient times into the modern world. I first encountered *The Book of Job* in a world literature course in my first year of undergraduate work and it has captivated me ever since. It has deepened and broadened with every reading. It addresses the perennial concerns that have shaped the human condition as no other.

I hold a three year Bachelor of Laws degree from Osgoode Hall Law School and currently practice almost exclusively as a criminal defense lawyer. With seventeen years at the bar, I have had some notable successes. In the case of *R. v. L.(S.R.) [1992] O.J. No.2305 (Ontario Court of Appeal)*, I was instrumental in bringing about a substantial rewriting of the Canadian law on aggravated assault. In the case of *R. v. Claus [1999] 139 CCC (3d) 47 (Ontario Superior Court) aff'd [2000] 149 CCC (3d) 336 (Ontario Court of Appeal)*, I was instrumental in bringing about a substantial rewriting of the Canadian law on solicitor-client privilege. Most recently, I was fortunate enough to defend a modern day Job, a man by the name of Jerome Kerrigan. He was wrongfully accused of a horrific crime, the death of his two grandchildren, and the case received months of national and international publicity. The case was tried in the court of public opinion and Mr. Kerrigan was ultimately vindicated in a court of law. This legal background has given me a deep appreciation of the lawsuit structure of *The Book of Job*.

I am a Senior Fellow at the *Centre for the Study of the Great Ideas,* (http://www.thegreatideas.org), an American think-tank based in Chicago. I owe an incalculable debt of gratitude to its founder Mortimer J. Adler and its president Max Weismann for their writings and their advice. I would not be the person I am without them. In and through their mentorship, I have become rationally persuaded of the truth of natural law ethics and Thomistic metaphysics. Both have profoundly influenced my understanding of the scriptures. This moral background has given me a deep appreciation of the moral dynamics in *The Book of Job*.

I would describe myself as an evangelical Christian, though not a fundamentalist. I believe the traditional doctrines of Trinity, Incarnation, substitutionary atonement, bodily resurrection, heaven and hell. I am denominationally Anglican, as much by temperament as by default. I value the high value it places on human reason. When I had searched for a spiritual home, the Reverends Joan Mitchell and Ed Swayze successively welcomed me into their home, St. Stephen's Anglican, Thunder Bay. They regularly encouraged my writings and preaching and I owe them a profound thanks. Years ago, two professors, Dr. Richard Berg of Lakehead University and Dr. Don Thompson of Laurentian University, read my early preaching on *The Book of Job* and strongly suggested I publish. I have ignored their sage advice for too many years. I now offer this book, in part, as a memorial to their good friendships.

I have elected to use the *New Revised Standard Version* of the *Bible* throughout this work. It is the only translation that is universally accepted by all three branches of the Christian faith: Orthodox, Catholic and Protestant.

I have elected to use Benjamin Foster's translation of the Babylonian *Enuma Elish* found in *Before the Muses: An Anthology of*

Akkadian Literature. The translation is crisp and clear. The notes are excellent. It is a good place to begin a fuller exploration of Babylonian mythology and I thank him and CDL Press for their permission in using quotations from that translation.

I have elected to use Nicolas Wyatt's translation of the Canaanite *Baal Cycle* found in *Religious Texts from Ugarit: The Words of Ilimiku and his Colleagues.* The translation is excellent. The notes are superb. It is a good place to begin a fuller exploration of Canaanite mythology and I thank him and The Continuum International Publishing Group (the successor to Sheffield Academic Press) for their permission in using quotations from that translation.

I would like to thank my wife Cindy, my good friend Max Weismann, Provincial Court Justice Paul Glowacki, Superior Court Justice Larry Kozak, Father Chris Rupert S.J., Dr. David Clines (author of *Job 1-20*, Word Biblical), Dr. Norman Habel (author of *Job*, Old Testament Library) and especially Dr. Gerald Janzen (author of *Job*, Interpretation) for their ongoing encouragement in this work and for their invaluable proof reading of the final draft. I absolve them of any failings this book might have and I take complete responsibility for the final form of this book. It is my hope and prayer that this commentary might be as satisfying for readers as *The Book of Job* has been for me.

This work *Putting God on Trial: The Biblical Book of Job* is the first in a trilogy. The second work is anticipated to be *Putting Jesus on Trial: The Gospels of Matthew, Mark, Luke and John.* The final work is anticipated to be *Putting Humanity on Trial: The Biblical Books of Genesis through Revelation.* Ideally, they will follow this work at one year intervals.

1: INTRODUCTION

A Theodicy

Widely praised as one of the greatest books ever written,[1] *The Book of Job* is a theodicy, an attempt to morally justify the ways of God to humankind. It is a most provocative theodicy for it is the story of the most righteous human being on earth putting God on trial for crimes against humanity and refusing to acquit God.

To the question of why there is evil in the world, *The Book of Job* offers a non-traditional answer.

(1) God created a world of undeserved and unremitted suffering in order the make the highest form of human love possible: a completely selfless love of men and women for God. Selfishness corrupts selfless love. If human beings know with certainty that God rewards those who love him, then they will serve God for what they can get from God. Undeserved evil is morally necessary in order to bring the existence of God into doubt and to sever any connection between righteousness and reward.

(2) God cannot reveal this explanation for evil in this life without defeating his own purpose in the creation of the world and the creation of men and women.

(3) God expects human beings to challenge God for the creation of such a world. Prima facie, it is an act of injustice to impose evil for reasons other than punishment or character development. The undeserved evil God sends is more punishment than any man or woman deserves. And the undeserved evil God sends destroys character more often than not. Human beings have a moral duty to challenge God for such evil. They have a natural need to know and a natural right to receive the explanation for evil in world. God expects human beings to stand up to him. They sin if they either prematurely condemn or prematurely acquit God for sending evil into the world. They must wait for the answer that only God can give.

(4) God will reveal that answer on the Day of the Final Judgment. At that time, God will resurrect all human beings to give them that answer. God will grant all human beings a special grace to understand the necessity and sufficiency of undeserved evil. God is

causally responsible for the evil in the world, but not morally blameworthy for it. At that time, all will know and understand God's purpose in the creation of a world of undeserved and unremitted suffering. And God will then judge all human beings on the selflessness of their love for God.

This Hegelian theodicy in *The Book of Job* has two real advantages over the traditional Augustinian and Irenean theodices which draw heavily on *The Book of Genesis* and *The Epistles of Paul*.

(1) It offers an explanation for the existence of undeserved evil in the world. Augustinian theodicies strain and break in their attempt to attribute all the natural and moral evils of the world to the acts of a single man and woman. Irenean theodicies strain and break in the face of evil that is so great it destroys character more often than not.

(2) And it offers an explanation for God's general practice of non-intervention in the world to prevent evil. Augustinian and Irenean theodices correctly posit the importance of freewill, but seriously stumble over the fact that the existence of freewill is consistent with a knowledge of God and God's intervention in the world. Free-will itself does not require God's non-intervention. However, a particular form of the exercise of free-will, a completely selfless love of men and women for God, probably does require God's non-intervention.

The Book of Job presents a new and engaging perspective based entirely on the existence of undeserved evil and a moral requirement that God not intervene to disclose the reason for evil in this world.

The Book of Job is a masterpiece in world literature, one that has stood the test of millennia. It is a highly integrated work with a profound message for those with eyes to see and ears to hear. The primary task of any interpreter of *The Book of Job* is to interpret the existing text before him and integrate seemingly disparate elements rather than abandoning the literary challenge and blaming the difficulty on a clumsy redaction of pre-existing texts.[2] I am more concerned with what is being said as opposed to how it may have come to be said. In any event, the received text can be read as a unity and I do read it that way. In its present form, it might be termed a "classic" text in the sense David Tracey argues for in the *The Analogical Imagination: Christian Theology and the Culture of Pluralism* (Crossroad Publishers, New York, 1991).

A Lawsuit Drama

The Book of Job presents that philosophical answer in poetry and prose through the vehicle of drama. As drama, *The Book of Job* is understandably a legal drama.[3] The moral issues of theodicy are easily translated into a legal framework of duties and rights. In fact, *The Book of Job* consists of a number of overlapping and interlocking trials. God puts Job on trial. Satan puts God on trial. God puts Job on trial a second time. Job's friends put Job on trial. Job puts his friends on trial. Everything builds to the climactic moment when Job puts God himself on trial and refuses to acquit God.

The Book of Job virtually opens with the God's trial of Job. The time is Rosh Hashanah, the first of the 10 Days of Awe. The place is heaven, the High Court of Heaven. God opens the books of life and reviews the lives of all men and women. He finds his servant Job to be sinless. In God's judgment, Job is "blameless and upright, one who fears God and turns from evil" at every juncture. He is humanity at its very best. He is the type of person all of us could be and should be. God's judgment sets the philosophical stage for all the action that follows. Because Job is sinless, the evil that will befall him is not punishment for sin. Because Job has no character flaw, the evil that will befall him is not for correction or character development.

Almost as soon as God's judgment on Job issues, Satan challenges the judgment. It is a profound three-fold challenge.

(1) First, God is wrong in his judgment on Job's goodness. Job is a sinner. He has sin in his life God missed. Job may intend the good, but his motive is selfishness. He serves God only for what he can get from God. Satan claims he can show God that hidden sin. Satan claims he can even get Job to curse God. Satan's challenge is a claim to the soul of Job.

(2) Second, God has lost his authority to judge. God is in error. God has passed false judgment. God is no longer a perfect being and should step down from his throne. Satan's challenge is a claim to the throne of heaven.

(3) Third, God is wrong about his plan for humankind. Human beings are not fit for relationship with God. They do not love God.

They seek only to manipulate God to get what they can from God. The very idea of a meaningful relationship between God and humankind is fundamentally wrong. Humanity should be destroyed as a failed project. Satan's challenge is a claim to destroy the earth and all in it.

With this challenge, there is silence in the heavenly court. Satan has put God himself on trial.

God picks up the gauntlet and elects trial by ordeal. He chooses Job as his personal champion to settle the issue of whether love for God can be completely disinterested. God directs Satan as his personal agent to inflict undeserved and unremitted evil upon his beloved servant Job. God's hands are tied. God cannot tell Job what has transpired. God cannot give Job the reason for his suffering, lest that give Job a selfish motive to continue his love for God.

God's trial by ordeal is truly an ordeal for Job. While it starts in heaven, the trial is played out on the earth during the 10 Days of Awe. Job is stripped of everything. God casts Job out his Eden into the wasteland that is the world as we know it. Unlike Adam, Job is expelled from his garden not for his sin but for his righteousness. Not surprisingly, Job struggles to keep faith with a loving God in the midst of this world of undeserved and unremitted suffering. He longs to know the reason behind evil in the world. Through five speeches on the Day of Atonement, Job turns that request into a demand. Through an Oath of Innocence, he institutes formal legal proceedings against God to provoke that answer. Job's claim is two-fold. God is the author of undeserved evil in the world. Human beings have the right to know the reason why God has sent such evil into the world. And Job stakes the propriety of his challenge on the integrity of his ways. He puts his eternal salvation on the line and demands that God answer him. If God fails to appear or appears but fails to give the required answer, then Job is morally and legally entitled to condemn God. The condemnation is by way of a curse. God's trial has built to a feverish pitch. Satan has promised that Job would curse God. And now, Job has set in motion to legal machinery to do it. In the eyes of Job's friends, this Oath of Innocence is blasphemy. But in the eyes of God, this Oath of Innocence is the pinnacle of righteousness.

To the surprise of all, God appears to Job. But, on the terms of his trial by Satan, God cannot give any direct answers to Job, lest those answers give Job a selfish motive to continue his love for God. Through two speeches, God reviews the natural and the mythological worlds, avoiding any discussion of the human world. God suggests the existence of a possible answer. But the suggestions are veiled. And God never broaches the subject of selfless love. God has been called to give a defense for his creation of this world. Instead, God rests his case having hinted at the existence of a defense, but having never presenting it. And with that act, God places before Job and all humankind a single question: will they condemn God that they themselves might be justified?

Job understands God's veiled suggestions and draws the proper inferences. Job chooses not to condemn God at this time but to continue to love God. He melts to his knees in worship. Yet Job refuses to retract his lawsuit. He refuses to withdraw his moral and legal claim to an explanation for evil in the world. He will neither prematurely acquit God nor prematurely condemn God. Job grants God the benefit of time to prepare a full and meaningful defense to the charges. Job gives God all of human history to work out his plan for evil in the world. The matter is adjourned to the Day of the Final Judgment for Job to hear from his Redeemer a third time. At that time, Job will pass his final judgment on God. If God fails to give a necessary and sufficient explanation for evil on the Day of the Final Judgment, then Job will condemn God. And he would be right in doing so. In a single moment, Job has become the perfect embodiment of the selfless love and moral integrity for which the world was created.

A moral not an aesthetic resolution

Many scholars find the legal metaphor of an Oath of Innocence inappropriate, though for different reasons.

Some liberal scholars[4] opt for an aesthetic, not a moral, resolution of the question of evil in the world. They find a sublime beauty in God's review of the animal and physical worlds, Behemoth and Leviathan. And it is certainly there. But that is all they find. They find no suggestions of a moral purpose in God's creation and control of evil. Indeed, they feel none could be forthcoming. God is beyond good and evil so no moral resolution is possible. Since no moral resolution is possible, a legal metaphor such as a lawsuit dramatizing the moral question is inappropriate. They interpret Job to understand that position. And they interpret him to retract the lawsuit in its entirety. They interpret the lawsuit metaphor to be inappropriate because there are no answers to the moral question of evil in the world. To the extent there is a scholarly consensus on *The Book of Job* and there probably is not such a consensus, this is the majority reading.

This author feels such liberal scholars miss a moral resolution for five reasons.

(1) First, they fail to give adequate weight to Satan's first speech in heaven setting out the moral solution. Selfless love is the reason God chooses to create a world of undeserved and unremitted suffering for Job and, by implication, for us. This sets the entire plot in motion. Their resolution however leaves this important point hanging such that the beginning and ending are completely disjointed.

(2) Second, they misinterpret Job's struggle with God to be a request for a restoration of his former position, rather than a request to know the reason behind evil in the world. As such, they see the moral issue Job raises to be nothing more than a retributive version of justice whereby righteousness is rewarded. This is not the moral right Job raises in his Oath of Innocence. The moral right is the right to know the reason behind evil in the world.

(3) Third, they fail to appreciate the moral restrictions under which God has to operate. God cannot reveal any moral answers directly without defeating his very purpose in the creation and control of evil. As a result, they miss the suggestions of moral purpose in God's two speeches and the inferences God would have Job draw.

(4) Fourth, they fail to fully appreciate the legal dynamics of the enforcement mechanism of Job's Oath of Innocence. In particular, they fail to appreciate the distinction between causal responsibility and moral blameworthiness. Thus, they do not understand God's comments concerning vindication and condemnation in his first speech to Job. And they do not understand Job's hesitation to proceed beyond his own vindication to a condemnation of God in Job's first speech to God. Ultimately, they fail to see Job's adjournment and continuation of his Oath of Innocence implied by the allusion to the story of Abraham and Sodom and Gomorrah in Job's final speech.

(5) Finally, they fail to give full expression to God's ultimate judgment on Job. Job and only Job spoke rightly about God. In the face of such a judgment, there is no room to deny the ultimate propriety of the moral and legal question as a way of framing humankind's encounter with God.

Some conservative scholars[5] opt for a moral resolution of the question of evil in the world, but their resolution is equally unsatisfying. They interpret Job's so-called excessive words in his speeches preceding the Oath of Innocence to be morally wrong. They interpret Job's raising of the Oath of Innocence to be a sin of presumption. While they accept God's two judgments on Job in heaven, they feel subsequent events show Job sinning. While God is not beyond good and evil, God is under no moral obligation to reveal any reason for sending evil into the world. Thus they would have Job retract his lawsuit in its entirety and repent morally for either his so-called excessive words, his raising of the lawsuit or both. They feel the legal metaphor is inappropriate because while there is an answer to the moral question of evil in the world, no human being has a right to that answer and God is under no duty to give that answer. To the extent there is a scholarly consensus on *The Book of Job* and there probably is not such a consensus, this is the minority reading.

This author feels such conservative scholars miss a satisfactory moral resolution for three reasons.

(1) First, they fail to understand the depth of Satan's challenge to God. It is not merely that Job will curse God. It is that God is wrong in his judgment on Job's goodness. God has missed sin in Job's life. Such scholars think their moral resolution is possible, because although Job sins, Job does not actually curse God. The problem they have is that their resolution actually makes Satan right in his challenge of God. Satan claimed Job was a sinner and they feel Job sinned. Thus Satan is in the right in his lawsuit with God and God should step down from his throne and destroy humankind.

(2) Second, they fail to give proper weight to Job's blamelessness and integrity. The raising of the Oath of Innocence is an expression of that blamelessness and integrity. It is what God expects of Job, though God cannot tell him that directly. If Job sins in raising the lawsuit against God, then the sin is blasphemy and God is seriously mistaken in his judgment of Job's blamelessness and integrity.

(3) Finally, they fail to give full expression to God's ultimate judgment on Job. Job and only Job spoke rightly about God. In the face of such a judgment, there is no room to attribute sin or wrongdoing to Job for either his so-called excessive words or for his Oath of Innocence. In the face of such a judgment, there is no room to deny the ultimate propriety of the moral and legal question as a way of framing humankind's encounter with God.

My personal interpretation charts a new middle course between these two-fold horrors: a liberal Scylla which places God beyond good and evil and a conservative Charybdis which attributes sin to Job, either for his so-called excessive words, his Oath of Innocence or both. I reject both streams of conventional scholarly interpretation, because they fail to integrate all the elements in *The Book of Job*.

(1) God has a moral reason for sending evil.

(2) Human beings have a need and a right to know that reason.

(3) God has a duty to give that reason. But God need not provide that reason here and now.

(4) However, God must provide that reason no later than the Day of the Final Judgment. An adjournment of Job's trial of God to that date and its continuation then is strongly implied. It is implied through the allusion to a Redeemer who stands up in court at the Final Judgment to plead Job's cause. It is implied through the allusion to the apocalyptic destruction of Leviathan at the Messianic banquet and the explanation of all things that follows. It is implied through the allusion to Abraham and his ongoing challenge.

The legal metaphor is highly appropriate. A satisfactory moral solution is only possible because of the distinction between casual responsibility and moral blameworthiness embedded in Job's Oath of Innocence. That distinction is central to the criminal law defense of justification or necessity. God may be causally responsible for the evil in the world, but not morally blameworthy for it. God has a necessary and sufficient reason for the evil and will ultimately give it. Job grants God that time without denying his need to know and without withdrawing his right to know. In this work, my intention is to present a single comprehensive and coherent interpretation of *The Book of Job* that preserves the moral integrity of both God and men and women.

An Interpretative Challenge

Interpreting *The Book of Job* is a profound struggle for all who read it and hope to understand it.

The book itself offers some help, though it is surprising how many readers manage to disregard the signs and lose their way. The book offers two interpretative aids.

(1) The first is God's judgment, repeated twice by God and once by the author, that Job is "blameless and upright, fearing God and turning from evil" on every occasion.

(2) The second is God's judgment that Job has spoken rightly in what he said about God.

These two aids bracket the work and set the parameters for any legitimate interpretation of the author's message.

(1) Any interpretation that calls Job's integrity into question for demanding that God give an answer as to why there is evil in world can be summarily ruled out as illegitimate.

(2) Any interpretation that calls the ultimate propriety of Job's moral question into question can be similarly and summarily ruled out as illegitimate.

Within those two parameters of interpretation, four things call for the closest examination a reader can muster:

(1) Satan's speech to God,

(2) Job's Oath of Innocence,

(3) God's two speeches to Job, and

(4) Job's two responses to God.

Only a proper handling of these four keys will unlock the treasures to be found in *The Book of Job*.

    The Book of Job demands much of its readers. In all the overlapping and intersecting lawsuits, the book invites the reader to judgment. It demands judgment on the part of the reader. It provokes judgment on the part of the reader. With its provocative language and anti-climaxes, it even tempts the reader to false judgment. And yet it condemns with the harshest judgment those who judge deceitfully or prematurely, showing bias either towards human beings or God. In many ways, *The Book of Job* is an abyss of eternal peril for as you look into it, it looks into you. More than any other biblical book, this book will tell you who you are by the choices it forces you to make.

2: A NEW LOOK AT GENESIS

Act 1 in *The Book of Job* might be entitled *A New Look at Genesis* for, within a canonical perspective,[6] it reworks the *Genesis* story. This time the ultimate responsibility for evil in the world rests on God's shoulders not Adam and Eve's shoulders.

Scene 1: Earth

A New Garden of Eden

The Book of Job opens onto a pastoral Eden, the land of Uz to the south and east of the Dead Sea. (Job 1:1) "Seven thousand sheep, three thousand camels, five hundred yoke of oxen, five hundred donkeys" graze the hillsides. And "very many servants" tend to their physical care. (Job 1-3) An ideal family lives there: a mom, a dad, "seven sons and three daughters". Their lives are lives of joy and celebration as evidenced by the many feasts. (Job 1:4) A devout father tends to their spiritual care. (Job 1:4) All is right with this world. The reader may hear echoes of an earlier Eden. "God saw everything that he had made, and indeed, it was very good." (Genesis 1:31)

A New Adam

Here we meet a new Adam. He is a mature human being, the man whose name is Job. (Job 1:1) The author places some emphasis on this point because the Hebrew text begins with the word for man "ish", "a man there was". This is a signifcant change in the normal Hebrew word order of verb-subject-object. Here the order is object-subject-verb.[7] The significance is found in the fact that there are only two genuine parallels to this inverted syntax and they are found in the opening lines of Nathan's parable (2 Samuel 12:1) and Joash's fable (2 Kings 14:9).[8] This syntax is an introductory Hebrew formula or idiom for the parable that follows, akin to the modern introductory phrase "once upon a time". Thus, the author *The Book of Job* is telling the reader from the start that this book is and should be read as a myth or parable about humankind.

As a new Adam, Job is not just Everyman. Job is the best humankind has to offer. He is truly and fully human. He is what all of us could be and should be. In the judgment of the author, Job is "blameless and upright, one who fears God and turns away from evil". (Job 1:1) Unlike the first Adam, Job is a completed work. "This man was the greatest of all the people of the east." (Job 1:3) Since the people of the east were proverbially regarded as wise,[9] Job is presented as the wisest of the wise. His decisions as to how to lead a moral life are something all of us should emulate. That is especially the case when he raises the Oath of Innocence against God. The Oath of Innocence is a formal lawsuit against God for bringing evil into the world.

As a new Adam, Job will not face a simple test of blind obedience. Job's test will require all the intellectual and moral resources a mature human being can muster. And that test will bring out the fullness of his name. The name "Job" means "where is my father."[10] In part, his struggle is the search for a loving father God in the midst of a world of undeserved and unremitted suffering. The fate of all humanity will rest on his choices.

The author's judgment on Job merits deeper examination. The terminology is the terminology of natural law. This may be the result of the international wisdom tradition of which *The Book of Job* is an important part. Or this may be the result of the author's personal background. Job is presented as a jurist (Job 29:7-17) and the author himself may have been a jurist.

Natural law is the ethical theory that moral rules, laws in the broadest sense of the term, are deduced or derived from an examination of the natural needs that constitute human nature. Natural law asserts that that single reason behind all the moral rules is human nature itself, specifically the natural needs that define human nature. There is a certain structure to how morals are deduced or derived from natural law. This three-fold structure is called a syllogism, meaning a way of rigorously reasoning things through. It begins with a major premise, an ethical principle. It proceeds with a minor premise, certain statements of fact. And it arrives at a conclusion which consists of certain moral rules. The logic is as simple as it is profound.

The following exposition of that framework is a tangential development out of those original texts so that modern readers can understand the basic parameters of natural law and the natural human need for truth. The ancient texts imply, support and sanction such a framework, even though the ancient Jews never fully articulated the philosophical foundations of such a framework.[11]

(1) The major premise of natural law is the basic ethical principle that "you ought to seek what's really good for you." This is a self-evident truth. Why? The opposite is unthinkable. It is unthinkable that "you ought to seek what's really *bad* for you". And, it is equally unthinkable that "you ought *not* to seek what's really good for you".[12]

(2) The minor premise consists of a number of statements of fact about what's really good.

Those statements are discovered through the insight that "what's really good is what fulfills a natural human need".[13] All animals, including humankind, have a nature or essence. It is what separates one kind of animal from another kind of animal. It is what allows an observer to know that a particular individual is a member of one particular kind of animal as opposed to another. A nature consists of a set of species-specific characteristics or potentialities for development within a certain direction and within a certain range. Another name for these "dynamic dispositional tendencies"[14] is natural needs or desires.[15]

(a) These natural needs are universal within a species in the sense that all members, without exception, have them.

(b) They are eradicable within a species in the sense that all members, without exception, have them at all points in their life.

(c) And they are irresistible within a species in the sense that they are constantly seeking fulfillment.[16]

Human nature consists of the set of species-specific potentialities or natural needs all human beings share which are universal, eradicable and irresistible. The natural needs are distinguishable from acquired wants or acquired needs.

The insight that "what's really good is what fulfills a natural need" is a self-evident truth. Why? There is no such thing as a wrong natural need. The very idea of a wrong natural need is unthinkable.

(a) We can imagine wrong wants. We can imagine wanting something that is bad for us as human beings. We can even imagine wanting it so strongly that we try to deceive ourselves and call it something good. Addictions are very good examples of such acquired needs. They are not universal, eradicable or irresistible. These acquired needs are not natural needs. They are not rooted in human nature itself.

(b) We can imagine wanting more of a good thing than is really good for us.

(c) We can imagine wanting less of a good thing than is really good for us.

But we can never imagine a wrong natural need. If it were wrong, then we would not, by nature, need it.[17]

Not many natural needs meet the three-fold criteria of universality, eradicability and irresistibility. Scholars agree that those natural needs or desires include:

(a) the desire to know the truth,

(b) the desire to enjoy beauty,

(c) the desire to seek goodness,

(d) the desire to be free,

(e) the desire for justice,

(f) the desire for pleasure,

(g) the desire to love and be loved,

(h) the desire to work and creatively express one's self,

(i) the desire for life, growth and health,

(j) the desire for food and drink,

(k) the desire for shelter and

(l) the desire for God.

Technically, the desire for God may be a separate desire or it may be included in the penumbra of the desires for truth, goodness and beauty. These are needs all human beings have. They possess them at all points in their lives. These desires demand fulfillment. They may be satisfied or denied for periods of time, but they never really go away. These needs are matters of objective fact and they constitute human nature.

Real goods fulfill natural needs or desires. These real goods are biological, economic, social, political, psychological and religious goods.

(a) The biological goods include life, health and vigor.

(b) The economic goods include a decent supply of the means of subsistence, living and working conditions that are conducive to health, medical care, opportunities for access to the pleasures of sense, the pleasures of play, aesthetic pleasures, opportunities for access to the goods of the mind through educational facilities in youth and adult life and enough free time from subsistence work, both in youth and adult life, to take full advantage of these opportunities.

(c) The political goods include liberty, peace, both civil and external, the political liberties of voting and holding office, together with the protection of individual freedom by the prevention of violence, aggression, coercion, or intimidation and justice.

(d) The social goods include equality of status, equality of opportunity and equality of treatment in all matters affecting the dignity of the human person.

(e) The psychological goods include the goods of personal association (family, friendship, and love), the goods of character (the cardinal virtues of prudence, justice, courage and temperance, and the theological virtues of faith, hope and love), and the goods of the mind (creativity, knowledge, understanding and wisdom).

(f) The religious goods include awe and wonder, repentance and forgiveness, gratitude and worship and a personal relationship with God.

All of these real goods are matters of objective fact.[18] Reasonable people reflecting on what it is to be human would agree that these are things people need for a good human life. The list may not be exhaustive, but it is very representative of the consensus that currently exists.

However, these real goods need ordering and proportioning so that they retain their overall goodness. That is the function of moral virtue. Moral virtue is the habit of rightly choosing the real goods that make for a good human life. The main virtues are the cardinal virtues: prudence, temperance, courage and justice.

(a) Prudence is the habit of rightly judging the means to obtaining those right ends.

(b) Temperance is the habit of resisting and limiting immediate pleasures for a future good.

(c) Courage is the habit of suffering pain or discomfort for a future good.

(d) Justice is the habit of concern for the good of others and community welfare.

While they may be analytically distinct, they are not existentially distinct. You cannot possess one without the others. These virtues are matters of objective fact.[19]

(3) The conclusion is a basic and comprehensive moral rule derived or deduced from the combination of a single self-evidently true ethical principle and those objectively true matters of facts.

(a) "You should pursue and possess all the real goods that every human being needs by nature,

(b) properly ordered and proportioned so that each good is really good for you as a human being, and

(c) all the apparent goods that you yourself might want as an individual,

(d) provided your pursuit and possession of those apparent goods does not interfere with your or anyone else's pursuit and possession of all the real goods every human being needs by nature.[20]

This is what constitutes the total good of men and women. This is what constitutes the good life. This is what constitutes happiness, for it is the pursuit and possession of everything you might rightly need or want such that you are lacking in nothing. This is what God intends in making humankind what it is. It is God's general revelation in creation. It is rationally discoverable by all men and women, regardless of time or place. (Romans 2:14-16) The author presents Job as one who has discovered that truth and made it his life.

The Bible itself is imbued with an ethic of natural law.[21] Most often, natural law is implicit, but every so often, it is made explicit. One would expect to find such explicit statements of natural law in portions of *The Bible* dealing with moral rules, because such statements are the articulations of the reason behind the rules. And that indeed is where the two formulations of it are to be found.

(1) In the Holiness Code, Moses expresses his understanding of the basic ethical principle of natural law. "You shall be holy for I the LORD your God am holy." (Leviticus 19:10)

The key word here is "holy". The Hebrew word behind it is "qodosh". It is virtually synonymous with the Hebrew word "tam" used to describe Job. "Qodosh" means "holy", "dedicated", "devoted", "separate", "set apart for a special purpose".[22] It describes three things:

(a) the perfect fulfillment of

(b) the purpose

(c) for which something exists or is used.

That purpose is found in the natural needs that define human nature.

To paraphrase, Moses is saying "you should perfectly fulfill the purpose for which you exist, just as the LORD your God perfectly fulfills the purpose for which he exists." The focus is on purpose within nature. The central ethical obligation is to perfectly fulfill the natural needs of men and women and to make one's self fully available to God for his purposes. This is the heart of Old Testament morality. All the rest is commentary on the real goods that make for a good human life.

(2) In the Sermon on the Mount, Jesus expresses his understanding of the basic ethical principle of natural law. "Be perfect, therefore, as your heavenly Father is perfect." (Matthew 5:6)

The key word here is "perfect". The Greek word behind it is "teleios". It is virtually identical with the Hebrew "tam" used to describe Job. "Teleios" means "perfect", "well-rounded", "whole", "sound", "mature", "complete".[23] It describes three things:

(a) the complete actualization of

(b) the potentialities

(c) that define the nature of something.

Those potentialities are found in the natural desires that define human nature. "Teleios" is a word that has a long history in Greek ethical philosophy, especially in the natural law writings of Aristotle. The focus again is on potentialities within nature.

Jesus is reworking and sharpening Moses' formulation of the basic ethical principle of natural law.

(a) Complete actualization corresponds to perfect fulfillment.

(b) Potentialities correspond to purpose.

(c) The nature of something corresponds to that for which something exists or is used.

To paraphrase, Jesus is saying that "you should be fully actualized, just as your heavenly Father is fully actualized". "You should be truly and fully human, just as your heavenly Father is truly and fully divine." The central ethical obligation is to fulfill the natural needs of men and women. It is an obligation to be all that you can be and to be the very best you can be. This is the heart of New Testament morality. All the rest is commentary on the real goods that make for a good human life.

Within this framework of natural law, evil is the "privation" of goodness. The good is the "integrity or perfection of being in all its orders: material, moral and spiritual". Evil "consists in a privation, in the fact that a certain being lacks a good it requires to enjoy the integrity of its nature."[24] To paraphrase Moses, evil is the frustration of the perfect fulfillment of the purpose for which something exists or is used. To paraphrase Jesus, evil is the frustration of the complete actualization of the potentialities that define the nature of something.

The ethical terminology used to describe Job- completion, wholeness, wellbeing- resonates with the ethic of natural law.

(1) Job is "blameless".

The Hebrew "tam" here means "whole", "complete", "sound", "lacking in nothing", "fully integrated", "blameless", "perfect".[25] The focus here is on human nature.

(a) Ideologically, "tam" covers the same ground as Moses' "qodosh". It describes the perfect fulfillment of the purpose for which a human being exists. It describes the perfect fulfillment of the natural needs that define human nature. Job is holy as the LORD his God is holy.

(b) Ideologically, "tam" covers the same ground as Jesus' "teleios". It is the complete and perfect actualization of all the natural desires that define human nature. Those actualizations are properly ordered and proportioned so that all the potentialities are fully integrated. Job is as truly and fully human as his heavenly father is truly and fully divine.

Job is humanity at its very best. His maturity verges on sinlessness.[26] In fact, "tam" is used to describe the sinlessness of Satan prior to his fall from grace. (Ezekiel 28:13) This single word governs all the other words that follow in the description of Job. They illustrate aspects of his blamelessness and are included within it.

(2) Job is "upright".

The Hebrew "yashar" here means "upright", "just", "righteous", "doing what is right and pleasing in the eyes of God".[27] It describes two aspects of moral virtue: justice and righteousness.

(a) Justice is one of the cardinal virtues, the hinge on which the moral life swings. Justice is rendering unto another that which is their due or right. Justice is primarily a negative virtue. It indicates that one's pursuit and possession of all the apparent goods a human being might want by nurture does not interfere with one's own or anyone else's pursuit and possession of all the real goods all human beings need by nature.

(b) Righteousness or love is one of the theological virtues. It is an extension and transformation of the cardinal virtue justice. Love is seeking the good of oneself or another. Love is primarily a positive virtue. It includes all the positive assistance one gives in helping others with their pursuit and possession of all the real goods all human beings need by nature. This positive "doing of what is right", as opposed to not "doing what is wrong", is what constitutes "righteousness".

Job is virtuous: just and loving.

(3) Job "fears God."

The Hebrew "yare Elohim" means the proper "awe", "reverence" and "honor" a human being should have towards Almighty God.[28]

(a) The "totum bonum" is the pursuit and possession of the package of real goods that makes a person truly and fully human. It is the "total good" of humankind. "Tam" draws out this dimension in Job.

(b) The "summum bonum" is the pursuit and possession of the "highest good" within that package, a personal relationship with God. "Yare Elohim" draws out this dimension in Job.

Job has it all. Job seeks first the kingdom of God and its righteousness and all has been added unto him.

(4) Job "turns from evil."

The Hebrew "sara ra" here means not only "withdrawing from evil" but "avoiding evil" and "keeping oneself far from" it in the first place.[29] The mature man or woman is not the one who never does wrong, but the one who is quick to realize he has done wrong, to be sorry for it, to do restitution and to amend his character. This is what's meant by withdrawing from evil. Unlike the first Adam, Job is not a person who fails to take personal responsibility for his actions and who tries to shift blame. Job is a mature Adam. However in Job's case, the emphasis in the phrase "turns from evil" is on the latter component: "avoiding evil" and "keeping oneself far from" it in the first place. Unlike the first Adam, Job is not one who blunders into sin. When he raises his Oath of Innocence against God, he will do it with the integrity of his being. For Job, the Oath of Innocence will be the only way he can avoid sinning. A follower of God must speak the truth at all costs.

The author's judgment on Job is one of the important sign posts for any journey through *The Book of Job*. It is a judgment God himself will endorse twice in the next three scenes. This three-fold judgment is a strong endorsement of the morality of natural law. In his general revelation to humanity rooted in the hearts of men and women, God has given human beings both the intellect to discern right from wrong and the free will to choose the good. And God has given human beings sufficient common grace to do both. It is vitally important that Job is not an Israelite. He has not had any special revelation from God such as might be found in the Old Testament or the New Testament. And yet he perfectly fulfills the natural moral law written in the hearts of all men and women. (Romans 2:14-16)

A New Fall

Yet in this paradise, there are suggestions of a coming Fall. Unlike the first Eden, these suggestions lie not in a serpent in the grass near a tree of knowledge. They are found in the hearts and minds of men and women. It is the sin of prematurely judging and condemning God. "It may be that my children have sinned, and cursed God in their hearts." (Job 1:5) This intimation of disaster foreshadows the events to follow that will drive the plot.

Scene 2: Heaven

High Court of Heaven

The scene shifts to heaven, to the Judgment Seat of Almighty God. All the heavenly beings have gathered to present themselves before the Lord. (Job 1:6) The time is Rosh Hashanah, the first of the 10 Days of Awe in the Jewish liturgical year.[30] The books of life are opened and an account is being taken of the lives of men and women. The life of one man stands out beyond all the rest. It is the man Job. In the words of Almighty God, "there is no one like him on the earth, a blameless and upright man who fears God and turns away from evil." (Job 1:8) God's judgment repeats the author's judgment from the first scene. Job is humanity at its very best.

And God's judgment here extends the author's judgment in the previous scene. "There is no one like him on the earth." (Job 1:8) His righteousness exceeds that of Abraham, Isaac and Jacob. His righteousness exceeds that of God's chosen people. There is no one like him. Throughout *The Bible*, this kind of praise is only used to describe two individuals: (1) God and (2) the incarnation of God- the man Jesus Christ. The prophet Isaiah repeatedly describes God as the one beside whom there is no other. (Isaiah 43:11; 44:6; 45:5) And the apostle John describes Jesus as the only man or woman in whom the glory of God's character found its fullness. (John 1:14-18) The writer of *The Epistle to the Hebrews* describes Jesus as one like us in every way, "yet without sin". (Hebrews 4:15) Job is in the very best of company. He is as truly and fully human as God is truly and fully divine. There is no one like him. Needless to say, this has to mean that Job is so righteous that he is neither worthy of punishment nor in need of character development. He is the best he can be. He is the best all of us can be.

Satan

Into this world comes a tempter. His name is "Satan". (Job 1:6) This proper name "Satan" is a modification of the common Hebrew noun "satan", which means "the accuser", "the slanderer".[31] His name is his title, and that title aptly describes his character. He is a liar, though the extent of his lies remains for other books of *The Bible* to develop. In any event, this is not the portrait of a faithful servant. As a member of the heavenly host and not yet an outside challenger, he seems to have unlimited access to God and the divine council. Having reviewed the lives of men and women "from going to and fro on the earth, and from walking up and down on it" (Job 1:7), Satan does not hesitate to question the justice of God when asked. For many scholars, the phrase "going to and fro" describes a member of the secret police of the ancient world.[32] Such persons were men who did not hesitate to wrongly accuse and wrongly condemn the innocent to death. This phrase darkens the portrait of a faithless servant. And as a "slanderer", Satan is not a just and impartial prosecutor of God's justice. He presents a profoundly different verdict on the life of Job and, by implication, the lives of all men and women. It is his charge that brings silence to the heavenly court.

"Does Job fear God for nothing? Have you not put a fence around him and his house and all that he has, on every side? You have blessed the work of his hands, and his possessions have increased in the land. But stretch out your hand now, and touch all that he has, and he will curse you to your face." (Job 1:9-11)

All await God's answer to this slander.

The accusation was devilish in both origin and design. It raises three issues for consideration: one explicit and two implicit.

(1) First, Satan's judgment brings into question God's judgment on Job. And it does so explicitly. God's judgment on Job is a judgment on his intentions. Job intends the good. Satan's judgment on Job is a judgment on his motives. Job intends the good for reasons of selfishness. He does not fear God for nothing. He serves God for what he can get from God: the good life. In short, Job does not really serve God. Job manipulates God. This motive is the hidden sin. Job is a sinner. Satan's challenge is a claim to the soul of Job.

Satan's claim here has two important elements. Job is a sinner. And Job is such a sinner that, given the right circumstances, Job will "curse" God "to his very face". Satan's prediction here may suggest a self-imprecation: "I'll be damned if he doesn't curse you to your face!"[33] If so, then, within a canonical perspective, *The Book of Job* may be presenting an alternate version of the fall of Satan. In any event, blessing and cursing, righteousness and rebellion, are for Satan two sides of the same coin. Because human beings serve God out of selfishness not selfless love, they are equally apt to curse God for the loss of their rewards as they are to bless God for the receipt of those rewards. It is vitally important to remember that the essence of Satan's claim is that God has missed sin in Job's character. Job was not blameless. If Job sins in any way in thought, word or deed short of actually cursing God, then Satan is right and God is wrong in his judgment on Job. The reason is simple. Plot reveals character. If Job sins in his test, then that sin is an expression of a pre-existing character flaw that God missed but Satan didn't miss.

(2) Secondly, Satan's judgment brings into question God's authority to judge. And it does so implicitly. If God is wrong in his judgment on Job, then God has erred. In this scene, God is called "LORD". This is the NRSV translation of the Hebrew "JHWH" which may also be transliterated as "YHWH". "Yahweh" is the personal name for God in the Old Testament. It is often left untranslated as YHWH.[34] This personal name is taken from God's self-disclosure to Moses in the burnish bush.

> "But Moses said to God, "If I come to the Israelites and say to them, 'The God of your ancestors has sent me to you,' and they ask me, 'What is his name? What shall I say to them? God said to Moses, "I AM WHO I AM." He said further, 'Thus you shall say to the Israelites, 'I AM has sent me to you.'" God also said to Moses, 'Thus you shall say to the Israelites, "The LORD, the God of your ancestors, the God of Abraham, the God of Isaac, and the God of Jacob, has sent me to you': This is my name forever and this my title for all generations." (Exodus 3:13-15)

In the Exodus revelation, God's name is given in three ways: "I AM WHO I AM", "I AM", and "LORD". All three forms are forms of the Hebrew word "to be". In Hebrew, "I AM WHO I AM" is "ehyeh asheh ehyeh", first person singular, present tense. In Hebrew, "I AM" is "ehyeh", a shortened form of the former, but again first person singular, present tense. In Hebrew, "LORD" is "jhwh", third person singular, present tense. It functions as a personal name, Yahweh. This self-designation by God is the designation of a perfect being. Scholars have seen in the use of the first "I AM" a reference to essence and in the use of the second "I AM" a reference to existence. Through this name, God declares himself to be the Supreme Being, a perfect being, a being whose essence is existence.[35] By definition, such a being is all-powerful, all-knowing, all-present and all-good. Certainly the ancient Jews understood the personal name of Yahweh to designate the perfect being God. If God is wrong in his judgment on Job, then God has ceased to be all-knowing. God has ceased to be a perfect being. The implication is clear. God should step down from his throne for God has lost the authority the one true God possess. Satan's challenge is a claim to the throne of heaven.

(3) Thirdly, Satan's judgment brings into question God's very purpose in the creation of humankind. And it does so implicitly. If Job is the very best humankind has to offer and God is wrong in his judgment on Job, then God is wrong in judgment on humankind. Human beings were created to freely love God. If men and women love God for what they can get from God, then their love for God is not genuine. It is manipulation not love. It is selfishness not self-giving. That selfishness may be short-term: the good life. Or that selfishness may be long term: an after-life, eternal life. If human beings cannot rise beyond selfishness, then a meaningful relationship with God is never possible in this life or the next. God is wrong in creating human beings in the first place. The entire human project is a failure and should be scrapped. Humankind itself should be destroyed. Satan's challenge is a claim to destroy the earth and all in it.

This three-fold judgment was a stroke of evil genius. With a single accusation, Satan had put God on trial. And he had done before the High Court of Heaven. In any event, this three-fold challenge carries with it profound implications for understanding Job's so-called excessive words and his Oath of Innocence. If Job sins in any way short of actually cursing God, then God has lost it all.

The 10 Days of Awe are the time in the Jewish liturgical year when human beings are called to repentance. They begin with the Jewish New Year, Rosh Hashanah and they end 10 days later with the

Day of Atonement. On Rosh Hashanah, God is said to pass judgment on humankind in heaven. Human beings are given 10 days to repent of their sins and amend their ways. On the Day of Atonement, God forgives those who repent. These two annual judgments foreshadow the one and Final Judgment to occur at the end of time.[36]

This subtle liturgical background arises out of the sequence of "one day" (Job 1:6), "one day" (Job 1:13), "one day" (Job 2:1) and "seven days and nights". (Job 2:13) It may be the author's intention that the *Book of Job* be read within that framework, though it is by no means explicit. Interestingly enough, within the Jewish liturgical year, the *Book of Job* is normally read on the Day of Atonement and that is the only time within the year that it is read. It certainly adds an ironic twist to the Days of Awe, a twist verging on demonic parody. It is not merely humankind that is on trial. God himself is on trial during these Days of Awe. On Rosh Hashanah, Satan passes a judgment on God in heaven calling into question God's judgment of Job, God's authority to judge and God's very purpose in creation. God has 10 days to consider his ways and to repent of his error in creating humankind. When on the Day of Atonement God appears to Job and refuses to repent and amend his ways, Job will pass a judgment that foreshadows the one and Final Judgment to occur at the end of time. This is what makes the Days of Awe truly awesome. God is on trial for his plan in creation.

Trial by Ordeal

This challenge would be difficult for God to answer. If God were to reject it out of hand on the grounds of his own omniscience, then the slander would forever remain unanswered in the court of public opinion. If God were to pick up the gauntlet, then God would have to risk everything.

The moral issue here turns on the connection between righteousness and reward. To settle the issue, God would have to create a world is which selfishness and selfless love develop separately. It would not be an Eden. It would be a Wasteland.

(1) It would have to be a world filled with undeserved and unremitted suffering.

(2) It would have to be a world where evil would triumph over good more often than not.

(3) It would have to be a world where suffering would destroy character more often than build it.

(4) It would have to be a world in which the very existence of God would be doubt. There could never be certainty that God rewards those who love him, either with abundant life or with eternal life. In fact, the evidence would have to weigh against it.

Only in such a world, the issue between God and Satan could be joined. If God were to accept the challenge, then he would have to create a world very much like our own. Yet in doing so, God would have to open himself to being cursed by the very creatures God loved so much.

Such is God's faith in humankind that God chooses to pick up the gauntlet. God elects trial by ordeal to establish the principle that righteousness can exist separately from reward. God chooses Job, humanity's best representative, to be his champion. This trial of God by ordeal will be an ordeal for Job. God specifically authorizes Satan as his agent to inflict evil on Job. "Very well, all that he has in your power; only do not stretch out your hand against him!" (Job 1:12)

There are two restrictions on this trial of Job: one explicit and one implicit.

(1) The explicit restriction that God places on Satan is that Job's life cannot be taken. The taking of Job's life would prevent a final determination of the issue. Job must be tested to the fullest degree.

(2) The implicit restriction that Satan places on God is that God is prohibited from explicitly giving Job the reason for suffering. The concern is that any disclosure of a reason behind suffering might give Job a selfish motive to worship God and ultimately to manipulate God.

If Job is truly the man God believes him to be, then Job will worship God regardless of what God might do for him. And so, Satan leaves the presence of God in heaven to create Hell on earth.

To the extent Job represents a new Adam and thereby all humankind, the author of *The Book of Job* is clearly presenting God as the ultimate cause of evil in the world. God is morally responsible for the decision to create a world of undeserved and unremitted suffering. While God may use natural or supernatural intermediaries, such intermediaries are secondary instrumental causes. God is the principal; they are his agents. They have no agency or power to act without God's permission and direction. In ancient and modern morality and law, the actions of an agent are attributable to the principal when those actions are either authorized, intended or foreseen by the principal. In *The Book of Job*, Satan's actions are clearly authorized and intended by God and probably foreseen. Thus any attempt to absolve God by attributing the evil to Satan alone is misguided. This father God is presented as a kind of godfather. Satan is his hit-man. Job and all of humankind is his mark or target.

Scene 3: Earth

Hell on Earth

The scene shifts to the earth, to the paradise of Uz, where Satan will execute the order of God to create Hell on earth. It is the next day, Day 2^{37} in the Days of Awe.

"One day when his sons and daughters were eating and drinking wine in the eldest brother's house, a messenger came to Job and said, "The oxen were plowing and the donkeys were feeding beside them, and the Sabeans fell on them and carried them off, and killed the servants with the edge of the sword; I alone have escaped to tell you. While he was still speaking, another came and said, "The fire of God fell from heaven and burned up the sheep and the servants, and consumed them; I alone have escaped to tell you. While he was still speaking, another came and said, "The Chaldeans formed three columns, made a raid on the camels and carried them off, and killed the servants with the edge of the sword; I alone have escaped to tell you. While he was still speaking, another came and said, "Your sons and daughters were eating and drinking wine in their eldest brother's house, and suddenly a great wind came across the desert, struck the four corners of the house, and it fell on the young people, and they are dead; I alone have escaped to tell you." (Job 1:12-19)

In a single day, Job has lost it all: his wealth, his friends, his family. God has removed his protective "fence"[38] around Eden. The marauding bands of Sabeans and Chaldeans have stormed in to plunder his world. A heavenly fire, reminiscent of God's judgment on Sodom and Gomorrah, has consumed his world. But this Eden was not Sodom. A whirlwind, the traditional symbol of God's personal presence, has destroyed those most dear to Job. While Satan may be the proximate cause of the moral and physical evil that destroyed Eden, the destruction is the handiwork[39] of God himself. His signature is the whirlwind. And in so far as Job is the representative of humankind, the author may be suggesting here that all the moral and physical evils of this world are either intentionally sent or intended by God as part of his plan in the creation of this world. In any event, God, not our new Adam, destroys Eden and creates the world we find ourselves in.

The only mercy God shows is that he spares the lives of four of Job's servants. They live only to tell Job the tragedy of it all. "I alone have escaped to tell you." And their appearance one after another only deepens the tragedy of it all. It is a small mercy indeed.

Job's Response

Job is stunned by the news. He tears his robe and shaves his head in an act of mourning for a tragedy beyond tragedy. Yet rather than collapsing at the news, Job "falls" to the ground to "worship" God. (Job 1:20) "Naked I came from my mother's womb, and naked shall I return there; the LORD gave, and the LORD has taken away; blessed be the name of the LORD." (Job 1:21)

The author's judgment is that Job has passed this part of his trial. "In all this, Job did not sin or charge God with wrongdoing." (Job 1:22) Job did not sin. The Hebrew word for "sin" here is "hata" which means to "miss the mark", "to miss the way". It describes anything less than perfection.[40] In the author's eyes, Job remains perfect in that he does not condemn God for evil in the world. In Job's eyes, God remains a perfect being, notwithstanding the fact that

God is the author of evil. Ironically, the godfather perfectly hits his "mark" or "target" Job. Yet Job does not charge God with wrongdoing. The Hebrew word for "wrongdoing" here, "tipla", means "folly", a folly that is invariably sinful.[41] While Job holds God causally responsible, Job does not think God is morally blameworthy.

The author is certainly tempting the reader at this point. Many readers think God has committed folly by this point and they anticipate Job will change his mind. This anticipated change of mind on Job's part helps push the plot forward.

Scene 4: Heaven

High Court of Heaven

The scene shifts once again to heaven, to the Judgment Seat of Almighty God. It is the next day, Day 3 in the Days of Awe.

Once again, the heavenly beings are gathered and the heavenly court is in session. Once again, Satan appears and announces he has come "from going to and fro on the earth, and from walking up and down on it." (Job 2:2) The suggestion is that Satan still persists in his wrongful accusation and condemnation of Job. So God asks him repeats the question he asked two days before. "Have you considered my servant Job? There is no one like him on the earth, a blameless and upright man who fears God and turns away from evil." (Job 2:3) Yet this time, God adds an important comment on Job's goodness and his own evil. "He still persists in his integrity, although you incited me against him, to destroy him for no reason." (Job 2:3)

It is important to understand Job's integrity. The Hebrew "tummah" here means "integrity", "perfection", "wholeness", "completion"[42]. It is derived from the same root as and is virtually the same as the word "tam" which has already been used three times to describe the blamelessness of Job: once by the author (Job 1:1) and twice by God himself (Job 1:8; 2:3) Both "tummah" and "tam" describe the complete and perfect human being. But "integrity" puts the emphasis on the "integration" of everything that makes for the good moral life. From this point forward in *The Book of Job*, "integrity" will become a quick summary of God's judgment that Job is "blameless and upright, fears God and turns from evil." And that integrity will become a centerpiece of Job's Oath of Innocence. The

Oath of Innocence is a formal indictment of God for crimes against humanity.

God's Confession

It is equally important to understand God's confession. God confesses to being causally responsible for the evil Satan inflicted. "You incited me against him to destroy him for no reason." (Job 2:3) God is not saying Satan destroyed Job. God is saying that he himself through Satan destroyed Job. God admits to being a party-to-the-offence, an accessory and a co-conspirator. Two additional points are worth noting.

(1) First, the evil in question is undeserved evil as evidenced by the verb. The Hebrew "sut" here means "to instigate", "entice", "seduce".[43] And the connotations are invariably negative. It is always incitement to do wrong, to do evil. In fact, the paramount example is Satan's incitement of David to place his trust in military force and conscription rather than in God. (1 Chronicles 21:1) There it was a grievous sin David is said to have committed. Here the author tempts the reader to find it was equally a grievous sin on God's part to accept Satan's incitement to evil.

(2) Second, although God says he acted for no reason, technically he had a reason. God chose to destroy Job to settle the question of whether human beings worship God for what they can they can get from him. The creation of a world filled with evil is presented as a necessary condition for the separation of selfishness from selfless love. Whether this reason is a sufficient reason to impose evil is an entirely different question. So God's reference to destroying Job for "no reason" has to be understood as a reference to Job's character. There was no character flaw or sin in Job that would merit punishment. There was no immaturity in Job that would suggest the need for character development. The evil God authorized was neither for punishment nor for character development. The evil God admits to doing is undeserved evil.

Satan

Still Satan is not satisfied. The evil inflicted was not as great as it could have been. He repeats and deepens the challenge. "Skin for skin! All that people have they will give to save their lives. But stretch out your hand now and touch his bone and his flesh, and he will curse you to your face." (Job 2:4-5)

Hell on Earth

Such is God's faith in humankind that God chooses to pick up the gauntlet a second time. God specifically authorizes Satan to inflict further evil on Job. "Very well, he is in your power; only spare his life." (Job 2:6) Once again, the only restriction that God places on Satan is that Job's life cannot be taken. The taking of Job's life would prevent a final determination of the issue. And so, Satan leaves the presence of God in heaven to create Hell on earth.

Scene 5: Earth

Hell on Earth

The scene shifts immediately to the earth. It is the same day, Day 2 of the Days of Awe.

This evil authorized by God is this time inflicted without delay. Perhaps Satan is so frustrated with Job's integrity that he cannot wait for another day. "So Satan went out from the presence of the LORD, and inflicted loathsome sores on Job from the sole of his foot to the crown of his head." (Job 2:7) In a very short time, these sores will become infected and filled with worms. (Job 7:4-6) The worms that would normally cover Job in death cover him in life. His life in this world is a living death, undeserved and unremitted. Those worms will gnaw his body and conscience and help drive him to his Oath of Innocence.

Although it was a natural evil, this evil had profound moral consequences. In the ancient world, leprosy was feared beyond all other things. This "contagion" was regarded as a living death. It deprived the sufferer of all feeling. It caused a gradual wasting away so that a person's body parts eventually fell off. The ancients mistakenly regarded this illness as a contagion and shunned the sufferer. They routinely expelled him or her from their cities and from all human contact.[44] It is not clear that Job's loathsome sores were leprosy. But for those around him, it did not matter. His disease was very much like leprosy, the AIDS of the ancient world. All precautions had to be taken and the sufferer isolated. This is the significance of the statement "Job took a potsherd with which to scrape himself, and sat among the ashes." (Job 2:8) Job has been expelled from human society, with only a potsherd to his name. Job has lost it all: his wealth, his friends, his family and now his health and all human contact. He sits in the ashes of the city dump. God has cast Job out of Eden. Unlike the first Adam, this Adam is not expelled from the garden for reasons of sin. God casts Job out of Eden precisely because this Adam is righteous. His test is whether he can maintain his righteousness in a world of undeserved and unremitted suffering.

The only one to come to Job is his wife. Curiously, Satan has spared her life, though perhaps not without reason. His wife comes to him and asks: "Do you still persist in your integrity? Curse God, and die." (Job 2:9) She is counseling God-induced suicide. Condemn God and let God strike you dead. It would appear through these comments that Job has lost the love of his very wife. This smallest of mercies continues the temptation.

Job's Response

Job is completely alone. All he has is his faith in God and it is being tested to the fullest. Yet Job persists in his integrity. "You speak as any foolish woman would speak. Shall we receive the good at the hand of God, and not receive the bad?" (Job 2:10) Unlike the first Adam, this Adam resists the temptation his Eve offers.

Job's comments on good and evil here are important.

(1) In a natural law framework, goodness is that which contributes to the fulfillment of the needs that define human nature. The Hebrew word for good "tob" (Job 2:10) brings out that meaning. "Tob" is the "state of happiness or well-being" that is the complete good of human beings.[45] It is a human being's integrity or perfection of being in all its orders: material, moral and spiritual.

(2) In a natural law framework, evil is the frustration of that original purpose for humankind. The Hebrew word for bad "ra-a" (Job 2:10) brings out that meaning. "Ra-a" has "a dual meaning of being wrong in regard to God's original and ongoing intention and detrimental in terms of its effects on

man."[46] Evil is the intentional frustration of God's original intention of goodness towards humankind. Evil is the privation of the goods a human being requires to enjoy the integrity of his or her nature.

In the eyes of the author of *The Book of Job*, God's authorship of evil is dialectical.

(1) His thesis is that God intends a first order good: an integrity of being, the complete actualization of all the potentialities that define the integrity of human nature.

(2) His antithesis is that God intends a first order evil which frustrates that good by depriving human beings of some or all of the real goods that make for an integrity of being.

(3) His synthesis is the production of a second order good. Evil is morally necessary to create a world in which a completely selfless love of human beings for God is possible.

At this point in time, Job can only express the paradox of evil, not resolve it.

The author's judgment is that Job has passed this part of his trial. "In all this, Job did not sin with his lips." (Job 2:10) God confesses to doing evil. (Job 2:3) And that confession is not dissimilar from the self-confession the prophet Isaiah records. "I form light and create darkness. I make weal and create woe. I the LORD do all these things." (Isaiah 45:7)

Yet the author's judgment on Job is tantalizing different from his early one. A single ambiguous phrase has been added: "with his lips". This phrase need not imply that Job has sinned in thought. Conventional Hebrew thinking is that the lips express the heart. The heart is the seat of intellect and free-will. The fact that Job has not sinned in word or deed is strong evidence that Job has not sinned in thought. It is not a sin to believe God is the author of evil. Yet the author tempts the reader to premature judgment. This temptation invites a close examination of the speeches that follow.

3: THE TRUTH ABOUT GOD NO ONE WANTED TO HEAR

Act 2 in *The Book of Job* might be entitled *The Truth about God No One Wanted to Hear* for, within a canonical perspective, it presents a dark *Gospel*. The bad news is God is the author of evil in the world. So says God's chief evangelist Job.

A Wasteland

The story continues here on earth. It is next day, Day 3 of the Days of Awe. Eden is now a Wasteland. Job's life has been reduced to ashes and Job himself is sitting on an ash heap that is a garbage dump outside the city. The gates of Hell have opened and our thinker Job is meditating on the meaning of life. He has not yet abandoned all hope.

Job's Three Friends

Into this world come Job's three friends: Eliphaz the Temanite, Bildad the Shuhite and Zophar the Naamathite. They may have lived in the general area. It was close enough that they "heard of all these troubles that had come upon him" and each of them set out from his own home." (Job 2:11) The terms Temanite, Shuhite and Naamathite suggest their ethnic background, not the lands from which they journeyed. It is extremely unlikely that they journeyed from different foreign lands, because it would be impossible to "meet together to go and console and comfort" Job. It is more likely they lived near Job. They heard of the all his troubles on Day 2 of the Days of Awe and arrived on Day 3 of the Days of Awe.

They come to offer the consolation and comfort of religious orthodoxy. (Job 2:11) Job is so disfigured by the tragedy that his friends barely recognize him. (Job 2:12) They attempt to share in his pain. "They raised their voices and wept aloud; they tore their robes and threw dust in the air upon their heads. They sat with him on the ground seven days and seven nights, and no one spoke a word to him, for they saw that his suffering was great." (Job 2:12-13) Theirs was a death watch.

A Whirlwind of Righteous Indignation

But Job will not go quietly into the night. Job sits with his friends seven days and seven nights. It is now the morning of the Day of Atonement, Day 10 of the Days of Awe.[47] Job's time of reflection is over. It is now the time for a final judgment.

And so, Job "opens his mouth" to "curse" the evil of it all. (Job 3:1-3) It is a moral challenge his three friends are quick to pick up. The word "curse" here is perhaps too strong. The Hebrew root actually means to "threat lightly" or with "contempt".[48] In any event, Job's friends regard it as a curse. Their comfort and consolation turns to confrontation. And the trial of Job by his three friends begins. Three cycles of six poetic speeches follow. An angry and opinionated youth joins the discussion at the very end. Job speaks 9 times; Eliphaz, 3; Bildad, 3; Zophar, 2 and Elihu, 1.

First Cycle of Speeches (Job 3:1-11:20)

(1) Job   (Job 3:1-3:26)
(2) Eliphaz   (Job 4:1-5:27)
(3) Job   (Job 6:1-7:21)
(4) Bildad   (Job 8:1-8:22)
(5) Job   (Job 9:1-10:22)
(6) Zophar   (Job 11:1-11:20)

Second Cycle of Speeches (Job 12:1-20:29)

(1) Job   (Job 12:1-14:22)
(2) Eliphaz   (Job 15:1-15:35)
(3) Job   (Job 16:1-17:16)
(4) Bildad   (Job 18:1-18:21)
(5) Job   (Job 19:1-19:29)
(6) Zophar   (Job 20:1-20:29)

Third Cycle of Speeches (Job 21:1-37:24)

(1) Job   (Job 21:1-21:34)
(2) Eliphaz   (Job 22:1-22:30)
(3) Job   (Job 23:1-24:25)
(4) Bildad   (Job 25:1-25:6)
(5) Job   (Job 26:1-31:40)
(6) Elihu   (Job 32:1-37:24)

All the speeches of Job and his friends are highly stylized poetry suggesting that book itself is parable or myth. Real persons do not speak in poetry, certainly not for 35 chapters. The participants rarely make extended arguments. In fact, they rarely respond directly to each other. Many of Job's speeches seem directed more to God than to his three friends. The three friends speak about God. Job speaks directly to God.

These three cycles of speeches constitute a whirlwind of righteous indignation. Bildad describes Job's speeches as "a great wind." (Job 8:2). Eliphaz describes them as "windy knowledge". (Job 15:2) And Job describes the speeches of all his friends as "windy words". (Job 16:3) They go round and round the issue of evil in the world. And they wear each other out. The only peace to be had is at the centre of the whirlwind. That peace is the answer that only God can give. Not surprisingly, when God appears to give an answer, he appears in a whirlwind.

Job's Complaint

Why? Why? Why? Why? Why? (Job 3:11-12,16,20,23) With this fivefold plaintive cry, Job opens this section of *The Book of Job*. [49]

Job pleads for answers from God. As a religious person, he "knows" God must have a "purpose" in sending that evil, but he cannot understand why God has "hidden" that purpose in his "heart" and not revealed it to his servants. (Job 10:13) As a rational being, Job needs those answers. "My days are past, my plans broken off, the desires of my heart...where then is my hope? Will it go down to the bars of Sheol? Shall we descend together into the dust?" (Job 17:11, 15-16) Without those answers, life is virtually meaningless.

(1) God has seemingly abandoned the righteous. The lives of good men and women are "hard service" here on earth. (Job 7:1) They are tested with evil morning, noon and night. (Job 7:17-18). The test is more than most can bear. In and through it all, God shows no partiality. "It is all one; therefore I say he destroys both the blameless and the wicked. When disaster brings sudden death, he mocks at the calamity of the innocent. The earth is given into the hand of the wicked; he covers the eyes of its judges- if it is not he, who then is it" (Job 9:22-24) God "despises the work of his hands".

(Job 10:3) "Who among all these does not know that the hand of the LORD has done this?" (Job 12:9) God treats his most beloved son Job as an "enemy" (Job 13:24) and an adversary. (Job 19:11)

(2) And God seemingly favours the wicked.

"Why do the wicked live on, reach old age, and grow mighty in power? Their children are established in their presence, and their offspring before their eyes. Their houses are safe from fear, and no rod of God is upon them. Their bull breeds without fail; their cow calves and never miscarries. They send out their little ones like a flock, and their children dance around. They sing to the tambourine and the lyre, and rejoice to the sound of the pipe. They spend their days in prosperity, and in peace they go down to Sheol. They say to God, 'Leave us alone! We do not desire to know your ways. What is the Almighty, that we should serve him? And what profit do we get if we pray to him?' Is not their prosperity indeed their own achievement? The plans of the wicked are repugnant to me. How often is the lamp of the wicked put out? How often does calamity come upon them? How often does God distribute pains in his anger? How often are they like straw before the wind, and like chaff that the storm carries away? You say, 'God stores up their iniquity for their children.' Let it be paid back to them, so that they may know it. Let their own eyes see their destruction, and let them drink of the wrath of the Almighty. For what do they care for their household after them, when the number of their months is cut off?" (Job 21:7-21)

The "wicked are spared in the day of calamity and are rescued in the day of wrath..." (Job 21:30)

(3) God has created this Hell on earth. So Job describes God as the Lord of the Underworld through a number of Ugaritic images and words.[50] The "arrows of the Almighty are in me; my spirit drinks their poison; the terrors of God are arrayed against me." (Job 6:4)

"He has torn me in his wrath, and hated me; he has gnashed his teeth at me; my adversary sharpens his eyes against me. They have gaped at me with their mouths; they have struck me insolently on the cheek; they mass themselves together against me. God gives me up to the ungodly, and casts me into the hands of the wicked. I was at ease, and he broke me in two; he seized me by the neck and dashed me to pieces; he set me up as his target; his archers surround me. He slashes open my kidneys, and shows no mercy; he pours out my gall on the ground. He bursts upon me again and again; he rushes at me like a warrior. I have sewed sackcloth upon my skin, and have laid my strength in the dust. My face is red with weeping, and deep darkness is on my eyelids, though there is no violence in my hands, and my prayer is pure." (Job 16:9-17)

God is portrayed as Resheph, the Canaanite Lord of the Underworld, the Lord of the arrow. Resheph is the god of pestilence, destruction, death and war.[51] He is the hungry one that is death itself. (Deuteronomy 32:23) The terrors he arrays are the minions of Hell itself. In and through such imagery, Job is goading God, much as Moses goaded God about how his destruction of the Israelites in Sinai would look to the Egyptians. (Exodus 32:12)

These three sets of declarations illustrate the so-called excessive words of Job. They are powerful expressions of God's authorship of evil. The ancient rabbis were inclined to excuse Job's inflammatory rhetoric. "A man is not held responsible for what he says when in distress."[52] Job is a man in distress, still mourning the children he has lost at God's hand. Modern conservative scholars are less inclined to be as charitable as the ancients. In any event, these so-called excessive words are fair comment on a world of undeserved and unremitted suffering and the creator of such a world.

Job agonizes that he is somehow being punished for a sin he has not committed. "Teach me, and I will be silent; make me understand how I have gone wrong." (Job 6:24) "I will say to God, Do not condemn me; let me know why you contend against me. Does it seem good to you to oppress, to despise the work of your hands and favor the schemes of the wicked? Do you have eyes of flesh? Do you see as humans see? Are your days like the days of mortals, or your years like human years, that you seek out my iniquity and search for my sin, although you know that I am not guilty..." (Job 10:6-7) Job has become the "laughingstock" of all the peoples for in and through it all, he continues to worship God. (Job 12:4)

Job's Road to an Oath of Innocence

Bewildered and tortured, Job turns to God time and time again for answers but none are forthcoming. In and through five speeches, Job turns his complaint into a demand. Five speeches map out that road to an Oath of Innocence. The Oath of Innocence is a formal lawsuit against God for crimes against humanity. Two of those speeches relate to the integrity of Job's ways. In one, Job reaches the height of Old Testament piety: "Though he slay me, yet will I trust him." In another, Job becomes a Kierkegaardian "knight of faith". Three speeches speculate about persons who might help Job settle his issue with God. In one, it is a mediator, who might bring the parties together. In another, it is a witness in heaven, who might testify to Job's righteousness. In another, it is a redeemer, a deliverer, who might free Job from the evil he endures. Together, these five speeches constitute an appeal to God, through God and against God

1. A mediator

The idea of a mediator surfaces in Job's third speech in the first cycle. Job's central problem is summoning God to answer.

"How can a mortal be just before God? If one wished to contend with him, one could not answer him once in a thousand. He is wise in heart, and mighty in strength --who has resisted him, and succeeded?-- he who removes mountains, and they do not know it, when he overturns them in his anger; who shakes the earth out of its place, and its pillars tremble; who commands the sun, and it does not rise; who seals up the stars; who alone stretched out the heavens and trampled the waves of the Sea; who made the Bear and Orion, the Pleiades and the chambers of the south; who does great things beyond understanding, and marvelous things without number. Look, he passes by me, and I do not see him; he moves on, but I do not perceive him. He snatches away; who can stop him? Who will say to him, 'What are you doing?' "God will not turn back his anger; the helpers of Rahab bowed beneath him. How then can I *answer* him, choosing my words with him? Though I am *innocent*, I cannot answer him; I must *appeal* for mercy to my *accuser*. If I *summoned* him and he answered me, I do not believe that he would listen to my voice. For he crushes me with a tempest, and multiplies my wounds *without cause*; he will not let me get my breath, but fills me with bitterness. If it is a contest of strength, he is the strong one! If it is *a matter of justice*, who can *summon* him? Though I am *innocent*, my own mouth would condemn me; though I am *blameless*, he would prove me perverse. I am *blameless*; I do not know myself; I loathe my life. It is all one; therefore I say, he destroys both the *blameless* and the wicked. When disaster brings sudden death, he mocks at the calamity of the innocent. The earth is given into the hand of the wicked; he covers the eyes of its judges-- if it is not he, who then is it? "My days are swifter than a runner; they flee away, they see no good. They go by like skiffs of reed, like an eagle swooping on the prey. If I say, 'I will forget my complaint; I will put off my sad countenance and be of good cheer,' I become afraid of all my suffering, for I know you will not hold me innocent. I shall be condemned; why then do I labor in vain? If I wash myself with soap and cleanse my hands with lye, yet you will plunge me into filth, and my own clothes will abhor me. For he is not a mortal, as I am, that I might *answer* him, that we should come to trial together. There is no *umpire* between us, who might lay his hand on us both. If he would take his rod away from me, and not let dread of him terrify me, then I would speak without fear of him, for I know I am not what I am thought to be. "I loathe my life; I will give free utterance to my *complaint*; I will speak in the bitterness of my soul. I will say to God, Do not *condemn* me; let me know why you *contend* against me. Does it seem good to you to *oppress*, to despise the work of your hands and favor the schemes of the wicked? Do you have eyes of flesh? Do you see as humans see? Are your days like the days of mortals, or your years like human years, that you seek out my iniquity and search for my sin, although you know that I am *not guilty*, and *there is no one to deliver out of your hand?*" (Job 9:14-10:7 Italics added for emphasis.)

The NRSV poorly translates "mediator" as "umpire". (Job 9:33) The Hebrew "yakah" is more properly translated "mediator" or "arbitrator". It is a legal word describing someone who can bring the parties together and negotiate a settlement. That person attempts to "convince", "convict", "rebuke" or "correct" one of the parties by "exposing their wrongdoing and calling them to repentance".[53] It can describe a judge acting outside his normal role, but it need not. It is often used in covenantal lawsuits where God seeks to resolve a complaint against his people without resorting to a full and formal legal condemnation. The emphasis here is on moral persuasion.

At this point in time, Job is not contemplating a formal lawsuit against God. He prefers an out of court settlement, an arbitration or mediation. But he soon dismisses this avenue as a dead end. There is no mediator between God and humankind to persuade God to answer him.

Yet this passage is remarkable for the sudden explosion of legal terminology that will frame Job's moral complaint against God. Job speaks of "sdq", winning a suit and being proven right (Job 9:2), being in the right and innocent. (Job 9:15,20:10:15) He speaks of "rs", being guilty (Job 9:22,29, 10:7,15), being declared or proven guilty. (Job 9:20; 10:2) He speaks of a "rib", a trial or lawsuit. (Job 9:19,32) He speaks of "mispat", litigation or justice. (Job 9:15) He speaks of a "mesopet", a legal adversary. (Job 9:15) He speaks of a "siah", a legal complaint or plea. (Job 9:27;10:1) He speaks of "dbr", stating one's case, charges or claims. (Job 9:14,35;10:1) He speaks of "ny", answering a complaint or charge (Job 9:3,14,15,32), or answering a summons. (Job 9:6) He speaks of "mokiah", a legal arbitrator. (Job 9:33) He speaks of "qr", summoning a person. (Job 9:16) He speaks of "y'd", arraigning a person. (Job 9:19) He speaks of the "tam", the blameless or guiltless. (Job 9:20,21,22) [54] This passage prepares the reader for the equally explosive Oath of Innocence to come. The Oath of Innocence is a formal indictment of God for crimes against humanity.

2. Though he slay me, yet will I trust him.

The idea of a formalized trial starts to take shape in Job's first speech in the second cycle.

"But I would speak to the Almighty, and I desire to *argue my case* with God. As for you, you whitewash with lies; all of you are worthless physicians. If you would only keep silent, that would be your wisdom! Hear now my *reasoning*, and listen to the *pleadings* of my lips. Will you speak falsely for God, and speak deceitfully for him? Will you show partiality toward him, will you *plead the case for God*? Will it be well with you when he searches you out? Or can you deceive him, as one person deceives another? He will surely rebuke you if in secret you show *partiality*. Will not his majesty terrify you, and the dread of him fall upon you? Your maxims are proverbs of ashes, your *defenses* are *defenses* of clay. "Let me have silence, and I will speak, and let come on me what may. *I will take my flesh in my teeth, and put my life in my hand. See, he will kill me; I have no hope; but I will defend my ways to his face. This will be my salvation, that the godless shall not come before him.* Listen carefully to my words, and let my declaration be in your ears. I have indeed prepared my *case; I know that I shall be vindicated.* Who is there that will *contend* with me? For then I would be silent and die. Only grant two things to me, then I will not hide myself from your face: withdraw your hand far from me, and do not let dread of you terrify me. Then call, and I will answer; or let me speak, and you reply to me. How many are my iniquities and my sins? Make me know my transgression and my sin. Why do you hide your face, and *count* me as your *enemy*?" (Job 13:3-24 Italics added for emphasis)

As a righteous person, Job knows God as a judge may be receptive to his pleadings, his reasoning and his case. Job is a righteous human being. And a righteous person he will pursue righteousness, even if it means confronting God himself.

Yet the very idea of putting God on trial is fraught with peril. God might destroy Job for the sin of presumption. Still Job is determined to push ahead. Again, the NRSV poorly translates the key phrase: "he will kill me; I have no hope". (Job 13:15 NRSV) The older KJV captures the sense more accurately: "though he slay me, yet will I trust him." (Job 13:15 KJV) Job understands that God may kill him for the sin of presumption, but he trusts that God will do otherwise. Job will continue to do the right thing, even if it means death in this life or the next. This is the height of Old Testament righteousness.

The KJV translation is to be preferred for three reasons.

(1) First, the immediate context calls for a positive affirmation of faith. "I will defend my ways to his face. This will be my salvation, that the godless shall not come before him...I know I shall be vindicated." (Job 13:15b-16,18) Job anticipates a positive response to his formalized plea and that can only result in hope, not

the absence of hope. Thus the NRSV translation "I have no hope" makes no sense contextually.

(2) Second, the language of the Hebrew text is somewhat confused and can easily be translated the way KJV does it. The confusion goes back to the language of the 10th century Hebrew Masoretic text. The choice is between two Hebrew words: "lo'" and "lo". The difference between the two words is a single (').

(a) In Hebrew, "lo'", that is "lo" with the ('), means "no". This is the textual reading that the 10th century Masoretic scribes used. This is what NRSV uses when it translates the line "he will kill me, I have no hope" (Job 13:15 NRSV).

(b) In Hebrew, "lo", that is "lo" without the ('), means "in him". The very same Masoretic scribes indicated in a margin note that they had real difficulty discerning the original text. It could either be "lo'" or "lo". They wanted to make it clear that "lo" represented an alternate reading and alternate tradition and could be the correct reading, even though they were choosing not to follow it. In fact, many other Hebrew manuscripts, some ancient, and the Hebrew oral tradition follow that alternate tradition.[55] This is what KJV uses when it translates the line: "though he slay me, yet will I trust" (Job 13:15 KJV) The trust is 'in him'.

It seems the original text cannot be known with certainty. The only way to decide the textual question is contextually. And there the KJV translation is distinctively better. A brilliant compromise was once offered to this textual problem by the Protestant theologian John Calvin and it is worth repeating. He would read the phrase as a rhetorical question "shall I not hope?"[56] expressing Job's great trust that God will ultimately answer his plea.

(3) Third, there exist two impressive Old Testament precedents for challenging God.

(a) In the story of Sodom and Gomorrah, Abraham challenges God seeking answers.

"Far be it from you to do such a thing, to slay the righteous with the wicked, so that the righteous fare as the wicked! Far

- 54 -

be that from you! Shall not the Judge of all the earth do what is just?" (Genesis 18:25)

And Abraham is successful in his challenge. After some discussion, God agrees to spare the lives of a righteous remnant.

(b) In story of the Israel's sin over the golden calf, Moses challenges God seeking answers.

"Why does your wrath burn hot against your people, whom brought out from the land of Egypt with great power and with a mighty hand? Why should the Egyptians say, 'It was with evil intent that he brought them out to kill them in the mountains, and to consume them from the face of the earth'? Turn from your fierce wrath; change your mind and do not bring disaster on your people. Remember Abraham, Isaac, and Israel, your servants, how you swore to them by your own self, saying to them, I will multiply your descendants like the stars of heaven, and all this is the land that I have promised to give to your descendants, and they shall inherit it forever.'" And the Lord changed his mind..." (Exodus 32:11-14)

He even cajoles God in the process. And Moses is successful in his challenge. God changes his mind and spares his people.

Like Abraham and Moses, Job realizes God may slay him for the sin of presumption, but Job hopes and trusts that God will do otherwise. The servant of God must speak the truth at all costs, even if it means challenging God. This is the highest expression of Old Testament piety, the piety of protest.

3. A witness or judge

The idea of a witness or a judge surfaces in Job's second speech in the second cycle. His lawsuit is taking shape. There may be no moral mediator between God and humankind but God has witnessed all the events that have happened. God could be a witness or a judge. As a witness, God could testify to Job's blamelessness. As a judge, God could uphold the right of a mortal to know the reason why there is evil in the world.

"O earth, *do not cover my blood*; let my outcry find no resting place. Even now, in fact, my *witness* is in heaven, and *he that vouches for me* is on high. My friends scorn me; my eye pours out tears to God, that he would maintain the *right* of a mortal with God, as one does for a neighbor. For when a few years have come, I shall go the way from which I shall not return." (Job 16:18-22 Italics added for emphasis)

This witness or judge could maintain Job's right to know the reason for evil. His right is a solid one. In natural law ethics, a right is a justified moral claim. The justification lies in the connection between duties, needs and rights.

(1) Every person has a basic moral duty to God, to others and to oneself to lead a good human life.

(2) By nature, they need certain things to fulfill that duty. Job needs the answer to why there is evil in the world in order to fulfill his duty to God.

(3) Job has a right to that knowledge, because there is no such thing as a wrong natural need.

That is what turns his moral claim into a moral right.[57]

4. A redeemer or advocate

The idea of a redeemer or advocate is added with Job's third speech in the second cycle. Again, that redeemer or advocate is God himself.

"Then Job answered: "How long will you torment me, and break me in pieces with words? These ten times you have cast reproach upon me; are you not ashamed to wrong me? And even if it is true that I have erred, my error remains with me. If indeed you magnify yourselves against me, and make my humiliation an argument against me, *know then that God has put me in the wrong*, and *closed his net around me.* Even when I cry out, *'Violence!'* I am not answered; I call aloud, but there is *no justice.* He has walled up my way so that I cannot pass, and he has set darkness upon my paths. He has stripped my glory from me, and taken the crown from my head. He breaks me down on every side, and I am gone, he has uprooted my hope like a tree. He has kindled his wrath against me, and *counts me as his adversary.* His troops come on together; they have thrown up siegeworks against me, and encamp around my tent. "He has put my family far from me, and my acquaintances are wholly estranged from me. My relatives and my close friends have failed me; the guests in my house have forgotten me; my serving girls count me as a stranger; I have become an alien in their eyes. I call to my servant, but he gives me no answer; I must myself plead with him. My breath is repulsive to my wife; I am loathsome to my own family. Even young children despise me; when I rise, they talk against me. All my intimate friends abhor me, and those whom I loved have turned against me. My bones cling to my skin and to my flesh, and I have escaped by the skin of my teeth. Have pity on me, have pity on me, O you my friends, for the hand of God has touched me! Why do you, like God, pursue me, never satisfied with my flesh? "O that my words were written down! O that they were inscribed in a book! O that with an iron pen and with lead they were engraved on a rock forever! *For I know that my Redeemer lives, and that at the last he will stand upon the earth; and after my skin has been thus destroyed, then in my flesh I shall see God, whom I shall see on my side, and my eyes shall behold, and not another.* My heart faints within me! If you say, 'How we will persecute him!' and, *'The root of the matter is found in him'; be afraid of the sword, for wrath brings the punishment of the sword, so that you may know there is a judgment."* (Job 19:1-29 Italics added for emphasis)

A redeemer might assist Job as a prosecuting attorney. The Hebrew word "goel" here means "advocate", "vindicator", "redeemer" or "deliverer."[58] It is an individual who is under a moral and legal obligation to protect the rights of another and to restore that individual to their former status. It was usually a relative, a "kinsman-redeemer". Historically, this redeemer would buy a person out of debt (Leviticus 19:25,29) or slavery (Leviticus 19:47-48). He would avenge wrongful killings. (Number 35:12, 2 Samuel 14:11) But he need not be a blood relative. Over time, God was understood to be the ultimate redeemer. It was God who redeemed his people from their bondage in Egypt. (Exodus 6:6; 15:13, Psalms 74:2) It was God who considered a person's affliction and delivered him from it.

(Psalms 119:154)   Unlike a mediator, a redeemer is under a moral and legal obligation to see justice done.

Job has been denied justice. "Know then that God has put me in the wrong." (Job 19:6) The Hebrew word "iwwet" here means "to bend" or "make crooked". In this legal context, it means "the denial of what is rightfully due."[59] Justice is rendering unto a person that which is their due or right. Job is rightfully due the reason for evil in the world.

Job "knows" he will get his answer no later than the Day of the Final Judgment. "I know my Redeemer lives, and that at the last, he will stand upon the earth; and after my skin has been thus destroyed, then in my flesh I shall see God, whom I shall see on my side, and my eyes shall behold, and not another." (Job 19: 25-26) The Day of Judgment is contemporaneous with the universal resurrection of the dead. It is the "last" day of human history. The dead shall be raised and stand before Almighty God in judgment. "After my skin has been...destroyed, then in my flesh I shall see God." (Job 19:26) The Hebrew "min mibbesari" here can mean either "from without" of my flesh, implying a disembodied state for Job, or as "from within" my flesh, implying an embodying state for Job, but the context requires an embodied state. Job will physically see God at his side and no other. The NRSV recognizes this with its translation "in my flesh". At that time, Job's redeemer will "stand" by his side. (Job 19:27) The Hebrew "gum" here is a legal term meaning to "stand up in court" as an "advocate".[60] Job's redeemer God will fulfill his own moral and legal obligations to Job and press Job's moral and legal claims against God in the High Court of Heaven. It is at that time that Job will be vindicated. He will "see God". (Job 19:26) He will be raised up from the ash heap to the right hand of God.

Job is building here on his earlier comments: "If mortals die, will they live again? All the days of my service I would wait until release should come. You would call, and I would answer you; you would long for the work of your hands. For then you would not number my steps, you would not keep watch over my sin; my transgression would be sealed up in a bag, and you would cover over my iniquity." (Job 14:14-17) He had vacillated on the possibility of an afterlife and a post-mortem vindication. But things have now changed and he lays a firm foundation in this passage. What was once the matter of a dream is now presented as a matter of fact: "I

know my Redeemer lives." (Job 19:25) Knowledge has replaced
opinion. In Job's eyes, the physical resurrection of the dead and the
Final Judgment are morally required as a matter of justice. The latter
entails the former. The resurrection of the dead and the Final
Judgment are the guarantee that all the moral questions of life will be
settled.

With that conviction in mind, Job warns his friends and the
reader about the dangers of prematurely acquitting God: "be afraid of
the word, so that you may know there is a judgment." (Job 19:29)
That judgment is the Final Judgment[61] that will clarify the issue for all
to see. That judgment will be a judgment in Job's favour. It is a
powerful testimony that Job is contemplating more than his own
personal resurrection. He envisions the resurrection of all the dead,
including his friends.

At this point, a trial date has been set: the Day of the Final
Judgment. And the main participants other than Job have been
revealed. Those parties form a legal trinity: three persons, one
lawsuit. The three persons are God the judge, God the advocate and
God the defendant. These three persons are one in the mystery of evil
and vindication. Job's complaint has become an appeal to God,
through God and against God.[62]

5. I should be acquitted forever by my judge.

The actual institution of a formal lawsuit is the subject of
Job's second speech in the third cycle. While Job contemplates his
ultimate vindication on the Day of Judgment, he wants his answer
here and now.

"Then Job answered: "Today also my complaint is bitter; his
hand is heavy despite my groaning. Oh, that I knew where I
might find him, that I might come even to his dwelling! I
would lay my *case* before him, and fill my mouth with
arguments. I would learn what he would answer me, and
understand what he would say to me. Would he *contend* with
me in the greatness of his power? No; but he would give heed
to me. *There an upright person could reason with him, and I
should be acquitted forever by my judge.* "If I go forward, he is
not there; or backward, I cannot perceive him; on the left he
hides, and I cannot behold him; I turn to the right, but I cannot

see him. But he knows the way that I take; when he has tested
me, I shall come out like gold. My foot has held fast to his
steps; I have kept his way and have not turned aside. I have not
departed from the commandment of his lips; I have treasured in
my bosom the words of his mouth. But he stands alone and
who can dissuade him? What he desires, that he does. For he
will complete what he appoints for me; and many such things
are in his mind. Therefore I am terrified at his presence; when
I consider, I am in dread of him. God has made my heart faint;
the Almighty has terrified me; If only I could vanish in
darkness, and thick darkness would cover my face!" (Job 23:1-
17 Italics added for emphasis)

And he believes he can get it with a formal lawsuit. "Would he
contend with me in the greatness of his power? No; but he would give
heed to me. There an upright person could reason with him, and I
should be acquitted forever by my judge." (Job 23:6-7)   His
confidence is high and rightfully so.   Job has previously been
declared "upright", once by the author (Job 1:1) and twice by God
(Job 1:8; 2:3) though he himself does not know that.

In spite of his fear and trembling, Job will push on his Oath
of Innocence. "What he desires, that he does. For he will complete
what he appoints for me; and many such things are in his mind.
Therefore I am terrified at his presence; when I consider, I am in
dread of him. God has made my heart faint; the Almighty has
terrified me." (Job 23:13-16)   In this moment, Job has become a
Kierkegaardian knight of faith. He will formally indict God for
crimes against humanity. He will defy conventional thinking to do
what he knows in his heart God requires, though none of his friends
will understand him. He walks in "fear and trembling" at the
enormity of the task before him. As a righteous person, Job knows
God would want him to raise the Oath of Innocence. And he knows it
with all the integrity of his being.

Job's Oath of Innocence

The Oath of Innocence is an ancient legal device, found in
Babylonian[63], Hittite[64] and Jewish[65] legal codes. It is not found in
Egyptian legal codes, since Egyptian law was never codified. The
word of the reigning Pharaoh was the law. However, it is found in
Egyptian mythology in the Final Judgment described in *The Book of*

the Dead.[66] So, it may have existed in the unwritten common law of Egypt.

The Oath of Innocence was a self-contained lawsuit involving a summary trial in absentia and two default judgments that issued virtually automatically. In all Ancient Near Eastern cultures, it was understood to have been given by God himself and reserved for those most difficult of cases where the defendant could not be found or if found, could not be compelled to come to court to answer the charges. Three features stand out.

(1) No formal court was required. The swearing of the Oath of Innocence created a court where God himself was the judge.

(2) No summons of a defendant was required. The swearing of the Oath of Innocence dispensed with the need for a summons.

(3) No witnesses were required. The confessions within the Oath of Innocence made by the deponent provided all the evidentiary testimony needed.

The Oath of Innocence could be used as a shield or as a sword. When a person such as Job was suspected of wrongdoing or was the victim of wrongdoing, that person could swear out an Oath of Innocence in the presence of God declaring his innocence and condemning the actual wrongdoer. And the Oath of Innocence would be accepted by any civil or criminal court as a final adjudication of the matters covered by the oath.[67]

The jurisdiction[68] for Job to put God on trial through an Oath of Innocence arises from the fact that there were no limits on who could be a defendant. It just had to be a person. And God guaranteed that he would hear the case. (1 Kings 8:31-32; 2 Chronicles 6:22-23; Deuteronomy 1:17)

1. Statement of Claim

Job's statement of claim is a simple one. God is the author of undeserved evil in the world. Job has a right to know the reason why. And God has taken away that right.

Job's raising of the Oath of Innocence instituted civil or criminal proceedings against God. Job was the first person in human history to ever raise this Oath of Innocence against God. The Oath of Innocence operated as a civil statement of claim or a criminal indictment of the actual wrongdoer. If the wrongdoer was not known or being known, could not be found, then the raising of the Oath of Innocence constituted proof of service on the wrongdoer. Job had finally found his way of summoning God. The wrongdoer was summoned by the oath to immediately appear before the court. The swearing of the Oath of Innocence instituted an immediate summary trial in absentia. The trial commenced the very moment the Oath of Innocence was sworn.

(1) Job opens his Oath of Innocence with an oath sworn in the presence of Almighty God.

"*As God lives, who has taken away my right,* and the Almighty, who has made my soul bitter, as long as my breath is in me and the spirit of God is in my nostrils, *my lips will not speak falsehood, and my tongue will not utter deceit.*" (Job 27:2-4 Italics added for emphasis)

As God is omnipresent, the oath is sworn on the ash heap on which Job sits and not in any temple. Job is always in the presence of God. The oath is sworn on the very life of God himself. Paradoxically, Job swears the oath by the very God who has wronged him. This is a clear indication that Job believes God has a reason for sending the evil in the first place. It is an act of great faith.

(2) Job's statement of claim begins with that actual act of swearing the oath, but continues beyond it.

"*God...has taken away my right,* the Almighty... has made my soul bitter... *Far be it from me to say that you are right; until I die I will not put away my integrity from me. I hold fast my righteousness, and will not let it go; my heart does not reproach me for any of my days.*" (Job 27:2-6 Italics added for emphasis)

Job is clearly putting his eternal life on the line here. The expression "far be it from me" is a weak translation of the Hebrew "halilah", which really means "I'm damned". [69] Job is saying "I'll be damned if

I do not demand an answer of God. I'll be damned if I ever let him off the hook without an answer." This passage has profound implications for understanding Job's second speech to God and precludes any withdrawal of the lawsuit.

(3) Later in the Oath of Innocence, he would add a very personal statement of the loss he has suffered through God's creation of a world of undeserved and unremitted suffering.

"But now they make sport of me, those who are younger than I, whose fathers I would have disdained to set with the dogs of my flock. What could I gain from the strength of their hands? All their vigor is gone. Through want and hard hunger they gnaw the dry and desolate ground, they pick mallow and the leaves of bushes, and to warm themselves the roots of broom. They are driven out from society; people shout after them as after a thief. In the gullies of wadis they must live, in holes in the ground, and in the rocks. Among the bushes they bray; under the nettles they huddle together. A senseless, disreputable brood, they have been whipped out of the land. "And now they mock me in song; I am a byword to them. They abhor me, they keep aloof from me; they do not hesitate to spit at the sight of me. Because God has loosed my bowstring and humbled me, they have cast off restraint in my presence. On my right hand the rabble rise up; they send me sprawling, and build roads for my ruin. They break up my path, they promote my calamity; no one restrains them. As through a wide breach they come; amid the crash they roll on. Terrors are turned upon me; my honor is pursued as by the wind, and my prosperity has passed away like a cloud. "And now my soul is poured out within me; days of affliction have taken hold of me. The night racks my bones, and the pain that gnaws me takes no rest. With violence he seizes my garment; he grasps me by the collar of my tunic. He has cast me into the mire, and I have become like dust and ashes. I cry to you and you do not answer me; I stand, and you merely look at me. You have turned cruel to me; with the might of your hand you persecute me. You lift me up on the wind, you make me ride on it, and you toss me about in the roar of the storm. I know that you will bring me to death, and to the house appointed for all living. "Surely one does not turn against the needy, when in disaster they cry for help. Did I not weep for those whose day was hard? Was not my soul grieved for the poor? But *when I looked for good, evil came; and when I waited for light, darkness came.* My inward parts are in turmoil, and are never still; days of affliction come to meet me. I go about in sunless gloom; I stand up in the assembly and cry for help. I am a brother of jackals, and a companion of ostriches. My skin turns black and falls from me, and my bones burn with heat. My lyre is turned to mourning, and my pipe to the voice of those who weep." (Job 29:1- 30:31 Italics added for emphasis.)

(4) The swearing of the claim is service of that claim on the alleged wrongdoer; in this case, God. Job has identified God as the wrongdoer in the opening sentence: "God...who has taken away my right". (Job 27:2)

However, Job deepens that identification. The answers he seeks are the answers only God has. So Job incorporates a traditional hymn to God into his oath. It is a hymn to wisdom. In Job's mouth, the wisdom in question becomes the answer to why there is evil in the world.

"Surely there is a mine for silver, and a place for gold to be refined. Iron is taken out of the earth, and copper is smelted from ore. Miners put an end to darkness, and search out to the farthest bound the ore in gloom and deep darkness. They open shafts in a valley away from human habitation; they are forgotten by travelers, they sway suspended, remote from people. As for the earth, out of it comes bread; but underneath it is turned up as by fire. Its stones are the place of sapphires, and its dust contains gold. "That path no bird of prey knows, and the falcon's eye has not seen it. The proud wild animals have not trodden it; the lion has not passed over it. "They put their hand to the flinty rock, and overturn mountains by the roots. They cut out channels in the rocks, and their eyes see every precious thing. The sources of the rivers they probe; hidden things they bring to light. "*But where shall wisdom be found? And where is the place of understanding?* Mortals do not know the way to it, and it is not found in the land of the living. The deep says, 'It is not in me,' and the sea says, 'It is not with me.' It cannot be gotten for gold, and silver cannot be weighed out as its price. It cannot be valued in the gold of Ophir, in precious onyx or sapphire. Gold and glass cannot equal it, nor can it be exchanged for jewels of fine gold. No mention shall be made of coral or of crystal; the price of wisdom is above pearls. The chrysolite of Ethiopia cannot compare with it, nor can it be valued in pure gold. *"Where then does wisdom come from? And where is the place of understanding? It is hidden from the eyes of all living*, and concealed from the birds of the air. Abaddon and Death say, 'We have heard a rumor of it with our ears.' *"God understands the way to it, and he knows its place. For he looks to the ends of the earth, and sees everything under the heavens. When he gave to the wind its weight, and apportioned out the waters by measure; when he made a decree for the rain, and a way for the thunderbolt; then he saw it and declared it; he established it, and searched it out. And he said to humankind, 'Truly, the fear of the Lord, that is wisdom; and to depart from evil is understanding.* "' (Job 28:1-28 Italics added for emphasis)

In Job's mouth, this hymn to wisdom becomes a poetic style of cause. It identifies the wrongdoer God as the object of the lawsuit. Only God has the answer. And only God can give it. Job "fears God and turns from evil". (Job 1:1,8; 2:3) This wise and understanding servant demands an answer from his master.

In adopting this hymn to wisdom, Job may be ironically playing off Eliphaz's earlier jibe.

"If you return to the Almighty, you will be restored, if you remove unrighteousness from your tents, if you treat gold like dust, and gold of Ophir like the stones of the torrent-bed, and if the Almighty is your gold and your precious silver, then you will delight yourself in the Almighty, and lift up your face to God. You will pray to him, and he will hear you, and you will pay your vows. You will decide on a matter, and it will be established for you, and light will shine on your ways." (Job 22:24-27)

Eliphaz had unknowingly tempted Job to manipulate God into restoring his former position by falsely repenting. Manipulation Satan had claimed was the essence of sin. In his Oath of Innocence, Job turns to God not in repentance, but in the integrity of his ways. This hymn and Eliphaz's earlier comments link precious stones and metals with a plea to God. Eliphaz had contemplated a successful plea. The "matter" "will be established for you." (Job 22:27) At this point, Job seems to be goading both Eliphaz and God. Ultimately, the matter will be "established" in Job's favour, though not in the way Eliphaz intended. Job will be declared by God to have spoken rightly about God. (Job 42:7-8) The Hebrew word "kuwn" there means "established with certainty".[70] It will be established that Job has a right to know the reason behind evil and God is the author of undeserved evil..

(5) In any event, Job drives home his service of the Oath of Innocence on God with his next to last words in the oath.

"Oh, that I had one to hear me! (*Here is my signature! let the Almighty answer me!*) Oh, that I had the indictment written by my adversary! Surely I would carry it on my shoulder; I would bind it on me like a crown; I would give him an account of all my steps; like a prince I would approach him." (Job 31:35-37)

Job's three friends are left speechless. It is a formal indictment of God for crimes against humanity.

Job signs his signature to the Oath of Innocence with a mark in the air. The Hebrew word here for "signature" is "tau" meaning a "mark". In the ancient Hebrew language, that mark was made through the sign of the cross: "+".[71] With his right hand, Job makes the sign of the cross in the air and swears by it.

Within a canonical perspective, Job's action reverberates down through the halls of scripture. Job is a suffering servant, a Christ figure. This moment is his garden of Gethsemane. But rather than saying "not my will but thy will be done", Job is saying the opposite: "let my will, not thy will, be done". Time will tell if his will is God's will. *The Book of Job* rewrites what will become an important part of *The Gospels of Matthew, Mark, Luke and John*. The righteous man or woman of God may be a suffering servant, but he or she need not be a lamb that goes silent to the slaughter.

2. Proof of Claim

The proof of that claim is accomplished by a series of self-imposed curses in the Oath of Innocence by which Job puts his temporal life and eternal salvation on the line. Ancient legal codes are very unclear as to whether the normal civil standard of proof was proof on a balance of probability and whether the normal criminal standard of proof was proof beyond a reasonable doubt. In any event, it did not matter. The swearing of the Oath of Innocence established proof beyond all possible doubt. It converted a summary trial into a summary default proceeding.

(1) Job's positive confession surfaces early in the Oath of Innocence. Job stands on his personal integrity, his blamelessness..

"As long as breath is in me and the spirit of God is in my nostrils, *my lips will not speak falsehood, and my tongue will not utter deceit...Until I die I will not put away integrity from me. I hold fast my righteousness, and will not let it go; my heart does not reproach me for any of my days.*" (Job 27:2-6 Italics added for emphasis.)

The raising of the oath is an expression of the integrity that God has already declared in heaven to be beyond reproach. (Job 1:8; 2:3)

Job deepens that positive confession with a recounting of his former life. Job was once a judge who did justice in both his personal and professional lives.

"Oh, that I were as in the months of old, as in the days when God watched over me; when his lamp shone over my head, and by his light I walked through darkness; when I was in my prime, when the friendship of God was upon my tent; when the Almighty was still with me, when my children were around me; when my steps were washed with milk, and the rock poured out for me streams of oil! When I went out to the gate of the city, when I took my seat in the square, the young men saw me and withdrew, and the aged rose up and stood; the nobles refrained from talking, and laid their hands on their mouths; the voices of princes were hushed, and their tongues stuck to the roof of their mouths. When the ear heard, it commended me, and when the eye saw, it approved; *because I delivered the poor who cried, and the orphan who had no helper. The blessing of the wretched came upon me, and I caused the widow's heart to sing for joy. I put on righteousness, and it clothed me; my justice was like a robe and a turban. I was eyes to the blind, and feet to the lame. I was a father to the needy, and I championed the cause of the stranger. I broke the fangs of the unrighteous, and made them drop their prey from their teeth. Then I thought, 'I shall die in my nest, and I shall multiply my days like the phoenix; my roots spread out to the waters, with the dew all night on my branches; my glory was fresh with me, and my bow ever new in my hand.' "They listened to me, and waited, and kept silence for my counsel. After I spoke they did not speak again, and my word dropped upon them like dew. They waited for me as for the rain; they opened their mouths as for the spring rain. I smiled on them when they had no confidence; and the light of my countenance they did not extinguish. I chose their way, and sat as chief, and I lived like a king among his troops, like one who comforts mourners."* (Job 29:2-25 Italics added for emphasis.)

Job consistently met the needs of those in need. He perfectly fulfilled the demands of justice and love. He now calls on God to do the same.

It is worth noting Job's allusion to the phoenix. (Job 29:18) In Ancient Near Eastern mythologies, the phoenix was a symbol of moral righteousness. Through its righteousness, it earned the right to a long life and the right to resurrection and eternal life. Every 500 to 1500 years depending on the myth, the phoenix would die in its nest, be renewed and reborn by a fire from God.[72] Job claims the moral righteousness that is the right to resurrection and eternal life.

(2) Job's negative confession occurs near the end of his Oath of Innocence. It consists of sixteen self-imposed curses. The gist of these curses is two-fold. It is as if Job is saying:

"If I have sinned in thought, word or deed, then let me be cursed forever. But if I have not sinned in thought, word or deed, then I reserve to myself the right to curse my enemy for what he has done to me."

Job is putting his temporal and eternal life on the line. Job has already indicated he would suffer the "unrelenting pain" of a hell to get that answer. (Job 6:10) And now he is preparing to condemn or damn God to such a metaphorical hell should he not get his answer.

1. *[If]* I have made a covenant with my eyes; how then could I look upon a virgin? What would be my portion from God above, and my heritage from the Almighty on high? Does not calamity befall the unrighteous, and disaster the workers of iniquity? Does he not see my ways, and number all my steps? (Job 31:1-4)

2. "If I have walked with falsehood, and my foot has hurried to deceit-- let me be weighed in a just balance, and let God know my integrity!— (Job 31:5-6)

3. if my step has turned aside from the way, and my heart has followed my eyes, and if any spot has clung to my hands; then let me sow, and another eat; and let what grows for me be rooted out. (Job 31:7-8)

4. "If my heart has been enticed by a woman, and I have lain in wait at my neighbor's door; then let my wife grind for another, and let other men kneel over her. For that would be a heinous crime; that would be a criminal offense; for that would be a fire consuming down to Abaddon, and it would burn to the root all my harvest. (Job 31:9-12)

5. "If I have rejected the cause of my male or female slaves, when they brought a complaint against me; what then shall I do when God rises up? When he makes inquiry, what shall I answer him? Did not he who made me in the womb make them? And did not one fashion us in the womb?" (Job 31:13-15)

6. "If I have withheld anything that the poor desired, or have caused the eyes of the widow to fail, or have eaten my morsel alone, and the orphan has not eaten from it-- for from my youth I reared the orphan like a father, and from my mother's womb I guided the widow— (Job 31:16-18)

7. if I have seen anyone perish for lack of clothing, or a poor person without covering, whose loins have not blessed me, and who was not warmed with the fleece of my sheep; (Job 31:21:19-20)

8. if I have raised my hand against the orphan, because I saw I had supporters at the gate; then let my shoulder blade fall from my shoulder, and let my arm be broken from its socket. For I was in terror of calamity from God, and I could not have faced his majesty. (Job 31:21-23)

9. "If I have made gold my trust, or called fine gold my confidence; (Job 31:24)

10. if I have rejoiced because my wealth was great, or because my hand had gotten much; (Job 31:25)

11. if I have looked at the sun when it shone, or the moon moving in splendor, and my heart has been secretly enticed, and my mouth has kissed my hand; this also would be an iniquity to be punished by the judges, for I should have been false to God above." (Job 31:26-28)

12.: "If I have rejoiced at the ruin of those who hated me, or exulted when evil overtook them-- I have not let my mouth sin by asking for their lives with a curse—(Job 31:29-30)

13. if those of my tent ever said, 'O that we might be sated with his flesh!'-- the stranger has not lodged in the street; I have opened my doors to the traveler—(Job 31:31-32)

14. if I have concealed my transgressions as others do, by hiding my iniquity in my bosom, because I stood in great fear of the multitude, and the contempt of families terrified me, so that I kept silence, and did not go out of doors—(Job 31:33-34)

15. "If my land has cried out against me, and its furrows have wept together; (Job 31:38)

16. if I have eaten its yield without payment, and caused the death of its owners; let thorns grow instead of wheat, and foul weeds instead of barley." (Job 31:39-40 Italics and paragraphing added for emphasis.)

A number of items here merit comment. The standard of social justice Job claims to have met is centuries, perhaps even millennia, ahead of its time. All human beings are created equal by

God. Every person, regardless of rank or wealth, is entitled to the equal benefit and protection of the law. (Job 31:13-15) The standard of personal righteousness Job claims to have met is very high. The sins denied are not merely deeds, but words and thoughts. This standard greatly exceeds the traditionally accepted Old Testament norm of morality.[73]

Perhaps, the most interesting passage is Job's denial that he has "concealed transgressions as others do." (Job 31:34) The actual Hebrew text reads "as Adam did".[74] This is clearly a reference to original sin. The essence of Adam's sin was that he failed to take personal responsibility for his actions and be forgiven on the spot by God. Job claims he does not do as Adam did and would not have done what Adam did. Within a canonical perspective, this is a profound rewriting of *The Book of Genesis* and a rejection of most formulations of the doctrine of original sin. Human beings can be perfect, both in terms of righteousness and justice. Job claims to be such a human being.

Job's negative confession has remarkable parallels to the Egyptian Oath of Innocence and notable differences.

In Egyptian mythology, the Oath of Innocence is found in the Egyptian Book of the Dead, dated to between 1500 and 1350 BC. The Oath of Innocence occurs in the context of the Final Judgment. The soul is ushered into the Halls of Maat. "Maat" means "order, truth, and justice" and it describes the natural moral order that underlies all of creation.[75] The soul appears before the high God Osiris, the Lord of the Underworld and the Judge of the dead.[76] Here the soul is asked to swear a formal Oath of Innocence. The oath is a negative one. It describes the sins a person has not committed. It is sworn in the presence of Osiris himself and the forty-two divine jurors that represent the forty-two districts in the land of Egypt.[77]

"Usekh-nemmt from Anu - I haven't committed sin.
Hept-khet from Kher-aha - I haven't committed robbery with violence.
Fenti from Kemenu- I haven't stolen.
Am-khaibit from Qernet - I haven't slain men and women.
Neha-her from Rasta - I haven't stolen grain.
Ruruti from heaven - I haven't purloined offerings.
Arfi-em-khet from Suat - I haven't stolen the property of God.

Neba, who comes and goest - I haven't uttered lies.
Set-qesu from Hensu - I haven't carried away food.
Utu-nesert from Het-ka-Ptah - I haven't uttered curses.
Qerrti from Amentet - I haven't committed adultery - I haven't lain with men.
Her-f-ha-f from thy cavern - I have made none to weep.
Basti from Bast - I haven't eaten the heart.
Ta-retiu from the night - I haven't attacked any man.
Unem-snef from the execution chamber - I am not a man of deceit.
Unem-besek from Mabit - I haven't stolen cultivated land.
Neb-Maat from Maati - I haven't been an eavesdropper.
Tenemiu from Bast - I haven't slandered no man.
Sertiu from Anu - I haven't been angry without just cause.
Tutu from Ati (the Busirite Nome) - I haven't debauched the wife of any man.
Uamenti from the Khebt chamber - I haven't debauched the wife of any man.
Maa-antuf from Per-Menu - I haven't polluted myself.
Her-uru from Nehatu - I have terrorized none.
Khemiu from Kaui - I haven't transgressed the law.
Shet-kheru from Urit - I haven't been wroth.
Nekhenu from Heqat - I haven't shut my ears to the words of truth.
Kenemti from Kenmet - I haven't blasphemed.
An-hetep-f from Sau - I am not a man of violence.
Sera-kheru from Unaset - I haven't been a stirrer up of strife.
Neb-heru from Netchfet - I haven't acted with undue haste.
Sekhriu from Uten - I haven't pried into matters.
Neb-abui from Sauti - I haven't multiplied my words in speaking.
Nefer-Tem from Het-ka-Ptah - I have wronged none - I have done no evil.
Tem-Sepu from Tetu - I haven't worked witchcraft against the king.
Ari-em-ab-f from Tebu - I have never stopped the flow of water.
Ahi from Nu - I have never raised my voice.
Uatch-rekhit from Sau - I haven't cursed God.
Neheb-ka from thy cavern - I haven't acted with arrogance.
Neheb-nefert from thy cavern - I haven't stolen the bread of the gods.

Tcheser-tep from the shrine - I haven't carried away the khenfu
cakes from the Spirits of the dead.
An-af from Maati - I haven't snatched away the bread of a
child, nor treated with contempt the city god.
Hetch-abhu from Ta-she (the Fayyum) - I haven't slain the
cattle belonging to the god."[78]

The sins denied are both ceremonial and moral. The ceremonial sins
are about ten in number, constituting almost a quarter of the entire
oath. The moral sins are almost exclusively sins of deed. There is
perhaps one sin of word, the cursing of God. It is a stark contrast to
Job's Oath of Innocence which consists entirely of moral sins. By
this oath, the soul puts its eternal life on the line. If the oath is false in
any respect, the person swearing the oath is eternally damned.

Once the Oath of Innocence is sworn, the heart of the person
is placed on the scales of justice and weighed against a feather of
truth.[79]   In Egyptian thinking, the heart represents the person. The
feather of truth represents Maat, the natural moral order. If the two
balance equally on the scales of justice, then the soul is vindicated.
Its life has been in accordance with the natural moral order.[80] And it
may proceed into the halls of the righteous for a favourable afterlife.[81]
Interestingly enough, Job has previously claimed "my heart does not
reproach me for any of my days" (Job 27:6) and asked in his negative
confession for the scales of justice: "let me be weighed in a just
balance and let God know my integrity!" (Job 31:6)

In Egyptian mythology, those who swear falsely and whose
lives are not in accordance with the moral order await a gruesome
fate. If the heart and the feather of truth do not balance equally on the
scales of justice, then the soul is condemned. Osiris sends it to a
chaos monster, Ammit, seated beside him. "Ammit" means the
"gobbler". Ammit is part crocodile, part lion and part hippopotamus,
representing the destructive powers of chaos. Ammit is seated beside
a lake of burning fire.[82]   The condemned soul is consumed by the
chaos monster and passes into non-existence.[83]   This aspect of the
Egyptian Oath of Innocence sets an ominous backdrop to Job's Oath
of Innocence. When God examines him in his second speech, the
chaos monster Leviathan is there beside God to devour Job if Job has
in any way sworn falsely in any aspect of his Oath of Innocence.

Egyptian theology never reached the height of ethical monotheism because of the corrupting power of magic. The essence of magic is power. The power in question is the power to overpower the gods and the demonic. Over time, magic corrupted the use of the Oath of Innocence in the Final Judgment and deprived it of its moral quality. Charms and spells were used to supplement the oath and overpower the gods, especially Osiris. A special heart scarab was always buried with the deceased. It "was thought to prevent the heart from owning up to any crimes the person had committed in life." This was important because the oath was sworn before the heart is weighed. The testimony of the heart might contradict the testimony of the lips. A correct recitation of the Oath of Innocence, using the proper pronunciation and tone,[84] coupled with the possession of a heart scarab was deemed magically sufficient to guarantee the soul a favourable judgment on the scales of justice. Through magic, things always balanced out.[85] Osiris, the god of judgment, became a rubber stamp. Morality was reduced to magical ritual. Job's Oath of Innocence is grounded in morality not magic. When God appears to answer Job, God is bound only by morality not magic.

3. Enforcement of claim

The enforcement of that claim is through a summary default procedure. When the actual wrongdoer, in this case God, did not show up and enter a defense to the Oath of Innocence, a two-fold summary default judgment would immediately issue.

(1) The first judgment was automatic. The person swearing the Oath of Innocence Job would be immediately vindicated of any suspected wrongdoing and the actual wrongdoer God would be immediately convicted of the alleged wrongdoing. That first judgment of vindication or justification was a finding of causal responsibility. Job would be found innocent of any responsibility in the evil that befell him. God would be found responsible for the undeserved evil that befell Job.

(2) The second judgment was almost as automatic, but it issued differently. The person swearing the Oath of Innocence, Job was legally entitled to proceed further and condemn the actual wrongdoer God. The condemnation was a curse separate from oath itself. That second judgment of condemnation was the actual imposition of blame, shame and guilt on the one causally responsible.

The person swearing the Oath of Innocence Job would then formally curse the wrongdoer God.

Both these were summary judgments were default judgments delivered "in absentia".

It should be remembered that God himself in giving the Oath of Innocence had promised that he would execute those summary default judgments. (1 Kings 8:31-32; 2 Chronicles 6:22-23)

That curse is foreshadowed early in the Oath of Innocence.

"May my enemy be like the wicked, and may my opponent be like the unrighteous. For what is the hope of the godless when God cuts them off, when God takes away their lives? Will God hear their cry when trouble comes upon them? Will they take delight in the Almighty? Will they call upon God at all times? I will teach you concerning the hand of God; that which is with the Almighty I will not conceal. All of you have seen it yourselves; why then have you become altogether vain?"(Job 27:7-12)

"This is the portion of the wicked with God, and the heritage that oppressors receive from the Almighty: If their children are multiplied, it is for the sword; and their offspring have not enough to eat. Those who survive them the pestilence buries, and their widows make no lamentation. Though they heap up silver like dust, and pile up clothing like clay-- they may pile it up, but the just will wear it, and the innocent will divide the silver. They build their houses like nests, like booths made by sentinels of the vineyard. They go to bed with wealth, but will do so no more; they open their eyes, and it is gone. Terrors overtake them like a flood; in the night *a whirlwind carries them off.* The east wind lifts them up and they are gone; it sweeps them out of their place. It hurls at them without pity; they flee from its power in headlong flight. It claps its hands at them, and hisses at them from its place." (Job 27:13-23 Italics added for emphasis)

If God fails to answer Job's claim, then Job can activate that curse. That is the nature of a trial in absentia and a summary default judgment. He does so by speaking the curse a second time. "Let the one who has wronged me be cursed now and forever." This was something Satan had prophesized Job would do; namely, curse God to his face. God would then execute that judgment by bringing that curse upon himself. And Job has put in place the legal machinery to activate that curse.

Elihu

Job's Oath of Innocence calls for an answer from God. Yet Elihu boldly steps forward to give an answer that only God can give.[86]

The author of *The Book of Job* tempts the reader to welcome what Elihu might say, by describing Job as "righteous in his own eyes". (Job 32:1) The reference to "in his own eyes" should not seduce the reader, though it is surprising how many readers go astray at this point. Job is righteous and he knows it. The author and God have declared him righteous three times already. Job has repeated that claim to integrity. He has bolstered it with an Oath of Innocence, whereby he has put his temporal and eternal life on the line. It is all staked on his righteousness. Job is righteous in his own eyes and rightly so. Yet many assume Job is a sinner to demand that God give an answer to the question of why there is evil in the world.

But from then on, the author of *The Book of Job* undercuts everything that Elihu has to say. Elihu is presented as a "Buzite". His lineage has contributed to his character. The Hebrew noun "buz" means "contemptuous" or "contemptible" and occurs several other times in *The Book of Job* (Job 12:5,21; 31:34) with that sense.[87] The reader is being warned that Elihu is "contemptuous" and "contemptible". The real deconstruction of everything Elihu has to say however is fourfold.

(1) The author introduces Elihu as an angry youth, frustrated with Job and his three friends.

"So these three men ceased to answer Job, because he was righteous in his own eyes. Then Elihu son of Barachel the Buzite, of the family of Ram, became *angry*. He was *angry* at Job because he justified himself rather than God; he was *angry* also at Job's three friends because they had found no answer, though they had declared Job to be in the wrong. Now Elihu had waited to speak to Job, because they were older than he. But when Elihu saw that there was no answer in the mouths of these three men, he became *angry*." (Job 32:1-5 italics added)

Anger and youth are not qualities valued in the wisdom traditions of the ancient world. In fact, since Elihu is described as "angry" four times and four is the symbolic number for fullness, the author is probably saying Elihu is out of control.

(2) The author then has Elihu describe himself as a windbag in the most comic of ways.

"Elihu son of Barachel the Buzite answered: "I am young in years, and you are aged; therefore I was timid and afraid to declare my *opinion* to you. I said, 'Let days speak, and many years teach wisdom.' But truly it is the *spirit* in a mortal, the breath of the *Almighty*, that makes for understanding....Therefore I say, 'Listen to me; let me also declare my *opinion*.'....I also will give my answer; I also will declare my *opinion*. For *I am full of words; the spirit within me constrains me. My heart is indeed like wine that has no vent; like new wineskins, it is ready to burst. I must speak, so that I may find relief*; I must open my lips and answer." (Job 32:6:-8, 10, 17-20 Italics added)

Elihu claims to be filled with the spirit of the Almighty (Job 32:8). Yet he describes himself as being filled with the spirit of wine to such an extent that he has to vent. (Job 32:18-20) There is rich irony here. The NRSV obscures the extent of the humour with its translation "the spirit within me constrains me." (Job 32:18b) The Hebrew there is literally "the spirit or wind of my belly swells." The spirit or wind that swells his belly is nothing but fermenting gas.[88] The venting of that gas and bloating is flatulence and defecation. Elihu is so bloated and puffed up by his arrogance that he is about to fart. This is not the description of God's chief spokesperson; it is the description of Satan's dupe. And it is a timeless way of saying that all Elihu's words are but flatulence or defecation. All Elihu has to say is crap for it is nothing more than the opinion of an arrogant youth with no respect for his elders.

(3) The author has Elihu contradict himself in a most serious way on the nature of what has to say. Elihu admits twice that what he

offers is opinion, not knowledge. (Job 32:6,17)   Elihu then turns around and claims he has the perfect knowledge only God could have. "For truly my words are not false; one who is perfect in knowledge is before you." (Job 36:4) Yet the reader knows or should know by then that all Elihu has to offer is opinion not knowledge. (Job 32:6,17) And that opinion is crap.

(4) The author has Elihu promise he will not show partiality (Job 32:21) and repeat the arguments of Job's friends. (Job 32:14) Yet that is precisely what he does. And those arguments will later be condemned by God himself. (Job 42:7-8)

(a) On the denial of Job's moral purity, Elihu claims: "You [Job] say 'I am clean without transgression; I am pure, and there is no iniquity in me...but in this you are not right." (Job 33:9,12)   That claim merely repeats Eliphaz's earlier two comments: "Can mortals be righteous before God?   Can human beings be pure before their Maker?" (Job 4:17) "What are mortals , that they may be clean? Or those born of woman, that they can be righteous?" (Job 15:14), Zophar's earlier comment: "For you say, 'My conduct is pure and I am clean in God's sight.' But oh, that God would speak and open his lips to you..." (Job 11:4-5) and Bildad's earlier comment: "How then can a mortal be righteous before God? How can one born of woman be pure?" (Job 25:4)

(b) On the nature of Job's character, Elihu claims: "Who is there like Job, who drinks up scoffing like water..." (Job 34:7) That claim merely repeats Eliphaz's earlier comment: "how much less one [Job} who is abominable and corrupt, one who drinks iniquity like water." (Job 15:17)

(c) On the importance of Job to God, Elihu claims: "If you [Job] have sinned, what do you accomplish against him [God]? And if your transgressions are multiplied, what do you do to him? If you are righteous, what do you give to him; or what does he receive from your hand?" (Job 35:6-7) That claim merely repeats Eliphaz's earlier comment: "Can a mortal be of use to God? Can even the wisest be of service to him? Is it any pleasure to the Almighty if you are righteous, or is it gain to him if you make your ways blameless?" (Job 22:2-3)

(d) On the denial of the legitimacy of Job's moral claim against God, Elihu claims: "Far be it from God that he should do wickedness and from the Almighty that he should do wrong...Of a truth, God will not do wickedly, and the Almighty will not pervert justice." (Job 34:10,12) "You [Job] say, 'I am in the right before God'...Job opens his mouth in empty talk, he multiplies words without knowledge." (Job 35:1,16) Those claims merely repeat Bildad's comment: "How long will you say these things, and the words of your mouth be a great wind? Does God pervert justice? Or does the Almighty pervert the right? (Job 8:2-3) and Eliphaz's comment: "Should the wise answer in windy knowledge and fill themselves with the east wind? Should they argue in unprofitable talk." (Job 15:1)

(e) On the punishment Job allegedly deserves, Elihu claims: "Would that Job were tried to the limit, because his answers are those of the wicked." (Job 34:36) That claim merely repeats Zophar's earlier comment: "Know then that God exacts of you less than your guilt deserves..." (Job 11:6) and Eliphaz's earlier comment: "Is not your wickedness great?" (Job 22:5)

In spite of his questionable credentials, Elihu condemns Job four times. Job is a sinner. It is blasphemy to force God's hand. It is blasphemy to demand that God give an answer to the question of why there is evil in the world.

(1) Elihu clearly rejects Job's blamelessness: his cleanliness and purity.

"You say, 'I am *clean, without transgression*; I am *pure*, and there is *no iniquity in me*. Look, he finds occasions against me, *he counts me as his enemy*; he puts my feet in the stocks, and watches all my paths.' "But in this you are not right. I will answer you: God is greater than any mortal. Why do you contend against him, saying, *'He will answer none of my words'*?" (Job 33:9-13 Italics added for emphasis)

Elihu clearly has Job's moral cleanliness and moral purity in mind as the companion phrases "without transgression" and "no iniquity" confirm. Elihu claims Job is in fact a man of iniquity, a sinner. His sin is his claim that God is the author of undeserved evil. Hence, God treats or "counts" him as his "enemy." (Job 33:10) However, Elihu predicts God will not answer any of the words of such a sinner. (Job 33:13) God will soon prove Elihu a false prophet on both points.

(2) A short time later, Elihu unwittingly adopts a position that Satan himself has presented in the first scene in heaven.

"Let us choose what is right; let us determine among ourselves what is good. For Job has said, 'I am innocent, and God has taken away my right; in spite of being right I am counted a liar; my wound is incurable, though I am without transgression.' Who is there like Job, who drinks up scoffing like water, who goes in company with evildoers and walks with the wicked? *For he has said, 'It profits one nothing to take delight in God.' "Therefore, hear me, you who have sense, far be it from God that he should do wickedness, and from the Almighty that he should do wrong.* For according to their deeds he will repay them, and according to their ways he will make it befall them. *Of a truth, God will not do wickedly, and the Almighty will not pervert justice.*"(Job 34:5-12 Italics added for emphasis)

Elihu cannot conceive of a selfless love for God free from selfishness. That was Satan's position. And Elihu is quick to pass judgment on Job for saying so. It would be an act of wicked and injustice for God not to reward the righteous. Through those words, Elihu has unwittingly condemned God.

(3) And a short time after that, Elihu describes Job as a wicked fool, deserving more evil than that which he has already suffered.

"Job speaks without knowledge, his words are without insight.' Would that Job were tried to the limit, because his answers are those of the wicked. For he adds rebellion to his sin; he claps his hands among us, and multiplies his words against God." (Job 34:35-37)

In Jewish theology, rebellion (disloyalty) is perhaps the greatest sin imaginable. Elihu describes Job as one of the greatest sinners imaginable. He merits one of the greatest possible punishments. This is a far cry from the consolation and comfort Job's friends first came to give.

(4) And Elihu ends his criticism of Job with a repetition of his earlier comments.

"Surely God does not hear an empty cry, nor does the Almighty regard it. How much less when you say that you do not see him, that the case is before him, and you are waiting for him! And now, because his anger does not punish, and he does not greatly heed transgression, Job opens his mouth in empty talk, he multiplies words without knowledge."....Surely God does not hear an empty cry, nor does the Almighty regard it. How much less when you say that you do not see him, that the case is before him, and you are waiting for him! And now, because his anger does not punish, and he does not greatly heed transgression, Job opens his mouth in empty talk, he multiplies words without knowledge." (Job 35:1-8, 13-16)

God will neither hear Job's cry nor give it any regard. Almost as he says this, the golden whirlwind can be heard and seen on the horizon (Job 37:1-2, 22-23). God has heard and attends to the cry of his beloved son Job.

Job has previously warned his friends, Elihu included, to show no deceit or partiality on behalf of God when discussing the question of why there is evil in the world.

"Hear now my reasoning, and listen to the pleadings of my lips. Will you speak falsely for God, and speak deceitfully for him? Will you show partiality toward him, will you plead the case for God? Will it be well with you when he searches you out? Or can you deceive him, as one person deceives another? He will surely rebuke you if in secret you show partiality. Will not his majesty terrify you, and the dread of him fall upon you? Your maxims are proverbs of ashes, your defenses are defenses of clay." (Job 13:6-12)

They are not to prejudge the case in favor of God. They have all done so, Elihu most of all.

Early in his speeches, Elihu promised: "I will not show partiality to any person or use flattery toward anyone. For I do not know how to flatter-- or my Maker would soon put an end to me!" (Job 32:21-23) Yet as with everything else, Elihu promises more than he delivers. Despite his promises, Elihu prematurely condemns Job and prematurely acquits God. In doing so, Elihu is condemned by the words of his own mouth. The evil in Job's life and in the world constitutes a prima facie case of wrongdoing on the part of God. Only God can answer those charges. Elihu flatters and damns himself when he thinks he can speak for God.

Elihu's comments here may be suggestive of his final fate. "Or my Maker would soon put an end to me!" (Job 32:21-23) As he describes the majestic coming of God, "his heart trembles and leaps out of its place." (Job 37:1) God is about to answer Job, something Elihu never dreamed possible. And Elihu probably suspects that a stern rebuke awaits him for his own presumption, a rebuke that will end his life. He is filled with the "terror" and the "dread" of which Job spoke. (Job 13:11) In such circumstances, it is probable this unstable youth flees the coming of his judge.

At least, Elihu disappears at this point in the book, never to reappear again. He is certainly not present for God's condemnation of Job's three friends. Were he present for that condemnation, that condemnation would certainly include him. His words were more vicious and more presumptuous than those of Job's friends. In all likelihood, this Judas has fled the scene of his crime. And failing to remain and take responsibility for his great sins, he is not in a position to be forgiven by God when Job ultimately asks for forgiveness for his friends.

4: PUTTING GOD ON TRIAL

Act 3 in *The Book of Job* might be entitled *Putting God on Trial* for, within a canonical perspective, it reworks the *Revelation* story. The Oath of Innocence trumpets a Final Judgment, a judgment on God himself. God is summoned to the bar of universal justice to give a defense for the world he has created.

God's Appearance in a Golden Whirlwind

To the astonishment of all, God appears before this court of justice. God appears in the form of a golden whirlwind. (Job 37:22; 38:1)

In part, the whirlwind is a cloak for God's own goodness. On the terms of God's own trial, God cannot fully disclose his purpose in creation. In part, the whirlwind mirrors the whirl of emotions in the three cycles of speeches that have immediately preceded it. This is the culmination of that discussion.

But more importantly, the golden whirlwind is a powerful mythological symbol for the divine control of evil. The mythological background is primarily the Babylonian myth of creation. And its use here intimates God's discussion of Leviathan to follow in his second speech to Job.

In Ancient Near Eastern creation myths, goodness is order; evil is chaos. The creation of the world and the creation of humankind is the imposition of order on chaos. Creation is not creation out of nothing, but rather creation out of chaos. The chaos consists of pre-existent physical materials which are inherently difficult to control. Those pre-existent materials are usually described in terms of water, probably because of its shapelessness. Those pre-existent materials are usually pictured as a sea monster or monsters within the water, though they represent the water itself. All the monsters are one: chaos. Any multiplication of monsters is merely for dramatic effect. The creation of the world is a divine struggle to impose order on this pre-existent chaos. That struggle is pictured through a combat motif in which the high God battles the chaos monsters, defeating them, killing some and imprisoning others. It is the triumph of good over evil. The world is created out of the body of a slain chaos monster. Land emerges out of the water. Form has been imposed on chaos. The primordial waters of chaos are then confined to the waters above the firmament (the heavens), to the waters below the firmament (the underworld) and to the waters surrounding the firmament (the oceans that circle the world). Humankind is then created out of the blood of a slain chaos monster. This is the poetic way of saying four things.

(1) Evil is all around us.

(2) Evil is deep within us.

(3) Evil is part of the very fabric of creation.

(4) And evil is part of God's very purpose in creation.

The Babylonian myth of creation typifies these Ancient Near Eastern creation myths.

In the the Babylonian myth of creation, the whirlwind is the identifying sign of the high God Marduk's triumph over evil. Marduk himself is draped in golden auras.

"His body was magnificent, fiery his glance,
He was a hero at birth,
he was a mighty one from the beginning!
….
He wore (on his body) the aura of ten gods,
had (them) wrapped around his head (?) too,
Fifty glories were heaped upon him.
Anu formed and produced the four winds,
He put them in his hand, "Let my son play!"[89]

Marduk holds in his hand the whirlwind and because he is golden, the whirlwind becomes a golden whirlwind. The phrase "Let my son play!" can mean "My son, let them whirl" referring to the winds.[90] Marduk is the storm God. The play in question is the imposition of order on chaos. The whirlwind is the identifying sign of the imposition of that order. "He fashioned dust, he made a storm bear it up, He caused a wave and it roiled Tiamat, Tiamat was roiled, churning day and night, The gods, finding no rest, bore the brunt of each wind."[91] Tiamat is the pre-existent evil that is chaos. When

Marduk goes to do battle with Tiamat, he takes a variety of weapons, the most important of which is the whirlwind.

> "He made the bow, appointed it his weapon,
> He mounted the arrow, set it on the string,
> He took up the mace, held it in his right hand,
> Box and quiver he slung on his arm.
> Thunderbolts he set before his face.
> With raging fire he covered his body.
> Then he made a net to enclose Tiamat within.
> He deployed the four winds that none of her might escape:
> South Wind, North Wind, East Wind, West Wind,
> Gift of his grandfather Anu, he fastened the net at his side.
> He made ill wind, whirlwind, cyclone.
> Four-ways wind, seven-ways wind, destructive wind, irresistible wind:
> He released the winds which he had made, the seven of them,
> Mounting in readiness behind him to roil inside Tiamat."[92]

The four winds, the seven winds circle together to create the irresistible ill wind, the whirlwind. The whirlwind is the vehicle by which Marduk defeats evil.

> "Tiamat and Marduk, sage of the gods, drew close for battle,
> They locked in single combat, joining for the fray.
> The Lord spread out his net, encircled her,
> The ill wind he had held behind him, he released in her face.
> Tiamat opened her mouth to swallow,
> He thrust the ill wind so she could not close her lips.
> The raging winds bloated her belly,
> Her insides were stopped up, she gaped her mouth wide.
> He shot off the arrow, it broke open her belly,
> It cut to her innards, it pierced her heart.
> He subdued her and snuffed out her life.
> He flung down her carcass, he stood his stand upon it."[93]

Tiamat is killed as she opens her mouth to swallow the high God. She swallows the whirlwind and is destroyed from within. Marduk shoots an arrow through her mouth and it pierces her heart and tears open her belly. Her innards fall out. She is dead. And Marduk takes his stand on her dead carcass. The author's introduction of this

Babylonian image of a golden whirlwind intimates the introduction of the chaos monster Leviathan in God's second speech. Leviathan is the Jewish reworking of the Tiamat myth.

Yet the whirlwind is a morally ambiguous image for Job. He has previously complained to God that "you have turned cruel to me; with the might of your hand you persecute me. You lift me up on the wind, you make me ride on it, and you toss me about in the roar of the storm. I know that you will bring me to death, and to the house appointed for all the living." (Job 30:21-23) The whirlwind had already taken the lives of Job's children. (Job 1:19) And in light of his Oath of Innocence, Job has to be apprehensive that God has come to personally take his own life.

To the astonishment of all, Job is not struck dead for his claim. It is a silent witness Job is in the right. To the astonishment of all, God does not enter a defense to the claim made by Job. God is prohibited, on the terms of his own trial with Satan, from explicitly giving Job the reason for his suffering, lest that in turn give Job and humanity a reason to worship God and ultimately to manipulate God for their own ends. God is on trial for his life and his very purpose in creation and his hands are tied. God is forced into a strategy of indirection.

God's First Speech

In his first speech, God reviews the created order at length, challenging the extent of Job's wisdom not his innocence or his integrity. God hints that there is a purpose in all things, his concern is ongoing and a human being should be ever mindful of his or her created status.

1. Physical World

Job has asked, indeed Job has demanded, that God explain his activity in the world. Specifically, Job has asked and demanded that God answer the question why is there evil in the world.

So God proceeds to describe his activity in the world. God first reviews the physical world through seven things:

(1) the foundations of the earth (Job 38:4-7),

(2) the sea (Job 38:8-11),
(3) Sheol (Job 38:12-21),
(4) the storehouses of snow and hail (Job 38:22-24),   ·
(5) the rain (Job 38:25-30),
(6) the heavens (Job 38:31-33) and
(7) the lightning (Job 38:34-38).

Opening Question: Then the *LORD* answered Job out of the whirlwind: "Who is this that darkens counsel by words without *knowledge*? *Gird up your loins like a man*, I will question you, and you shall declare to me. (Job 38:1-3 Italics added for emphasis and clarification.)

Physical World

1. Foundations of the Earth: "Where were you when *I laid the foundation of the earth*? Tell me, if you have *understanding*. Who *determined its measurements*--surely you *know*! Or who *stretched the line upon it*? On what were its bases sunk, or who *laid* its cornerstone when the morning stars sang together and all the heavenly beings shouted for joy? (Job 38:4-7 Italics added for emphasis and clarification.)

2. Sea: "Or who *shut in the sea with doors when it burst out* from the womb? when I *made* the clouds its garment, and thick darkness its *swaddling band*, and *prescribed bounds for it, and set bars and doors, and said, 'Thus far shall you come, and no farther, and here shall your proud waves be stopped'?* (Job 38:8-11 Italics added for emphasis and clarification.)

3. Sheol: "Have you *commanded the morning* since your days began, and *caused the dawn to know its place*, so that it might take hold of the skirts of the earth, and the wicked be shaken out of it? It is changed like clay under the seal, and it is dyed like a garment. Light is withheld from the wicked, and their uplifted arm is broken. "Have you entered into the springs of the sea, or walked in the recesses of the deep? Have the gates of death been revealed to you, or have you seen the gates of deep darkness? Have you *comprehended* the expanse of the earth? Declare, if you know all this. "Where is the way to the dwelling of light, and where is the place of darkness, that you may take it to its territory and that you may discern the paths to its home? *Surely you know*, for you were born then, and the number of your days is great! (Job 38:12-21 Italics added for emphasis and clarification.)

4. Storehouses of snow and hail: "Have you entered the storehouses of the snow, or have you seen the storehouses of the hail, which *I have reserved* for the time of trouble, for the day of battle and war? What is the way to the place where the light is distributed, or where the east wind is scattered upon the earth? (Job 38:22-24 Italics added for emphasis and clarification.)

5. Rain: "Who has *cut a channel for the torrents of rain*, and a way for the thunderbolt, *to bring rain on a land where no one lives, on the desert, which is empty of human life, to satisfy the waste and desolate land, and to make the ground put forth grass*? "Has the rain a father, or who has begotten the drops of dew? From whose womb did the ice come forth, and who has given birth to the hoarfrost of heaven? The waters become hard like stone, and the face of the deep is frozen. (Job 38:25-30 Italics added for emphasis and clarification.)

6. Heavens: "Can you *bind the chains of the Pleiades, or loose the cords of Orion*? Can you *lead forth the Mazzaroth* in their season, or can you *guide the Bear with its children*? Do you *know the ordinances of the heavens*? Can you *establish their rule on the earth*? (Job 38:31-33 Italics added for emphasis and clarification.)

7. Lightning: "Can you lift up your voice to the clouds, so that a flood of waters may cover you? Can you send forth lightnings, so that they may go and say to you, 'Here we are'? *Who has put wisdom in the inward parts, or given understanding to the mind*? Who has the *wisdom* to number the clouds? Or who can tilt the waterskins of the heavens, when the dust runs into a mass and the clods cling together? (Job 38:34-38 Italics added for emphasis and clarification.)

2. Animal World

God then reviews the animal world through seven things:

(1) the wild lions (Job 38:38-41),
(2) the wild goats (Job 39:1-4),
(3) the wild ass (Job 39:5-8),
(4) the wild ox (Job 39:9-12),
(5) the wild ostrich (Job 39:13-18),
(6) the war horse (Job 39:13-18) and
(7) the birds of prey (Job 39:26-30).

Animal World

1. Wild Lions: "Can you hunt the *prey for the lion*, or *satisfy the appetite of the young lions*, when they crouch in their *dens*, or lie in wait in their covert? Who provides for the raven its prey, when its young ones cry to God, and wander about for lack of food? (Job 38:39-41 Italics added for emphasis and clarification.)

2. Wild Goats: "Do you know when the *mountain goats* give birth? Do you observe the calving of the deer? Can you number the months that they *fulfill*, and do you know the time when they give birth, when they crouch to give birth to their offspring, and are *delivered* of their young? Their young ones *become strong*, they *grow up* in the open; they *go forth*, and do not return to them. (Job 39:1-4 Italics added for emphasis and clarification.)

3. Wild Ass: "Who has let the *wild ass go free*? Who has *loosed the bonds of the swift ass*, to which I have given the steppe for its home, the salt land for its dwelling place? It scorns the tumult of the city; it does not hear the shouts of the driver. It ranges the mountains as its pasture, and it searches after every green thing. (Job 39:5-8 Italics added for emphasis and clarification.)

4. Wild Ox: "Is the wild ox willing to *serve you*? Will it spend the night at your crib? Can you tie it in the furrow with ropes, or will it harrow the valleys after you? Will you depend on it because its strength is great, and will you hand over your labor to it? Do you have faith in it that it will return, and bring your grain to your threshing floor? (Job 39:9-12 Italics added for emphasis and clarification.)

5. Wild Ostrich: "The ostrich's wings flap wildly, though its pinions lack plumage. For it leaves its eggs to the earth, and lets them be warmed on the ground, *forgetting* that a foot may crush them, and that a wild animal may trample them. It *deals cruelly with its young*, as if they were not its own; though its labor should be in vain, yet it has no fear; because God has made it forget wisdom, and given it no share in understanding. When it spreads its plumes aloft, it laughs at the *horse and its rider*. (Job 39:13-18 Italics added for emphasis and clarification.)

6. War Horse: "Do you give the *horse* its *might*? Do you clothe its neck with mane? Do you make it leap like the locust? Its *majestic snorting* is terrible. *It paws violently, exults mightily; it goes out to meet the weapons. It laughs at fear, and is not dismayed; it does not turn back from the sword. Upon it rattle the quiver, the flashing spear, and the javelin. With fierceness and rage it swallows the ground; it cannot stand still at the sound of the trumpet. When the trumpet sounds, it says 'Aha!' From a distance it smells the battle*, the thunder of the captains, and the shouting. (Job 39:13-18 Italics added for emphasis and clarification.)

7. Birds of Prey: "Is it by your *wisdom* that the *hawk soars*, and spreads its wings toward the south? Is it at your command that the eagle mounts up and makes its nest on high? It lives on the rock and makes its home in the fastness of the rocky crag. *From there it spies the prey; its eyes see it from far away. Its young ones suck up blood; and where the slain are, there it is.*" (Job 39:26-30 Italics added for emphasis and clarification.)

Concluding Question: And the LORD said to Job: "Shall a *faultfinder contend with the Almighty*? Anyone who argues with God *must respond*." (Job 40:1-2 Italics added for emphasis and clarification.)

Seven is a symbolic number and this is a symbolic review of all in the physical and animal worlds that God intends to reveal.

Significantly, God deliberately chooses not to review the human world. While his descriptions are extensive and often beautiful, they are entirely irrelevant to question at hand- God's moral activity in the creation of evil in the human world. At first glance, the whirlwind appears to be nothing more than a windbag. God goes round and round the world missing the moral point at every turn.

God seems to be making only one point. Job is ignorant and should be every mindful of his created status in challenging God. God hammers home that point time and time again- thirty five times in all. "Who is this that darkens counsel by word without knowledge?" (Job 38:1) "Declare to me" (Job 38:3) "Where were you?" (Job 38:4) "Who determined" (Job 38:5) "Have you" (Job 38:12) "Have you" (Job 38:16) "Have you" (Job 38:17) "Have you" (Job 38:18) "Declare, if you know all this" (Job 38:18) "Where is the way" (Job 38:19) "Surely you know" (Job 38:21) "Have you" (Job 38:22) "What is the way" (Job 38:24) "Who has" (Job 38:25) "Can you" (Job 38:21) "Can you" (Job 38:32) "Do you know" (Job 38:33) "Can you" (Job 38:33) "Can you" (Job 38:34) "Can you" (Job 38:35) "'Who has" (Job 38:36) "Can you" (Job 38:39) "Do you know" (Job 39:1) "Do you observe" (Job 39:1) "Can you" (Job 39:2) "Who has" (Job 39:1) "Who has" (Job 39:1) "Can you" (Job 39:10) "Will you" (Job 39:11) "Do you" (Job 39:12) "Do you" (Job 39:19) "Do you" (Job 39:19) "Do you" (Job 39:20) "Is it" (Job 39:26) "Is it" (Job 27) Yet God's point is of limited worth. Job has never claimed omniscience.

And Job has never questioned God's sovereignty. In fact, he gave at least three extended speeches on God's sovereignty. (Job 9:5-13; 12:7-15; 26:5-14) He acknowledges God performs "great things beyond understanding, marvelous things without number" (Job 9:10) and these things are but the "outskirts of his ways" (Job 26:14).

(a) On the subject of the physical world, Job has already acknowledged that God has created and is sovereign over (1) the foundations of the earth (9:8; 26:7 cf. 38:4-7), (2) the sea (Job 7:12; 26:8 cf. 38:8-11), (3) Sheol (Job 9:6-7; 7:9-10 cf. 38:12-21), (4) the rain (Job 12:15; cf. 38:25-30), (5) the heavens (Job 9:9 cf. 38:31-33), (6) the lightning and thunder (Job 26:14 cf. 38:34-38).

(b) On the subject of the animal world, Job has already acknowledged that God has created and is sovereign over (1) the wild lions (Job 10:16; 12:10 cf. 38:38-41), (2) the wild asses (Job 24:5 cf. 39:5-8); (3) the war horse (Job 10:13; 19:12 cf. 39:19-25) and (4) the birds of prey (Job 9:26; 39:26-30).

Virtually every question God puts to Job, Job has already answered in his prior speeches.

In his Oath of Innocence, Job has testified that God is the author of undeserved evil in the world and that human beings have a right to know the reason why. Those are the issues. God's defence might legitimately include a cross-examination of the plaintiff Job. But God is brow-beating the witness Job on a point that is irrelevant to the question at hand. In the entire *Bible,* this first speech is the longest speech God ever gives. It leaves Job and many a reader wondering what is God up to here and in the world.

On the terms of his own trial with Satan, God cannot give direct answers. Somehow whatever answer God does give is tied to the created status of men and women. Job certainly does not know what has happened in heaven. And God cannot tell him without defeating the very purpose of creation. God has to be harsh and evasive with Job. God cannot appear loving, lest Job find in kind words a reason to love God. If this is love, then it is the toughest love possible.

It should be noted that God's description of the physical animal worlds is a creation account. It begins with the statement "where were you when I laid the foundation of the earth?" (Job 38:4) What follows is a description of the physical and animal worlds as they were from their foundation. Of particular interest is God's comment "can you hunt the prey for the lion, or satisfy the appetite of the young lions...?" (Job 38:39) God has built into the very structure of things an almost Darwinian struggle for existence and the chaos that entails. This is a profound rewriting of the *1 Isaiah's* understanding of *The Book of Genesis* where the lion originally lay down with lamb in a time of primal innocence. (Isaiah 11:6-7) In *The Book of Job*, the lion has always eaten the lamb since the "foundation of the earth". (Job 38:4) Death in the natural world is not a result of Adam and Eve's sin.

God's description of the physical and animal worlds finds some interesting parallels in *Psalms 104* and *89*. Both psalms link the natural world with the mythological world. And God's use of similar language in his first speech should prompt the discerning reader to expect the appearance of Leviathan in God's second speech.

(1) *Psalm 104* is a myth of creation modeled on an earlier Egyptian myth of creation involving the high God Ra. However, the psalmist seems to have had before him a Canaanite copy of that myth, as evidenced by the use of a number of Canaanite words and images within this psalm.[94] Egypt and Canaan had extensive trading relations, so the cross-fertilization seems likely. Genesis 1 may have been modeled on this psalm itself, as the order of creation is quite close.[95] The date of composition is unknown.

"Bless the LORD, O my soul. O LORD my God, you are very great. You are clothed with honor and majesty, wrapped in light as with a garment. You *stretch out the heavens* like a tent, you set the beams of your chambers on the waters, you make the clouds your chariot, you ride on the wings of the wind, you make the winds your messengers, fire and flame your ministers. *You set the earth on its foundations*, so that it shall never be shaken. *You cover it with the deep as with a garment*; the waters stood above the mountains. At your rebuke they flee; at the sound of your thunder they take to flight. They rose up to the mountains, ran down to the valleys to *the place that you appointed for them. You set a boundary that they may not pass*, so that they might not again cover the earth. You make spring gush forth in the valley; they flow between the hills, giving drink to every wild animal; the *wild asses* quench their thirst…From your lofty abode *you water the mountains; the earth is satisfied* with the fruit of your work. You cause the *grass* to grow for the *cattle*…The high mountains are for the *wild goats*…You have make *the moon mark the seasons; the sun knows its time* for setting…The *young lions creep roar for their prey, seeking their food from God*. When the sun rises, they withdraw and lie down in their *dens*…Yonder is the *sea*, great and wide, *creeping things innumerable* are there, living things both small and great. There go the ships, and *Leviathan* that you formed to *sport* in it. These all look to you to give them their food in due season; when you give to them, they gather it up; when you open your hand, they are filled with good things." (Psalm 104:1-11,13-14,18-19,21-22, 25-28 Italics added for emphasis.)

Echoes of the Babylonian myth of creation can be heard in the emergence of the land out of the waters that "covered the earth." The cosmic battle has been demythologized to a very great degree. It is by God's "rebuke" not his weaponry that the waters of the deep flee. The imposition of order is by fiat command. Chaos is given a role to play in the world, but that role is dramatically circumscribed. "They...ran to the place that you appointed for them. Yet set a boundary that they may not pass." (Psalm 104:8-9) This language of boundaries, limits and appointed places will reoccur in God's first speech to Job. "Who shut in the sea with doors, when it burst out from the womb?- when I made the clouds its garment, and thick darkness its swaddling band, and prescribed bounds for it, and set bars and doors, and said, 'Thus far shall you come, and no farther, and here shall your proud waves be stopped?" (Job 8-10)

The author of *The Book of Job* may have known this psalm. The order of creation in this hymn: stretching out the heavens, covering them with clouds, fixing the foundations of the earth and rebuking the raging sea is repeated in Job's first words in the third speech in the third cycle. They precede his Oath of Innocence.

"With whose help have you uttered words, and whose spirit has come forth from you? The shades below tremble, the waters and their inhabitants. Sheol is naked before God, and Abaddon has no covering. *He stretches out Zaphon over the void,* and hangs the earth upon nothing. *He binds up the water in his thick clouds,* and the cloud is not torn open by them. He covers the face of the full moon, and spreads over it his cloud. *He has described a circle on the face of the waters, at the boundary between light and darkness.* The pillars of heaven tremble, and are astounded at *his rebuke. By his power he stilled the Sea; by his understanding he struck down Rahab. By his wind the heavens were made fair; his hand pierced the fleeing serpent. These are indeed but the outskirts of his ways; and how small a whisper do we hear of him!*" (Job 26:4-14 Italics added for emphasis)

In many ways, God's first and second speech to Job play off this introduction to Job's Oath of Innocence. Much of the language and many of the images will be repeated. The idea of a providential control of chaos is deepened with the repeated image of a covering garment. (Psalm 104:6; Job 38:9) God treats the chaos as his child, presumably rearing it for a special purpose. That purpose involves the effortless control that is play. God brings up this child through play. God is said to "sport" with Leviathan, that chaos monster of the deep. (Psalm 104:26) The Hebrew here "lesaheq bo" is admittedly ambivalent and can be read either as "sport in it" meaning the sea or "sport with it" meaning the dragon. The NRSV opts for the former, but the latter seems preferable. A similar expression, "hatesheq bo" occurs in God's second speech to Job where it is clear the meaning is "sport with it". "Will you *play with it* as a bird, or will you put it on lease for your girls." (Job 41:5) This latter usage should dictate in our understanding of the passage at hand.[96] God's final purpose for this child, Chaos, is never stated, but presumably it involves the giving of something good in due season. (Psalm 104:27-28) At least, there is a "whisper" that that might be the case.

(2) *Psalm 89* presents that myth of creation once again. The heavenly council has its Babylonian and Canaanite counterparts, but God's kingship is never in question. God is the creator of all things, not the fashioner of pre-existent things.

"For who in the skies can be compared to the LORD? Who among the heavenly beings is like the LORD, a God feared in the *council of the holy ones*, great and awesome above all that are around him? O LORD God of hosts, who is as mighty as you, O LORD? Your faithfulness surrounds you. You rule the *raging of the sea*; when its waves rise, you still them. *You crushed Rahab like a carcass*; you scattered your enemies with your mighty arm. The heavens are yours, the earth also is yours; the world and all that is in it—you have founded them." (Psalm 89:6-11 Italics added for emphasis.)

The chaos monster is retained, under one of its Hebrew names Rahab. "Rahab" means "boisterous one".[97] But there is no suggestion of a violent battle. Whenever the waves of chaos rise, God effortlessly stills them.

The author of *The Book of Job* may have known this psalm. The reference to God stilling the waves of the Sea, Rahab, reoccurs in Job's third speech in the first cycle, the one where he contemplates a mediator.

"He is wise in heart, and mighty in strength- who has resisted him and succeeded? he...who alone *stretched out the heavens* and *trampled the waves of the Sea*, who made the *Bear and Orion, the Pleiades*, and the chambers of the south; who does great things beyond understanding, and marvelous things without number. Look, he passes by me, and I do not see him; he moves on, but I do not perceive him. He snatches away; who can stop him? Who will say to him, 'What are you doing?' God will not turn back his anger; the helpers of Rahab bowed beneath him. How then can I answer him?" (Job 9:4-14)

In many ways, God's first and second speech to Job play off this introduction to Job's hope for a mediator. Much of the language and many of the images will be repeated.

3. Purpose and Providence

A deeper reading of God's first speech reveals two important points.

(1) First, God's language in his review of the physical world suggests purpose. It is the language of order, purpose, constancy and control. The foundations of the world were laid as an architect would. "Measurements" were taken (Job 38:5), survey "lines" "stretched out" (Job 38:5), a "cornerstone" laid (Job 38:6). The sea was subjected to "prescribed bounds" (Job 38:10), shut in with "bars and doors" (Job 38:10). "Thus far shall you come, and no farther." (Job 38:11) The morning light was "commanded" to reappear every morning. (Job 38:12) "Reserves" were placed in the storehouses of the snow and hail. (38:23) "Channels" "were cut" for the rain. (Job 38:25) Order was imposed in the heavens. Some things were "bound in chains". (Job 38:31) Some had their "cords" "loosed". (Job 38:31) Some things were "led forth". (Job 38:32) "Ordinances" were made (Job 38:38:33) and "rule" was "established". (Job 38:33) There is a certain "wisdom" or "understanding" (Job 38:36) in the nature of the physical order.

(2) Second, God's language in his review of the animal world suggests providence. God "satisfies the appetites" of the young lions. (Job 38:39) God hears the young ravens and answers their "cry". (Job 38:41) God gives "freedom" to the wild ass. (Job 39:5) God frees the ostrich from "fear". (Job 39:16) God gives "might" and

"majesty" to the war horse. (Job 39:19-20) God enables the birds of prey to "soar" to the heights they do. (Job 39:26) God's concern is purposeful and on-going.

Yet these suggestions are veiled and can be read otherwise. The language of providential purpose here is tinged with a lack of concern for the human world and with a certain hostility towards it. The rain that falls is not described as falling on the agricultural fields where it is needed by human beings. The rain falls "on a land where no one lives, on the desert, which is empty of human life, to satisfy the waste and desolate land." (Job 38:26) There is an inherent "cruelty", even stupidity, in how the ostrich deals with its young. (Job 39:16) The "terrible snorting" of the war horse foreshadows the wars that bring death to men, women and children. (Job 39:20,25) The birds of prey are there to "suck up" their blood. (Job 39:30)

At best, these are all suggestions of possible purpose and providence. God may be suggesting that Job should not only see purpose and providence in the natural and animal worlds, but that he should infer a similar purpose and providence exists in the human world. They are insights and inferences that Job might reasonably draw, but they are insights and inferences that he need not draw.

Job's First Response

In God's first speech, God has focused on the vast grandeur of creation. But Job has asked a question concerning justice, not power. And God had seemingly dodged the question, belittling Job's intelligence but not his integrity. Job's response is worth noting.

"See, I am of small account; what shall I answer you? I lay my hand on my mouth. I have spoken once, and I will not answer; twice, but will proceed no further." (Job 40:3-5 Italics added for emphasis.)

With some irony, Job accepts the irrelevance of it all and throws it back at God as a defense. "See" God, in comparison to the vast grandeur of creation, "I am of small account". Why would you God ever expect one of such "small account" as I to declare to you the things you ask? "I lay my hand on my mouth," perhaps to conceal my laughter, certainly because there is nothing more to say. The issue is not power, but justice. On that point, "I have spoken once" in my Oath of Innocence and "I will not answer" until you have addressed the moral question I raised.

Job's comment about "proceeding further" is pregnant with dramatic meaning. The meaning lies in the distinction between causal responsibility and moral blameworthiness found in the two default judgments in his Oath of Innocence. God has not entered a defense. A finding that God is causally responsible for undeserved evil has issued. All that remains is for Job to make a finding of moral blameworthiness against God. All that remains is for Job to condemn God by way of a curse not giving an explanation for evil in the world. Job seems to hesitate. He is forcing God's hand and giving God one final chance to say something concerning God's creation and control of evil.

God's Second Speech

God picks up on Job's hesitation to "proceed...further" in his Oath of Innocence to a "condemnation" of God. Having suggested a purpose in creation in his first speech, God now suggests a moral purpose in the creation and control of evil. That purpose is expressed through the cross-cultural myth of Leviathan where Leviathan is the embodiment of evil in the world. And that purpose finds its completion in the Jewish reworking of the myth.

Opening Question: Then the LORD answered Job out of the whirlwind: "Gird up your loins like a man; I will question you, and you declare to me. *Will you even put me in the wrong? Will you condemn me that you may be justified?* (Job 40:6-8 Italics added for emphasis and clarification.)

General Comments: Have you an arm like God, and can you thunder with a voice like his? "Deck yourself with majesty and dignity; clothe yourself with glory and splendor. Pour out the overflowings of your anger, and look on all who are proud, and abase them. *Look on all who are proud, and bring them low; tread down the wicked where they stand. Hide them all in the dust together; bind their faces in the world below.* Then I will also acknowledge to you that your own right hand can give you victory. (Job 40:9-14 Italics added for emphasis and clarification.)

Behemoth: "*Look at Behemoth,* which I made just as I made you; it eats grass like an ox. Its strength is in its loins, and its power in the muscles of its belly. It makes its tail stiff like a cedar; the sinews of its thighs are knit together. Its bones are tubes of bronze, its limbs like bars of iron. "*It is the first of the great acts of God-- only its Maker can approach it with the sword.* For the mountains yield food for it where all the wild animals *play.* Under the lotus plants it lies, in the covert of the reeds and in the marsh. The lotus trees cover it for shade; the willows of the wadi surround it. Even if the river is turbulent, it is not frightened; it is confident though Jordan rushes against its mouth. *Can one take it with hooks or pierce its nose with a snare?* (Job 40:15-24 Italics added for emphasis and clarification.)

Leviathan: "*Can you draw out Leviathan with a fishhook,* or press down its tongue with a cord*? Can you put a rope in its nose, or pierce its jaw with a hook? Will* it make many supplications to you? *Will* it speak soft words to you? *Will it make a covenant with you to be taken as your servant forever? Will you play with it as with a bird, or will you put it on leash for your girls? Will traders bargain over it? Will they divide it up among the merchants? Can you fill its skin with harpoons, or its head with fishing spears?* Lay hands on it; think of the battle; you will not do it again! Any hope of capturing it will be disappointed; were not even the gods overwhelmed at the sight of it? No one is so fierce as to dare to stir it up. *Who can* stand before it? *Who can* confront it and be safe? --under the whole heaven, who? "I will not keep silence concerning its limbs, or its mighty strength, or its splendid frame. *Who can* strip off its outer garment? *Who can* penetrate its double coat of mail? *Who can* open the doors of its face? There is terror all around its teeth. Its back is made of shields in rows, shut up closely as with a seal. One is so near to another that no air can come between them. They are joined one to another; they clasp each other and cannot be separated. Its sneezes flash forth light, and its eyes are like the eyelids of the dawn. From its mouth go flaming torches; sparks of fire leap out. Out of its nostrils comes smoke, as from a boiling pot and burning rushes. Its breath kindles coals, and a flame comes out of its mouth. In its neck abides strength, and terror dances before it. The folds of its flesh cling together; it is firmly cast and immovable. Its heart is as hard as stone, as hard as the lower millstone. When it raises itself up the gods are afraid; at the crashing they are beside themselves. Though the sword reaches it, it does not avail, nor does the spear, the dart, or the javelin. It counts iron as straw, and bronze as rotten wood. The arrow cannot make it flee; slingstones, for it, are turned to chaff. Clubs are counted as chaff; it laughs at the rattle of javelins. Its underparts are like sharp potsherds; it spreads itself like a threshing sledge on the mire. It makes the deep boil like a pot; it makes the sea like a pot of ointment. It leaves a shining wake behind it; one would think the deep to be white-haired. *On earth it has no equal, a creature without fear. It surveys everything that is lofty; it is king over all that are proud."* (Job 41:1-34 Italics added for emphasis and clarification.)

1. The mythological world: Behemoth- Leviathan

Leviathan is a cross-cultural symbol of evil incarnate. The image is found in the Babylonian myth of creation, the Canaanite myth of recreation and the Jewish myth of apocalypse.

"Leviathan" is a proper name. It means "twisting one" as befits a serpent.[98] And Leviathan is a supernatural serpent, much like Satan. Leviathan is the Jewish chaos monster Rahab by another name. Leviathan is the Canaanite chaos monsters Litan, Yam and Mot by another name. Most scholars believe that the Leviathan gets his name from this Canaanite chaos monster Litan. Litan is Yam by another name. The Ugaritic word for Litan "ltn" and the Hebrew word for Leviathan "liwyatan" are almost identical linguistically. And the Ugaritic word for "writhing" or "fleeing" "brh" and the Hebrew word for "writhing" or "fleeing" "bariah" are almost identical linguistically.[99] Leviathan is the Babylonian chaos monsters Tiamat, Qingu and their offspring by another name.

Leviathan is "behemoth", because "behemoth" is a common not a proper noun. It is not a personal name and is never mentioned anywhere else in the Old Testament nor in the pagan mythologies of the Ancient Near East. The Hebrew word "behemoth" means "the great beast", "the beast par excellence".[100] It is a plural noun used with singular verbs as the verses which follow indicate. It is the "plural of majesty" or the "plural of fullness".[101] Such plurals were regularly used to describe the one true God and their usage here indicates an intentional contrast. The plural of majesty suggests that Leviathan claims a kingship that is God's alone. The plural of fullness suggests that Leviathan embodies all the attributes of evil in their perfection. It may even suggest a plurality of modalities or persons within the one evil. If so, all the predators of the earth, human and otherwise, are but the incarnations or manifestations of this one beast.

Some scholars believe Behemoth is a chaos monster separate from Leviathan. If so, then Behemoth is probably the Jewish reworking of the Canaanite chaos monster Atik. In the Canaanite myth of recreation, the high God Baal's sister claims to have defeated both Yam and Atik.

> "Surely I smote the Beloved of El, Yam?
> Surely I exterminated Nahar, the mighty god?
> Surely I lifted up[102] the dragon
> I overpowered him?
> I smote the writhing serpent,
> Encircler[103]- with-seven heads!
> I smote the Behoved of El, Arsh,
> I finished off El's calf, Atik,
> I smote El's bitch, Fire,
> I exterminated El's daughter, Flame.
> I fought for the silver,
> I took possession of the gold
> of those who drove Baal from the heights of Saphon,
> knocking him like a bird from his perch,
> (who) drove him the throne of his kingship,
> from the back-rest,
> from the siege of his dominion."[104]

The chaos monster Yam is a "dragon", a "writhing serpent", an "Encircler with seven heads". This seven headed dragon is the chaos water that encircles the earth. Yam is the Canaanite Leviathan. Atik is a mythological bull calf. From other Canaanite myths, Atik appears to be the chaos monster that ravages the land as a wild bull might. If Yam is Leviathan, then presumably Atik is Behemoth.

If so, Satan, Behemoth and Leviathan form a kind of unholy trinity in *The Book of Job*. Three persons, one chaos monster. Within a canonical perspective, they foreshadow the three chaos monsters of *The Book of Revelation*. There, the sky dragon is Satan. (Revelation 12:1-18) The composite monster from the sea is the Antichrist. (Revelation 13:1-10) And the composite monster from the earth is the False Prophet. (Revelation 13:11-17) Three persons, one evil.

The Ancient Near Eastern chaos monster was always pictured as a supernatural dragon.[105]

(1) This fire-breathing dragon has many heads, many eyes, many teeth, a huge mouth and many horns. The exact number varies from culture to culture. The many eyes and the many heads represent knowledge. The knowledge in question is the "intention" to bring about evil.

(2) The many teeth represent appetite. The appetite in question is the "desire" to bring about evil.

(3) The many horns and the fire represent power. The power in question is the "ability" to bring about evil.

(4) While it normally lives in the sea and represents it, this dragon has wings and can fly. It rules the sea, the land and the air. This power of flight represents a certain kind of omnipresence. The omnipresence in question is the "pervasiveness" of evil. It can strike anywhere and at anytime.

(5) This dragon is heavily armored with many scales on its body and rows of back plates and spines along its undulating back and tail. The many scales and back plates represent a certain kind of invincibility. The invincibility in question is the "difficulty" in subduing and ultimately destroying evil.

(6) This dragon is a supernatural twisting serpent. The twisting or crooked body represents the "twisted" and forever "twisting" nature of evil.

That is the literary meaning of the dragon image.

Leviathan is clearly a primordial chaos monster, a dragon.[106] It is a fire-breathing dragon. "Its sneezes flash forth light, and its eyes are like the eyelids of the dawn. From its mouth go flaming torches;

sparks of fire leap out. Out of its nostrils comes smoke, as from a boiling pot and burning rushes. Its breath kindles coals, and a flame comes out of its mouth." (Job 41:9-21) It is a heavily armored dragon with impenetrable scales on its body and rows of back plates and spines along its undulating back and tail. "I will not keep silence concerning its limbs, or its mighty strength or its splendid frame? Who can strip off its outer garment? Who can penetrate its double coat of mail....Its back is made of shields in rows, shut closely together as with a seal. One is so near to another that no air can come between them. They are joined one to another; they clasp each other and cannot be separated." (Job 41:12-17) The fire and the armor suggest invincibility. "On earth it has no equal, a creature without fear. It surveys everything that is lofty; it is king over all that are proud." (Job 41:33-34) This proud chaos monster is a king, a king ever ready to expand his kingdom. He continually surveys the "lofty" heavens looking for a chance to do evil and overturn the rule of God. "Its heart is as hard as stone, as hard as the lower millstone." (Job 41:25) It will never change.

2. Creating the dragon

Leviathan is "the first of the great acts of God." (Job 40:19) It is a created being, like Job. (Job 40:15) The evil it represents is created evil, undeserved evil created by God. Evil is "the first of the great acts of God". In fact, the Hebrew here "re sit darke el" may very well mean this evil is "the finest demonstration of God's power" since the Ugaritic root "drkt" can mean "dominion" or "power".[107] That would mean God's creation and control of evil is "the finest demonstration of his power", a clear indication of purpose. God's purpose is the creation of good in the midst of evil.

This description of Leviathan as "the first of the ways of God" is a deliberate reworking of Proverbs 8:22 which posits wisdom, not evil, as the "first of his acts of long ago." In the eyes of the author, God's shrewd and considered plan or purpose in the world (Job 42:2b) involves a deep, even dark, wisdom that is the mystery of evil and its role in the world. In terms of mythic image and its reference, I had often thought Leviathan a good metaphor for, among other things, the beauty and ugliness of the evolutionary process which produced the human body, as opposed to the human mind. Life feeds on life and death is in the world long before Adam.

The author of *The Book of Job* is rewriting both the Babylonian myth of creation and *The Book of Genesis* on two points.

(1) Evil is created by God.

(2) Evil is in the world before the fall of humankind..

It is worth looking at those two other myths for similarities and differences.

In the Babylonian myth of creation, evil is pre-existent.

In that myth, the world was created out of the body of a slain chaos monster. When the high God Marduk divided Tiamat,

"Half of her he set up and made as a cover, heaven.[108]
He stretched out the hide and assigned watchmen,
And ordered them not to let her waters escape.
He crossed heaven, he inspected (its) firmament.[109]
He made the position(s) for the great gods,
He established (in) constellations the stars, their likenesses.
He marked the year, described its boundaries,
He set up twelve months of three stars each.
After he had patterned the days of the year,
He fixed the position of Neberu to make the (star') relationships.
Lest any make an error or go astray,
He established the position(s) of Enlil and Ea in relation to it.[110]
He opened up gates on both (side of her) ribs,
He made strong bolts to left and right.
In her liver he established the zenith.
He made the moon appear, entrusted (to him) the night.[111]
....
He set down her head and piled [   ][112] upon it,
He opened underground springs, a flood was let flow(?).
From her eyes he undammed the Euphr[ates] and Tigris,
He stopped up her nostrils, he left...
He heaped up high-peaked mo[unt]tains from (?) her dregs.
He drilled through her waterholes to carry off the catchwater.
He coiled up her tail and tied it as(?) 'The Great Bond.'[113]
...
He set her crotch as the brace of heaven,

Spreading [half of] her as a cover, he established the earth.
[After] he had completed his task inside Tiamat,
[He spre]ad his net, let all (within) escape,
He formed (/?) the...[   ] of heaven and netherworld."[114]

In Ancient Near Eastern thinking, the universe was tri-partite: heaven, earth and the underworld. The earth was a disk sitting on water, surrounded by water. The earth is created out of Tiamat. The remains of Tiamat are confined to three places: the heavens, the oceans surrounding and encircling the earth and the underworld below. The reference to heaven is direct here: "half of her he set up and made as a cover, heaven." The reference to the surrounding and encircling oceans is direct as well though some readers might miss it: "He coiled up her tail and tied it as(?) 'The Great Bond.'" The surrounding waters are the bond that holds the heavens, the earth and the underworld together.[115] The reference to the underworld is found in the eyes that are the springs of the Euphrates and Tigris rivers. From the underworld, water comes forth onto the earth.

Echoes of this creation of the world might be heard early in *The Book of Genesis.*

"And God said, 'Let there be a dome in the midst of the water, and let it separate the waters from the waters.' So God made the dome and separated the waters that were under the dome from the waters that were above the dome. And it was so. God called the dome Sky. And there was evening and morning, the second day. And God said, 'Let the waters under the sky be gathered together into one place and it was so. God called the dry land Earth, and the waters that were gathered together he called Seas. And God saw that it was good." (Genesis 1:6-10)

And echoes of this creation of the world might even be heard in God's first speech to Job, with its references to "establishing" the heavens and setting "boundaries" therein.

""Where were you when I laid the foundation of the earth? Tell me, if you have understanding. Who determined its measurements--surely you know! Or who stretched the line upon it? On what were its bases sunk, or who laid its cornerstone when the morning stars sang together and all the heavenly beings shouted for joy? Or who shut in the sea with doors when it burst out from the womb?-- when I made the clouds its garment, and thick darkness its swaddling band, and prescribed bounds for it, and set bars and doors, and said, 'Thus far shall you come, and no farther, and here shall your proud waves be stopped'? Have you commanded the morning since your days began, and caused the dawn to know its place, so that it might take hold of the skirts of the earth, and the wicked be shaken out of it?... Can you bind the chains of the Pleiades, or loose the cords of Orion? Can you lead forth the Mazzaroth in their season, or can you guide the Bear with its children? Do you know the ordinances of the heavens? Can you establish their rule on the earth? Can you lift up your voice to the clouds, so that a flood of waters may cover you? Can you send forth lightnings, so that they may go and say to you, 'Here we are'?'" (Job 38:4-13, 31-35)

Such intimations foreshadow the appearance of Leviathan in God's second speech to Job.

The poetic point being made by the Babylonian poet in his description of the creation of the world is a very simple one.

(1) Chaos is evil.

(2) Evil is all around us. Evil is above us, beside us and beneath us, just as the waters of chaos are.

(3) Evil is part of the very fabric of creation.

(4) Evil is a part of the high God Marduk's plan in the creation of the world.

In that Babylonian myth, humankind was created out of the blood of a slain chaos monster.[116] In Ancient Near Eastern thinking, the blood is the life. The life is the character of a human being. Human beings takes their lives, their character from their parents. Qingu is the father of all men and women. Tiamat is their mother. The blood of the evil ones flows in their veins.

The poetic point being made by the Babylonian poet in his description of the creation of humankind is a very simple one.

(1) Chaos is evil.

(2) Evil is deep within us. Evil flows within our veins. Evil shapes our life and our character.

(3) Evil is part of the very fabric of our being.

(4) Evil is part of the high God Marduk's plan in the creation of humankind.

In *The Book of Genesis,* evil comes into the world with the fall of men and women. Adam is created out of the "dust of the earth" and the spirit or "breath" of God. (Genesis 2:7) He is awakened to a truly human life through a kiss from God. It is God's love that animates Adam. His parents are mother earth and father God. He takes his body from the earth. But he takes his mind, his intellect and free will, from God himself. That is what it is to be made in the "image" and "likeness" of God. (Genesis 1:26) Unlike any other animal, human beings are capable of apprehending the immaterial concepts of good and evil and choosing accordingly. Human beings are created neither good nor evil. Their natural orientation is towards the good, for that is what makes for a truly and fully human life. But they become good or evil through their choices. They are evil not by nature, but by nurture.

In *The Book of Genesis*, the evil of the chaos monster is not put into the heart of human beings by God. Human beings take the chaos monster into themselves through their choices. In the story of Adam and Eve, the chaos monster appears in a diminutive form, a serpent in the grass. The serpent tempts them to do evil and when they fall, they acquire a second parent, that serpent. They become the offspring of Satan. They become evil by nurture. With the repeated choice of evil, they become less and less human, more and more bestial. And for all appearance sake, they acquire a second nature. Chaos now reigns in their being. Their passions are no longer subordinate to their reason and life becomes a struggle to impose order on chaos. That is the meaning of original sin. It is the loss of the original justice that was the subordination of the passions to reason.[117] The moral point of the Babylonian poet remains. Evil is deep within us. Evil is part of who and what we have become. We are all little monsters at heart.

The moral point being made by the author of *The Book of Job* is similar yet different. While evil is part of the fabric of creation, human beings are not corrupted to the point they cannot choose good over evil. In fact, they are capable of the perfect goodness that is the completely selfless love of a man or woman for God.

The ancient Jewish poets adopted the Babylonian and Canaanite myths of a cosmic conflict between the high God and the chaos monster to a monotheistic framework. The imagery is retained but transformed. Creation ceases to be a struggle with the divine and the demonic. Creation is now understood as creation through fiat command. And in time, that creation through fiat command will deepen to be understood as creation out of nothing. In the meantime, the imagery of a primordial sea monster is retained and demythologized to various degrees. Creation is no longer a life and death struggle between a high God and a chaos monster. Creation is the creation and control of that monster and the evil it represents by an all-powerful, all-present, all-knowing and all-good God. Re-creation is the continuing control of that monster by that one true God. Any challenge to the civilized order, whether it is a force of nature or a human force, is always regarded as a re-emergence of that primordial chaos. The threat may be economic as seen in the annual death of vegetation. Or the threat may be political as seen in the frequent wars and rebellions. The defeated chaos monster is behind all these threats to civilization. The chaos monster has escaped its prison and seeks to destroy the human world.

The ancient Jewish conception of time was linear, not cyclical. God was beyond space and time and the author of both. God was not an expression of or identical with Mother Nature, as were the pagan gods of Babylonia and Canaan, and was not subject to the recurring cycles of nature. In the Canaanite myth of recreation, the high God Baal's victories over the chaos monsters Yam, Litan and Mot are only temporary. The high God is a fertility god closely chained the cycles of the nature. As the vegetation dies every year, the high God is annually defeated by the chaos monster and descends into the underworld. But as the vegetation returns each New Year, the high God is annually reborn and overpowers that chaos monster. The pattern repeats itself for all eternity. There is no final resolution to the conflict. While a polytheistic god might be able to control a pre-existent chaos monster to a certain degree, a monotheistic God could have a purpose in creating such a thing, perfectly controlling it and ultimately destroying it.

The great Jewish genius was in the reworking of the Babylonian myth of creation and the Canaanite myth recreation into a Jewish myth of an apocalypse where God's purpose in evil could be accomplished and explained. Redemption was pictured not only as a temporary defeat of the monster, but as its complete and utter destruction. At the end of human history, God will intervene and destroy the dragon once and for all. It and the evil it represents will never reappear to trouble the moral and natural orders.

The myth of Leviathan finds in highest development in the writings of the Jewish prophet Isaiah. In the full myth, three elements are consistently conjoined:

(1) God's capture of the chaos dragon and his drawing it out of the water by hooks, snares or nets,

(2) a Messianic feast, and

(3) a symposium following the meal when God would answer all questions.

One follows the other sequentially in time. The presence of any one of these three elements suggests the presence of the other two and events to follow.

In Isaiah's reworking of the myth, a Messianic banquet is thrown by God the Messiah. All the peoples of the world are invited to it. At that banquet, the body of the chaos dragon that has been captured and drawn from the water is served as the main course. All the people of the world consume the roast beast. The animals of the world feed on the scraps from the table. This Messianic banquet will mark the end of time. It will usher in a new creation, a new heavens and a new earth whether there is neither pain nor suffering. Part and parcel of that removal of all suffering is an explanation of all things by God the Teacher immediately following the meal.

It was a poetic way of saying there will come a time when the evil around us, the evil within us will be finally purged and destroyed. The dragon represents that evil, all sorts of evil. In its most horrific form, the dragon is a personification of death. The dragon is the person Death. The death of Death is the creation of new life, now and forever. The communal eating of the dragon at the Messianic feast is a kind of sacramental acceptance of the new life God offers at the end of time, an eternal life in a completely transformed world. The ancient Jews transformed the Ancient Near Eastern myths of creation and re-creation into a myth of the coming apocalypse. The communal eating of the chaos dragon by the animals and people of the world is the symbol of that new creation, that new heavens and new earth.

The author of *The Book of Job* expects the discerning reader to see these suggestions of a final resolution to the moral problem for they are embedded in the myth of Leviathan itself. God expects Job to see the very same suggestions with his choice and description of Leviathan in his second speech to Job.

(1) Leviathan implies the Isaian apocalypse.

(2) And the Isaian apocalypse implies the existence of a defense through a symposium where God answers all questions, though the nature of the defense is never articulated.

This legitimacy of this interpretation requires a date of composition for *The Book of Job* subsequent to *1 Isaiah*, probably sometime within the 7th or 5th centuries B.C. Since most conventional scholars opt for a date of composition or final redaction within between the 7th and 5th centuries B.C.,[118] this interpretation seems possible.

(1) Job is presented as a non-Israelite, but not necessarily a pre-Israelite. While it is often assumed Job lives in a patriarchal age more or less contemporaneously with Abraham in the 19th-17th centuries B.C., it is important to remember that the "patriarchal world" continued well into the mid-1st millennium B.C. in lands to the east and south of Israel. Uz may have been such a land. Uz would be to Israel as a third world country would be to a first world country. Both Uz and Israel could have existed contemporaneously, but not necessarily contiguously. Thus, the real life setting of Job could be within the timeframe of the 6th-5th centuries B.C.

(2) *The Book of Job* is profoundly counter-cultural and the absence of any reference to Jewish ritual may merely reflect a counter-cultural

preference for myth over ritual and not an early date. Similarly, the absence of any reference to the Exile may merely reflect a counter-cultural preference for myth over history and not an early date.

(3) Job is clearly aware of all the mythologies of the Ancient Near East including those of Israel, without regarding any particular mythology as special revelation for him. In that respect, Job is in the position of many a modern reader. Myth is an embodiment of the hopes and dreams of all humankind and the occasion for insight for those who have eyes to see and ears to hear. God inspires all great poets and touches the hearts of their audience. God presents Job and the reader with *1 Isaiah*'s reworking of the Leviathan myth and invites both to explore the "redemptive analogies" found therein. That redemption is not merely the redemption of men and women, but the redemption of God. That redemption is a time for God's destruction, explanation and justification of evil.

3. Capturing the dragon

The first aspect of the Jewish reworking of the Leviathan myth is the capture of the dragon.

God tells Job that God and God alone can draw Leviathan from the chaos waters. Seven times God promises he will do it: by "hooks", "snare", "draw", "fishhook", "cord", "rope", "hook". "Can one take it with hooks or pierce its nose with a snare? Can you draw out Leviathan with a fishhook, or press down its tongue with a cord? Can you put a rope in its nose, or pierce its jaw with a hook?" (Job 40:24-41:2) The number seven here has symbolic import. It is the perfection of divine power. Only God can destroy the chaos monster. Drawing the monster from the waters is the first part of its destruction.

No lesser divine or semi-divine being can control, let alone destroy the evil that Leviathan represents.

"Any hope of capturing it will be disappointed; were not even the gods overwhelmed at the sight of it? No one is so fierce as to dare to stir it up. *Who can* stand before it? *Who can* confront it and be safe? --under the whole heaven, who?" (Job 41:9-11) "When it raises itself up the gods are afraid; at the crashing they are beside themselves. Though the sword reaches it, it does not avail, nor does the spear, the dart, or the javelin. It counts iron as straw, and bronze as rotten wood. The arrow cannot make it flee; slingstones, for it, are turned to chaff. Clubs are counted as chaff; it laughs at the rattle of javelins." (Job 41:25-29)

Here, God is drawing on the Babylonian myth of a cosmic struggle between good and evil, where even the gods themselves are dumb struck.

In the Babylonian myth of creation, the god of wisdom Ea is "struck dumb with horror and sat stock still" at the rebellion of the chaos monster Tiamat.[119] Ea goes to his grandfather Anshar and tells him the bad news of a demonic horde.

"They are massing around her, ready at Tiamat's side
Angry, scheming, never laying down night and day,
Making warfare, rumbling, raging,
Convening in assembly, that they might start hostilities,
Mother Huber,[120] who can form everything,
Added countless invincible weapons,
gave birth to monster serpents,
Pointed of fang, with merciless incisors (?),
She filled their bodies with venom for blood.
Fierce dragons she clad with glories,
Causing them to bear auras like gods, (saying)
"Whoever see them shall collapse from weakness!
Wherever their bodies make onslaught,
they shall not turn back!"
She deployed serpents, dragons, and hairy hero-men,
Lion monsters, lion men, scorpion men,
Mighty demons, fish men, bull men,
Bearing unsparing arms, fearing no battle.
Her commands were absolute, no one opposed them.
Eleven indeed on this wise she created."[121]

This demonic refrain will be repeated four times in the poem to heighten the fear of the gods. Anshar orders Ea and Anu in turn to destroy Tiamat, but both:

'...stopped, horror-stricken, then turned back....
Her strength is enormous, she is utterly terrifying,

She is reinforced with a host, none can come out against her.
Her challenge was not reduced,
it was so loud (?) against me,
I became afraid at her clamor, I turned back."[122]

Even the high God Marduk is dumb struck as he approaches that evil.
Tiamat cast her own spell on him and "his tactic turned to confusion,
His reason was overthrown, his actions panicky."[123]

No human being such as Job can destroy the evil Leviathan
represents. *"Look on all who are proud, and bring them low; tread
down the wicked where they stand. Hide them all in the dust
together; bind their faces in the world below.* Then I will also
acknowledge to you that your own right hand can give you victory."
(Job 40:12-14) Only God can destroy it.

This destruction of Leviathan by drawing it out of the water
finds some interesting parallels in *Psalm 74, Ezekiel 29* and *32.*

(1) *Psalm 74* is a lament incorporating both a myth of
creation and a myth of re-creation. As in the Canaanite myth of re-
creation, the emissaries of the chaos monster have occupied and
devastated the holy place of God. This violent act has upset the moral
order. This psalm is a plea, a petition, that God restore or recreate
that moral order.

"O God, why do you cast us off forever? Why does your anger
smoke against the sheep of your pasture" Remember your
congregation which you acquired long ago....Your foes have
roared within your holy place; they set up their emblems there.
At the upper entrance they hacked the wooden trellis with axes.
And then, with hatchets and hammers, they smashed all its
carved work. They set your sanctuary on fire; they desecrated
the dwelling place of your name, bringing it to the ground.
They said to themselves, "We will utterly subdue them"; they
burned all the meeting places of God in the land. Yet God my
King is from of old, working salvation in the earth. *You
divided the sea by your might; you broke the heads of the
dragons in the waters. You crushed the heads of Leviathan;*
you gave him as food for the creatures of the wilderness. You
cut openings for springs and torrents; you dried up ever-
flowing streams. Yours is the day, yours also the night; you

established the luminaries and the sun. You have fixed all the bounds of the earth; you made summer and winter." (Psalm 74:1-2,4-8,12-16 Italics added for emphasis.)

The hope is that this "King from of old" will act as he did in the times "of old" and once again subdue the powers of chaos. They are a threat to his kingship and he needs to restore that kingship. Only God can restore the moral order. Echoes of the Babylonian myth of creation can be heard in the references to the "dividing of the sea" and "the openings for springs and torrents" which recall the splitting of Tiamat and the creation of the Tigris and Euphrates from the eyes of her body. Echoes of the Canaanite myth of re-creation can be heard in the reference to a multi-headed Leviathan which recalls the seven headed Litan.

(2) *Ezekiel 29* describes the tyrannical Pharaoh, king of Egypt, as a chaos dragon living in the waters of the Nile.

"Mortal, set your face against Pharaoh king of Egypt, and prophesy against him and against all Egypt; speak, and say, Thus says the Lord GOD: I am against you, *Pharaoh king of Egypt, the great dragon sprawling in the midst of its channels*, saying, "*My Nile is my own; I made it for myself.*" *I will put hooks in your jaws, and make the fish of your channels stick to your scales. I will draw you up from your channels, with all the fish of your channels sticking to your scales. I will fling you into the wilderness, you and all the fish of your channels; you shall fall in the open field, and not be gathered and buried. To the animals of the earth and to the birds of the air I have given you as food.*" (Ezekiel 29:3-5 Italics added for emphasis.)

This chaos dragon regards himself as the lord of creation. "My Nile is my own; I made it for myself." (Ezekiel 29:3) Herein lies a threat to the created order that recalls the Canaanite myth of re-creation. Inherent in this refusal to accept one's created status lies a claim to deity or at least to the kingship that is God's alone. Just as the Canaanite chaos monster Mot is flung into the wilderness, this chaos dragon will be similarly overthrown.

(3) *Ezekiel 32* continues the thought as it describes the Pharaoh, king of Egypt, as both a "dragon in the seas" and a "lion among nations". Echoes of the Canaanite myth of re-creation can be

heard here. A voracious lion is how Mot, the Canaanite dragon of death, describes himself. His appetite is such that it consumes the earth and all in earth.

"Mortal, raise a lamentation over *Pharaoh king of Egypt,* and say to him: *You consider yourself a lion among the nations, but you are like a dragon in the seas; you thrash about in your streams, trouble the water with your feet, and foul your streams.* Thus says the Lord GOD: In an assembly of many peoples *I will throw my net over you; and I will haul you up in my dragnet. I will throw you on the ground, on the open field I will fling you, and will cause all the birds of the air to settle on you, and I will let the wild animals of the whole earth gorge themselves with you.* I will strew your flesh on the mountains, and fill the valleys with your carcass. *I will drench the land with your flowing blood* up to the mountains, and the watercourses will be filled with you. When I blot you out, I will cover the heavens, and make their stars dark; I will cover the sun with a cloud, and the moon shall not give its light. All the shining lights of the heavens I will darken above you, and put darkness on your land, says the Lord GOD. I will trouble the hearts of many peoples, as I carry you captive among the nations, into countries you have not known. I will make many peoples appalled at you; their kings shall shudder because of you. When I brandish my sword before them, they shall tremble every moment for their lives, each one of them, on the *day of your downfall.*" (Ezekiel 32:2-10 Italics added for emphasis.)

Once again, the imagery of drawing the chaos monster out of the waters and the feeding on the body of the monster are conjoined. The one follows the other. This time there is the suggestion that defeat may be everlasting. The dragon will be "blotted out." The "day of his downfall" sounds like the day of the Final Judgment. The sun, moon and stars go dark. Darkness covers the land. Most of the inhabitants of the nations of the earth "tremble" and shudder at this Day of Judgment.

4. Eating the dragon at the Messianic Feast

The second aspect of the Jewish reworking of the Leviathan myth is the eating of the dragon at the Messianic banquet where God is the Messiah. The fullest expression of that is found in the writings of the prophet Isaiah.

"On this mountain the LORD of hosts will make for all peoples a feast of rich food, a feast of well-aged wines, of rich food filled with marrow, of well-aged wines strained clear. *And he will destroy on this mountain the shroud that is cast over all peoples, the sheet that is spread over all nations; he will swallow up death forever. Then the Lord GOD will wipe away the tears from all faces*, and the disgrace of his people he will take away from all the earth, for the LORD has spoken. *It will be said on that day, Lo, this is our God; we have waited for him, so that he might save us.* This is the LORD for whom we have waited; let us be glad and rejoice in his salvation." (Isaiah 25:6-9 Italics added for emphasis.)

"On that day the LORD with his cruel and great and strong sword will punish Leviathan the fleeing serpent, Leviathan the twisting serpent, and he will kill the dragon that is in the sea." (Isaiah 27:1 italics added for emphasis.)

The time is the end of human history. The dead of the world are summoned to a Messianic feast. The shroud of death which is "the shroud that is cast over all peoples, the sheet that is spread over all nations" is lifted by God himself. (Isaiah 25:7) A universal resurrection of the dead has been accomplished. This final resurrection is contemporaneous with a Final Judgment.

"Leviathan the fleeing serpent", "Leviathan the twisting serpent", Leviathan "the dragon that is in the sea" will be judged. He will be killed once and forever. (Isaiah 27:1) The dragon represents that evil, all sorts of evil. In its most horrific form, the dragon is a personification of death. The dragon is the person Death. The death of Death is the creation of new life, now and forever. On that day, God will "swallow up death forever." (Isaiah 25:7) This death of Death is the creation of a new earth and a new heaven. On that day, God removes all "tears". God wipes away all "disgrace". (Isaiah 25:8) This is the day of salvation for which all peoples have "waited". (Isaiah 25:9)

The communal nature of the Messianic feast strongly suggests the participants partake of the dead body of the chaos dragon. They eat what the host eats. This communal eating of the dragon is a kind of sacramental acceptance of the new life God offers at the end of time, an eternal life in a completely transformed world. This communal participation is implied but never explicitly stated. All that is required in my interpretation is that Job infer that God will "swallow up" Leviathan in a final judgment to end all human history.

Still, it may be interesting to explore later understandings of this passage to gain a more canonical perspective to communal participation. Later Jewish tradition, apocryphal, pseudepigraphical and rabbinic, has the body of the dragon being consumed by the participants in the Messianic banquet. It makes explicit what was merely implicit in *1 Isaiah*.

(1) The apocrypha means "things that are hidden". It refers to fifteen or so Jewish works written in Greek that were not included in the Hebrew canon of the Bible, but which were included in early Greek translations of that Hebrew canon. For the most part, Jews inside Israel did not accept those works as authentic; Jews outside Israel did. The Orthodox and Catholic[124] branches of Christianity generally accept them as authentic; the Protestant branch does not. Many of the early church fathers did accept them as authoritative.

(a) *2 Esdras* is one such apocryphal work, probably written in the first century A.D.[125] For our purpose, it is important in that it reveals the common Jewish understanding of Isaiah's apocalypse. It refers to the eating of the chaos dragon at the Messianic banquet.

"Upon the *fifth day* thou saidst unto the seventh part, where the waters were gathered that it should bring forth living creatures, fowls and fishes: and so it came to pass. For the dumb water and without life brought forth living things at the commandment of God, that all people might praise thy wondrous works. Then didst thou ordain *two living creatures*, the one thou calledst *Enoch*, and the other *Leviathan*; And didst separate the one from the other: for the seventh part, namely, where the water was gathered together, might not hold them both. Unto *Enoch* thou gavest one part, which was *dried up* the third day, that he should dwell in the same part, wherein are a thousand hills: But unto *Leviathan thou gavest the seventh part, namely, the moist; and hast kept him to be devoured of whom thou wilt, and when.*" (2 Edras 6:47 Italics added for emphasis.)

It was always God's intention to kill the dragon. The dragon was "kept" alive only for the Messianic banquet to be devoured by "whom thou wilt and when." It makes clear what is already fairly clear in the Isaian Apocalypse; namely, that human beings consume the dead body of the chaos dragon at the same time God does.

(2) The pseudepigrapha means "falsely written". It refers to a large number of Jewish works written in Greek that purported to be from God, but which works were not accepted by the majority of Jews living inside or outside of Israel as either canonical or authoritative. They are not part of the Hebrew or Christian scriptures in any way.

(a) *2 Baruch* is one such pseudepigraphical work, probably written early second century A.D. [126] For our purpose, it is important in that it reveals the common Jewish understanding of Isaiah's apocalypse. It refers to the eating of the chaos dragon at the Messianic banquet.

"And he answered me and said to me: '*That which will happen at that time bears upon the whole earth. Therefore, all who live will notice it.* For at that time I shall only protect those found in this land at that time. And it will happen that when all that which should come to pass in these parts has been accomplished, *the Anointed One will begin to be revealed. And Behemoth will reveal itself from its place, and Leviathan will come from the sea, the two great monsters* which I created on the fifth day of creation and *which I shall have kept until that time. And they be nourishment for all who are left.* The earth will also yield fruits then thousandfold. And on one vine will be a thousand branches, and once branch will produce a thousand clusters, and one cluster will produce a thousand grapes, and one grape will produce a cor of wine. *And those who are hungry will enjoy themselves and they will, moreover, see marvels every day.*" (2 Baruch 29:1-7 Italics added for emphasis.) [127]

It makes clear what is already fairly clear in the Isaian Apocalypse; namely, that "all" human beings "who are left" consume the dead body of the chaos dragon at the same time God does.

(b) *I Enoch* is another such pseudepigraphical work, probably written between the second century B.C. and the first century A.D.[128] For our purpose, it is important in that it reveals the common Jewish understanding of Isaiah's apocalypse. It refers to the eating of the chaos dragon at the Messianic banquet.

> "*On that day, two monsters* will be parted- one monster, a female named *Leviathan,* in order to dwell in the abyss of the ocean over the fountains of water; and (the other) a male called *Behemoth,* which hold his chest in an invisible desert who name in Dundayin, east of the garden of Eden, wherein the elects and the righteous dwell....And the angel of peace who was with me said to me, "*These two monsters are prepared for the great day of the Lord (when) they shall turn into food.* So that the punishment of the Lord of the Spirits should come down upon them in order that the punishment of the Lord of the Spirits should not be issued in vain but slay the children with mothers and the children with their fathers, when the punishment of the Lord of the Spirits comes down upon everyone. After that there shall be the judgment according to his mercy and his patience." (1 Enoch 60:7-8, 24-26 Italics added for emphasis.)[129]

(3) The rabbis were local teachers in the synagogues of Israel following the return of the Jewish people from the captivity in Babylon in the sixth century B.C. They established an oral tradition, preserving and passing on the teaching of one generation to the next. Those teachings include common understandings of scripture. As various points in time, those oral traditions were converted to writing. The *Mishnah* converted some oral traditions to writing in the second century A.D.[130] *The Jerusalem and Babylonian Talmuds* converted some oral traditions to writing in the fourth and sixth centuries A.D. respectively.[131] And the *Midrash Rabbah* converted some oral traditions to writing in the fifth through seventh centuries A.D.[132] The precise dating of any oral tradition is very difficult. It may be very early or it may be very late.

(a) *The Midrash Rabba on Leviticus* preserves an oral rabbinic tradition concerning the common Jewish understanding of Isaiah's apocalypse. It refers to the eating of the chaos dragon at the Messianic banquet.

> "R. Judan b. R. Simeon said: *Behemoth* and the *Leviathan* are to engage in a wild-beast contest before the righteous in the Time to Come, and whoever has not been a spectator at the wild-beast contests of the heathen nations in this world will be accorded the boon of seeing one in the World to Come. How will they be *slaughtered*? Behemoth will, with its horns, pull Leviathan down and rend it, and Leviathan will, with its fins, pull Behemoth down and pierce it through...R.Berekiah said in the name of R. Isaac: In the Time to Come, the *Holy One, blessed be He, will make a banquet for his righteous servants, and whoever has not eaten nebelah[133] in this world will have the privilege of enjoying it in the World to Come.*" (Midrash Rabba Leviticus 13:3 Italics added for emphasis.)[134]

The rabbis were especially concerned with ceremonial law, including the proper killing and eating of food. A concern had been expressed that the slaughter of the chaos monsters Leviathan and Behemoth may not have been in accordance with proper ritual. The concern is dismissed. This passage makes clear what is already fairly clear in the Isaian Apocalypse; namely, that God's "righteous servants" consume the dead body of the chaos dragon at the same time God does.

The Isaian Apocalypse is a new Exodus.

> "Awake, awake, put on strength, O arm of the LORD! Awake, *as in days of old, the generations of long ago! Was it not you who cut Rahab in pieces, who pierced the dragon? Was it not you who dried up the sea, the waters of the great deep; who made the depths of the sea a way for the redeemed to cross over?* So the ransomed of the LORD shall return, and come to Zion with singing; everlasting joy shall be upon their heads; they shall obtain joy and gladness, and sorrow and sighing shall flee away. I am he who comforts you...You have forgotten the LORD, your Maker, who *stretched out the heavens and laid the foundations of the earth*...Thus says your Sovereign, the

LORD, your God who pleads the cause of his people." (Isaiah 51:9-13, 22 Italics added for emphasis.)

God will interfere in human affairs to do in the near future what he has done in the "generations of long ago." The old Exodus foreshadows the new and final Exodus. God will free his people from the chaos of their world. This prophecy of a future death of the chaos monster carries with it the promise of full and final destruction to that evil. The death of that dragon will inaugurate a new "redemption" that will bring "everlasting joy" and "gladness". All "sorrow and sighing" shall fall away. God the Redeemer will finally "plead the cause" of his people and justice will be established for all to see. God the Redeemer will finally "plead the cause" of Job himself.

The Isaian development of the myth of Leviathan into a Messianic feast was a poetic way for the ancients to say three things.

(1) Evil is all around us, deep within us.

(2) The time will come when that evil within us will be purged and destroyed.

(3) Evil is not God's final purpose in creation.

In God's second speech to Job, the scholar Tur-Sinai finds a reference to this Messianic feast of *1 Isaiah*. The NRSV obscures the allusion with its translation: "can you fill its skin with harpoons, or its head with fishing spears?" (Job 42:41:7) Tur-Sinai would clarify the allusion with his own translation: "couldst thou stud his body with cloves, with fish-onions his head?"[135] "Harpoons" have been replaced by "cloves"; "fishing spears", by "fish-onions."

"If Job thus appears to be questioned as to the filling of the body of Leviathan, which had been bought and divided by food-hoarders or merchants, then this inquiry would seem to refer to the preparation of Leviathan's body for cooking. In that case, *bslsl* is not *slsl* with prepositional *b,* but *bslsl* with *b* as a radical, meaning a kind of seasoning (small) onions, like *bslswl* in the Mishna. The omission of another, prepositional *b*- if at all necessary- may be due to the frequent phenomenon of haplography or haplology, as *byt prsh* for *bbyt prsh* etc. The mention of small onions in connection with the cooking of the fish seems quite natural.- It follows that *sbwt* is likewise a condiment, probably clove, *Naglein* (= *skwt* Accadian, *shikkatu* "pin, nail" etc.)."[136] (the transliteration from Hebrew to English is mine)

The image is that of a stuffed and roasted beast. Since Leviathan is a sea monster, the image is that of a stuffed and roasted fish.

Tur-Sinai finds additional support for his view in what he sees as an earlier reference to a stuffed and roasted fowl. "And having caught him, would you bind him and hand him to your maidservants, so that they might prepare him for your table?- *spwr* is here a general term for any edible fowl, as e.g. in Deuteronomy 14:11, and in Canaanite inscriptions."[137]

There are many good reasons to adopt Tur-Sinai's understanding of the passage.

(1) First, the amendments are minor. It is easy to understand how such a corruption in the transmission of the text could have occurred.

(2) Second, his interpretation makes good sense in terms of the surrounding verses. God has been talking about the preparation of a special meal connected with Leviathan. The image of stuffing an animal for cooking is strong.

(3) Third, his interpretation accords with the common Jewish understanding that Leviathan would be served up as the main course at the Messianic banquet at the end of human history.

This is especially the case when one remembers the structure of that apocalyptic myth. The capture of the chaos dragon by hooks and by net is immediately and invariably followed by a feast, a feeding on the dead body of the dragon, by the animals and peoples of the world. The verses that closely precede these focus on the capture of the chaos dragon by hooks. "Can one take it with hooks or pierce its nose with a snare? Can you draw out Leviathan with a fishhook, or press down its tongue with a cord? Can you put a rope in its nose, or pierce its jaw with a hook?" (Job 40:24-42:2) And the verse that immediately precedes this passage focuses on food preparation in the market. "Will traders bargain over it? Will they divide it up among the merchants?" (Job 42:6) Certainly, the "dividing" up of the monster by the fish mongers of the market can mean "cut up" in preparation for a meal. (Job 41:6) The preceding verse describes an edible fowl (Job 41:5), a bird that one might play with, but a bird that is normally meant for eating.

In any event, Tur-Sinai's insights are not necessary to this interpretation. God's seven-fold reference to the capture of the dragon Leviathan entails its ultimate destruction and an answer to all things. This is the apocalyptic structure of the Jewish myth of Leviathan. It is a myth of purpose, God's purpose in the creation, control, destruction and justification of evil.

This ultimate destruction of evil is a significant advance on the Babylonian myth of creation and the Canaanite myth of recreation.

In the Babylonian myth of creation, the high God Marduk's victory over evil is temporary. The strong suggestion is the evil will re-emerge. God and human beings have the joint responsibility for continuing that struggle. The gods "made Marduk's destiny highest, they prostrated themselves...They established him forever for lordship of heaven and netherworld....He shall do the same on earth as what he brought to pass in heaven."[138] Marduk will continue to battle an evil that he cannot completely destroy. Human beings will assist. God's will, Marduk's will, is to be done on earth as it is in heaven. Our struggle on earth is a divinely imposed burden. It is the struggle to impose order on chaos that is the history itself. It is never ending. And so the myth ends.

In the Canaanite myth of recreation, the high God Baal and the chaos monsters Yam and Mot reach a compromise, a mutual co-existence. Each will retain their separate kingdoms. "Divine <M>ot was afraid: the Beloved of El, the hero was in dread. Mot started at her voice. [He lifted up his voice and cried:] Let Baal be installed [on the throne of] his kingship, on [the back-rest, on the siege of] his dominion!"[139] Together they sit down to a communal meal to seal the peace. "Shapsh, you rule the chthonian gods; lo, mortals are your company. Kothar is your associate, and Hassis is your companion. In the sea of Arsh and the dragon, Kothat-and-Hasis, steer (the bark)!, Pilot (the ship), Kothar-and-Hasis."[140] The realms of order and chaos are both preserved. Chaos is not destroyed for ever. The dragon that is in the sea Yam remains alive. An accommodation is reached between the forces of order and the forces of chaos. Baal's counselors Kothar and Hasis drive off chaos' enemies. The conflict continues, though in a muted form. The high God Baal may control death, but he can never defeat it once and for all. And so the myth ends.

5. Explaining the dragon at the Symposium to follow

The third aspect of the Jewish myth of an apocalypse is the explanation for evil that follows in the Symposium after the Messianic banquet. This is where the justification for evil is given to all humankind. Again, the prophet Isaiah has the best exposition of that Symposium. It is a time when God the Messiah sits down and explains all things to all people.

"*Whom will he teach knowledge*, and to whom will he explain the message? Those who are weaned from milk, those taken from the breast? For it is precept upon precept, precept upon precept, line upon line, line upon line, here a little, there a little." Truly, with stammering lip and with alien tongue he will speak to this people, to whom he has said, "This is rest; give rest to the weary; and this is repose"; yet they would not hear. Therefore the word of the LORD will be to them, "Precept upon precept, precept upon precept, line upon line, line upon line, here a little, there a little;" in order that they may go, and fall backward, and be broken, and snared, and taken." (Isaiah 28:9-13 Italics added for emphasis.)

"*On that day the deaf shall hear the words of a scroll, and out of their gloom and darkness the eyes of the blind shall see.* The meek shall obtain fresh joy in the LORD, and the neediest people shall exult in the Holy One of Israel. *For the tyrant shall be no more, and the scoffer shall cease to be; all those alert to do evil shall be cut off-- those who cause a person to lose a lawsuit, who set a trap for the arbiter in the gate, and without grounds deny justice to the one in the right.*" (Isaiah 29:18-21 Italics added for emphasis.)

"Therefore the *LORD waits to be gracious* to you; therefore he will rise up to show mercy to you. For the LORD is a God of justice; blessed are all those who wait for him. Truly, O people in Zion, inhabitants of Jerusalem, you shall weep no more. *He will surely be gracious to you at the sound of your cry; when he hears it, he will answer you. Though the Lord may give you the bread of adversity and the water of affliction, yet your Teacher will not hide himself any more*, but your eyes shall see your Teacher. And when you turn to the right or when you turn to the left, your ears shall hear a word behind you, saying, "This is the way; walk in it."" (Isaiah 30:18-21 Italics added for emphasis.)

This is the moment for which the "weary" have "waited". This is the moment in which God gives the explanation for why there is evil in the world. The Lord has given the "bread of adversity" and the "water of affliction", but God the Teacher no longer hides himself or his purposes in creation. God answers all questions at this time. That is the time God will answer Job's question as to why God created a world of undeserved and unremitted suffering.

The author of *The Book of Job* may have had this passage before him. For it curiously makes reference to a person much like Job. That person is "one" involved in a "lawsuit" who was "in the right" but "denied justice" at the time. (Isaiah 29:21) On the terms of God's trial by Satan, God could not in this life answer Job and give him the reason for evil in the world. Job is denied justice in this life. But in eternity, the need for that restriction is no longer present, the trial having ended. So in eternity, that restriction will be lifted. At that moment, the Lord will hear the sound of Job's cry, and answer it. At that moment, God will fulfill the requirements of justice and reveal his hidden purpose (Job 10:13-14) in creation. At that moment, God will give a full and final explanation to all and to Job as to why there is evil in the world.

There is nothing in either the Babylonian myth of creation or the Canaanite myth of recreation that even remotely compares to this explanation and justification for the existence of evil.

In his appearance and his two speeches, God reveals himself and his intentions through the literary imagery of myth. It is not so much revelation as the occasion for the insight and inference.

6. Condemnation and Justification

Will you even put me in the wrong? Will you condemn me that you may be justified? (Job 40:7-8 Italics added for emphasis and clarification.)

God has picked up on Job's hesitation to "proceed further". In the context of Job's Oath of Innocence, that can only mean Job's hesitance to proceed beyond his own vindication to a condemnation of God brought about by a curse. The mere swearing of the oath has vindicated Job. God's appearance and the fact that God has not struck him dead has vindicated Job. Job is justified. The question is whether Job fully understands that fact. A condemnation of God for wrongdoing is neither logically nor legally necessary at this point. Job is vindicated and God has been found causally responsible for undeserved evil. As yet, God has not been found to be morally blameworthy for that evil. The question is whether Job will pass a premature judgment blaming and condemning God and depriving God of the chance to work out his purpose in bringing evil into the world. God expects Job to walk that razor's edge.

God suggests a moral purpose in his review of the mythological world. The image of Leviathan carries with it two time frames: the beginning of time and the end of time.

(1) The beginning of time is the creation and control of the chaos monster. There is an efficient cause for evil in the world.

(2) The end of time is the destruction of that chaos monster and an answering of all questions. There is a final cause for evil in the world.

Through the myth of Leviathan, God is subtly drawing Job's attention to the beginning of time and the end of time. From the beginning of time symbolized by the creation of the dragon to the end of time symbolized by the destruction of that dragon, God claims to be in control of that evil and to be using it for his own purpose.

At best, these are all suggestions.

(1) Job should infer from God's creation and control of evil an ultimate purpose for that evil.

(2) Job should infer from God's ability to capture the dragon and draw it out of the waters the two further Jewish developments of the myth: namely, a Messianic feast symbolizing the full and final destruction of evil and God as Teacher sitting down with humankind after that meal to answer all questions including the question of why there is evil in the world. These three elements of the Jewish apocalypse follow one after another and the presence of one suggests the presence of all three.

(3) Moreover, Job should infer that that ultimate explanation will be a rational demonstration and justification of the need for evil in the world.

These are inferences that Job might reasonably draw, but they are inferences that he need not draw.

In his second speech to Job, God never mentions what that moral purpose is.

(1) He never mentions what has transpired in heaven.

(2) He never mentions a special second order good, a particular type of selfless love, which might justify a massive first order evil, this world of undeserved and unremitted suffering.

(3) He never explains how and why the one might justify the other.

God rests his case, so to speak, having hinted at the existence of a defense, but having never presented it.

And in doing so, God deliberately opens himself to the condemnation that is the second default judgment in the Oath of Innocence. In doing so, God puts Job and humankind to the ultimate test. Will we condemn God so that we ourselves might be justified? Will we condemn God so that we ourselves might be vindicated?

Job's Second Response

In his second and final response, Job appears to have understood God's strategy of indirection.

"Then Job answered the LORD: "*I know that you can do all things, and that no purpose of yours can be thwarted.* 'Who is this that hides counsel without knowledge?' Therefore I have uttered what I did not understand, things too wonderful for me, which I did not know. 'Hear, and I will speak; I will question you, and you declare to me.' *I had heard of you by the hearing of the ear, but now my eye sees you*; therefore *I despise myself, and repent in dust and ashes.*" (Job 42:1-6 Italics added for emphasis and clarification.)

1. I understand your purpose.

"*I know that you can do all things, and that no purpose of yours can be thwarted.. I had heard of you by the hearing of the ear, but now my eye sees you..*" (Job 42:2 Italics added for emphasis.)

Job finds purpose in God's two speeches. Job has understood the suggestions of purpose and providence in God's first speech. And Job has understood the suggestion of a final purpose in God's creation and control of evil in God's second speech.

(1) The Hebrew word for "purpose" here is "mezimma", meaning "considered plan". It is often associated with wisdom and prudence but there is a certain shrewdness to it.[141] That shrewdness may evidence a sophisticated or nuanced approach to God's goodness. At least, the author may be suggesting the same.

(2) The Hebrew word for "thwarted" here is "batsar", meaning "cut off".[142] "Cut off" usually means death. So in Job's thinking, God's purpose in life cannot be thwarted by even death itself. God's purpose in life cannot be defeated by the person Death that is Leviathan itself.

God had commanded Job to listen and he has listened attentively to everything that God had just spoken and left unspoken, with the consequence that he now "saw" or "understood" the existence of a possible answer. The "hearing by the ear" refers to the two sets of speeches God has just delivered and not to any prior revelation received secondhand.[143] Job has learned something through God's second speech, but it is not God's sovereignty over the evil that is Leviathan. Job had much earlier in his speeches acknowledged that God was sovereign over Leviathan. (Job 9;8,13; 26:12) Through the Leviathan motif, Job has learned two things.

(1) He has learned that there will be an end to the undeserved evil that is Leviathan.

(2) He has learned that there will be an explanation for that evil.

Those two insights explain Job's comments "I uttered what I did not understand". (Job 42:1)

Job knows that God has not answered his ethical question: why do the innocent suffer, why do I suffer. But God's coming to Job, in the midst of his suffering, deepens his understanding. For all God's blustering, Job finds in it evidence that God cares. Whatever the purpose of suffering may be, it is not punishment and it is not correction. He has seen the face of God and lived. No formal declaration of innocence is required, though one has issued. God has not entered a defense and Job is vindicated or justified through his Oath of Innocence.

However, evidence that God cares is not sufficient evidence to acquit God on the charges facing him. The mere fact that God is with those who suffer is no justification for God having caused the suffering in the first place. At best, God's ex-post facto compassion may be relevant to sentence, but not to guilt. The trial of God must continue.

Job temporarily grants God the benefit of the doubt, which in this case is the benefit of time. Whatever that purpose may be, God should have the opportunity to bring it to fruition. Job grants God all of human history to work out his purpose for evil in the world. At the end of human history when all the evidence will be in, God will be able to present a full and meaningful defense, a defense of justification or necessity. Job will not thwart that purpose by prematurely passing judgment on God and blaming him for the undeserved evil in the world.

2. I despise premature judgment; I melt to my knees in worship.

"Therefore I *despise* myself, and repent in dust and ashes." (Job 42:6 Italics added for emphasis.)

A proper interpretation of this passage turns on the meaning of an extremely rare Hebrew word *"em'as"*, which only occurs once in Jewish literature, here in this passage. It stands alone in the received Hebrew text. The word "myself" is not in the Hebrew text. Some translations add it as part of their interpretation of the word *"em'as'*, but the addition is only as good as the interpretation . The meaning of *"em'as"* depends on whether the verbal root from which it is probably derived is either (1) *"ma'as"* or (2) *"masas"*.[144]

(1) The first root *"ma'as"* means "to despise" or "to reject".[145] A majority of translations and scholars, including NRSV, derive *"em'as"* from the root *"ma'as"*. In this respect, they follow the 10th century Hebrew Masoretic text. The marginal note in the Hebrew Masoretic text makes reference to the fact that the original document read *"em'as"*. The meaning was unclear. So the scribes transcribed it as *"ma'as"* to bring out their interpretation.

(2) The second root *"masas"* means "to sink down" or "to melt".[146] A significant minority of translations and scholars derive *"em'as"* from the root *"masas"*. In this respect, they follow a marginal note in the same 10th century Hebrew Masoretic text and the 5th century Greek Septuagint text. The marginal note in the Hebrew Masoretic text indicates that while they have used *"ma'as"*, a variant reading is *"masas"*.

This author's interpretation of *The Book of Job* is compatible with either translation of the word *"em'as"* and the author of *The Book of Job* may have used or invented such a rare word to imply both meanings.

(1) If the word is to be understood as "to despise", then what Job despises is not himself. Job despises premature judgment, especially a premature pronunciation of the condemnation that is the second summary default judgment of his Oath of Innocence. He grants God all of human history to finish his plan for evil in the world.

(2) If the word is to be understood as "to melt", then Job "melts" or falls to his knees in worship, maintaining a healthy respect for God and for himself. God has twice asked him to stand up, to "gird himself". (Job 38:3; 40:7) That is the proper position of a litigant. But this is also the Day of Atonement, the day when the devout worshipper falls to his knees. There are only two days in the Jewish liturgical year when a Jewish believer actually bows the knee before God; this is one.[147] Having given God the benefit of the doubt or the benefit of time, Job "melts" to his knees. He assumes the position he assumed days before when "he fell to the ground and worshipped." (Job 1:20) "In all this, Job did not sin or charge God with wrongdoing." (Job 1:22)

3. I change course. I am comforted in my vindication and delay any condemnation.

"Therefore I despise myself, and *repent* in dust and ashes." (Job 42:6 Italics added for emphasis.)

A proper interpretation of this passage turns on the meaning of the Hebrew word "*naham*". "Naham means either (1) "to change course" or (2) "to comfort or be comforted".[148]

Again, this author's interpretation of *The Book of Job* is compatible with either interpretation of the word.

(1) If the word is to be understood as "changing course", then Job "changes course" with respect to the enforcement mechanism of his Oath of Innocence. When God appeared to Job and did not enter a defense, Job was automatically vindicated in his two-fold claim that God is the author of undeserved evil in the world and that he had a right to know the reason why. On the terms of the Oath of Innocence, he was morally and legally entitled to "proceed further" to a condemnation of God by way of curse. And without any suggestions of a possible answer to the question of evil in the world, he had intended to condemn God. But such suggestions of moral purpose in evil were forthcoming in God's second speech. So Job rightly changes his mind and changes the course of his prosecution of God. Job does not and cannot retract or withdraw his Oath of Innocence. That would be to

prematurely acquit God. That would be a sin. There is a prima facie case for God to answer that has not been answered. Evil cannot be simply dismissed as something other than it is. God would not allow such partiality in judgement to go unpunished. Job adjourns the Oath of Innocence to the Day of Judgment so that he might hear from Redeemer a third time. (Job 19:25-29) The adjournment is implied in the phrase "in dust and ashes".

(2) If the word is to be understood as "being comforted", then Job is "comforted" in two ways. First, when God appeared to Job and did not enter a defense, Job was automatically vindicated in his two-fold claim that God is the author of undeserved evil in the world and that he had a right to know the reason why. Second, Job is "comforted" that God has come to him in the midst of his suffering. It is evidence that God cares. It is evidence that persuades Job to adjourn his Oath of Innocence, to wait for God's final answer. God has not abandoned Job. God has not abandoned humankind. Whatever is the reason for evil in the world, it is not punishment or character development. Still the evidence of God's presence is not sufficient evidence to acquit God on the charges facing him. The mere fact that God is with those who suffer is not, in and of itself, a justification for God having caused the suffering in the first place. God's ex-post facto compassion may be relevant to sentence but not to guilt. Job adjourns the Oath of Innocence to the Day of Judgment so that he might hear from his Redeemer a third time. (Job 19:25-29) The fact that God cares encourages Job to believe he will ultimately get that answer. The adjournment is implied in the phrase "in dust and ashes".

"Naham" can be translated "repent" but only in the loosest possible sense and a potentially misleading sense in this context. The New Oxford Annotated Edition of the NRSV adds an important editorial note to its translation of the word "naham" as "repent":

"Repent, a verb that is often used to indicate a change of mind on the Lord's part (Exodus 32:14; Jeremiah 18:8, 10). Here it does not mean repentance for sin (see vv. 7-8, where Job is said to have spoken what is right)."[149]

Shub" is the normal Hebrew word for a repentance that involves a confession of wrongdoing or sin.[150] "Shub" means "turning away from sin and returning to God through repentance."[151] The author of *The Book of Job* has carefully chosen his words. He has deliberately chosen "naham" as opposed to "shub". The author is tempting the inattentive reader to premature judgment. He is tempting the reader to find that Job is confessing sin, either for his so-called excessive words, his Oath of Innocence or both. Nothing could be further from the truth.

Job never confesses sin. He never confesses to having wrongfully used excessive language. He never confesses to having wrongfully instituted his Oath of Innocence. And he never retracts or withdraws his Oath of Innocence. God would later say Job was right in everything he said. (Job 42:7-8) In the face of such a judgment, there is no room to attribute sin or wrongdoing to Job for either his so-called excessive words or his Oath of Innocence. If Job were actually confessing sin of any sort, then Job would be damned on the terms of his Oath of Innocence. The Oath of Innocence once sworn cannot be withdrawn as having been wrongfully instituted. If Job were actually confessing sin of any sort, then Satan would be proven right in his challenge of God. And the consequences would be enormous. God would be proven wrong in his three judgments on Job. (Job 1:8-9; 2:3; 42:7) God should step down from his throne. And all of humankind should be destroyed as a failed project.

4. In dust and ashes, I continue the lawsuit and adjourn the matter to the Final Judgment.

"Therefore I despise myself, and repent *in dust and ashes*."
(Job 42:6 Italics added for emphasis.)

In[152] dust and ashes, I adjourn the Oath of Innocence to the Final Judgment to hear from my Redeemer a third time.

In part, "dust and ashes" are the condition of human beings in this world. They are but dust and ashes in a world of suffering. But it is a world Job accepts. He does not now ask for any other world. He does not ask for a restoration of his former condition. The dust heap, the ash heap, on which he now sits, is where he is content to remain. He himself is on the verge of death, soon to become dust and ashes.

Job will not condemn God nor ask God to change his ways to suit Job's needs. This is the one of the deepest surrenders imaginable.

But more importantly, the phrase "dust and ashes" implies a continuation of Job's lawsuit with a certain defiance.

That continuing challenge and defiance is its association with Abraham's challenge of God. When Abraham challenged the Lord God of the universe, the "judge of all the earth", to "judge rightly" concerned Sodom and Gomorrah and to slay not the "righteous with the guilty" (Genesis 18:22-33), he described himself as "dust and ashes".

"Then the LORD said, 'How great is the outcry against Sodom and Gomorrah and how very grave their sin! I must go down and see whether they have done altogether according to the outcry that has come to me; and if not, I will know.' So the men turned from there, and went toward Sodom, while Abraham remained standing before the LORD. Then Abraham came near and said, 'Will you indeed sweep away the righteous with the wicked? Suppose there are fifty righteous within the city; will you then sweep away the place and not forgive it for the fifty righteous who are in it? Far be it from you to do such a thing, to slay the righteous with the wicked, so that the righteous fare as the wicked! Far be that from you! Shall not the Judge of all the earth do what is just?' And the LORD said, 'If I find at Sodom fifty righteous in the city, I will forgive the whole place for their sake.' Abraham answered, 'Let me take it upon myself to speak to the Lord, *I who am but dust and ashes.* Suppose five of the fifty righteous are lacking? Will you destroy the whole city for lack of five?' And he said, 'I will not destroy it if I find forty-five there.' Again he spoke to him, 'Suppose forty are found there.' He answered, 'For the sake of forty I will not do it.' Then he said, 'Oh do not let the Lord be angry if I speak. Suppose thirty are found there.' He answered, 'I will not do it, if I find thirty there.' He said, 'Let me take it upon myself to speak to the Lord. Suppose twenty are found there.' He answered, 'For the sake of twenty I will not destroy it.' Then he said, 'Oh do not let the Lord be angry if I speak just once more. Suppose ten are found there.' He answered, 'For the sake of ten I will not destroy it.' And the LORD went his way, when he had finished speaking to Abraham; and

Abraham returned to his place." (Genesis 18:20-33   Italics added for emphasis)

Seven times, this man of "dust and ashes" continues his challenge of God: (1) "Will you indeed sweep away the righteous with the wicked." (Genesis 18:23); (2) "Far be it from you...Far be it from you." (Genesis 18:25); (3)"Suppose five of the fifty righteous are lacking? (Genesis 18:28); (4) "Suppose forty are found there?" (Genesis 18:29); (5) "Suppose thirty are found there?" (Genesis 18:30); (6) "Suppose twenty are found there?" (Genesis 18:31); (7) "Suppose ten are found there?" (Genesis 18:32) Like Job, Abraham was demanding that God give answers for his moral activity in the world. Thus, the phrase "dust and ashes" describes the person who has the moral courage to challenge God and to continue his challenge of God, even in the face of God's possible anger. (Genesis 18:30,32)

In fact, the context may even make that linkage even stronger. The exchange between God and Abraham is preceded by God's comment: "'Shall I hide from Abraham what I am about to do [namely, destroy Sodom and Gommorah]...No, for I have chosen him that he may charge his children and his household after him to keep the way of the LORD by doing justice." (Genesis 18:17-19) Thus it would seem that "doing justice" can mean challenging God and God gives human beings the opportunity "to keep the way of the LORD" by doing so.

The phrase "dust and ashes" implies Job is continuing his challenge of God. Its use here should not be read as an indication of capitulation on Job's part. Whenever Old Testament writers wish to indicate a hopeless resignation, they always use either the word "dust" or "ashes", but never the two words together. The phrase "dust and ashes" is associated with a fiery challenge of God and the discerning reader should see that Job has not lost his fire in the belly. Abraham's challenge of God may not have been expressed in terms of a formal lawsuit, but it has all the elements of a covenantal dispute. The phrase "dust and ashes" is strong literary evidence that Job is not withdrawing the lawsuit. He is not backing down. He is merely changing course as to its prosecution. Instead of condemning God here and now, he postpones and adjourns the consideration of a condemnation to a later date. Combining piety with protest, Job now continues to challenge God with his patience and his silence.

The phrase "dust and ashes" only occurs in one other place in the entire *Bible*. "He has cast me into the mire and I have become like dust and ashes." (Job 30:19) At first glance, it might appear that Job 30:19 is the proximate literary context within which to interpret Job 42:6. However, I do not believe this is the case. Things make sense in terms of context. The context is not merely physical proximity but thematic relevance. Abraham's challenge of God and Job's second speech are forensic or court-room speech involving dialogue with God. Hence, Job 42:6 should be read in light of Genesis 18:27. The existence of the phrase "dust and ashes" in Job 30:19 may complicate my argument; but I do not believe it subverts it. Arguably, Job 30:19 is a restatement of an earlier comment by Job: "If I wash myself with soap and clean my hands with lye, yet you will plunge me into filth, and my own clothes will abhor me." (Job 9:30-31) That earlier statement occurs in the first prolonged 'courtroom' scene: Job's speech concerning a mediator. Hence, Job 30:19 is not without a forensic dimension and may even provide collateral support to my interpretation. All three uses of "dust and ashes" are forensic and the allusion to Genesis 18:27 best fits the forensic dynamic of Job's second speech. [153]

The discerning reader may see in the phrase "dust and ashes" a further reference to the "earth", literally the "dust", upon which Job's Redeemer will stand to render judgment in Job's favour on the Day of Judgment. (Job 19:25-27) In that earlier context, that "earth" is the person Job reduced to ashes. That blood-stained "earth", that blood-stained "dust and ashes", cries out for justice. It is Job's moral claim to an answer for why there is evil in the world. Job's Redeemer will hear that cry for justice and press Job's claim in the High Court of Heaven long after Job is dead. Job knows he will have his answer on the Day of the Final Judgment. (Job 19:25-29) The trial date has been set. The author of the *Book of Job* is here connecting Job's continuing challenge of God with an anticipated final judgment in Job's favour.

On the dynamics of his Oath of Innocence, Job cannot withdraw the lawsuit without being damned and putting Satan in the right. He can however adjourn the condemnation that is part of the enforcement mechanism of the Oath of Innocence. An adjournment would be consistent with a continuing challenge. And the appropriate time for that adjournment would be the trial date which has already been set. (Job 19:25-29) That is what is artfully being done through the phrase "dust and ashes", a phrase pregnant with the idea of an ongoing challenge. The lawsuit is adjourned to the Day of the Final Judgment. This is the deepest surrender God knew possible. This is the selfless love and moral integrity for which the world was created. This is what preserves the moral integrity of God and men and women..

Within a canonical perspective, *The Book of Job* rewrites an important part of *The Book of Revelation*. On the Day of the Final Judgment, the trial of God will precede the trial of humanity. When all human beings appear before the Judgement Seat of God, a preliminary motion will be made to the jurisdiction of the court. No judge who is himself a criminal may pass judgement on humanity. In fact, that preliminary motion has already been made. Job made it through his Oath of Innocence. That question must be settled before God can judge all humankind. God's trial by Job will continue then and God will complete his defence. It is Job's conviction that God's final answer to the question of why there is evil in the world will settle all doubts, wipe away all tears. When all is known and understood, all will bow the knee before the Lord. God will then assume the great white throne of judgment and judge humanity on the selflessness of their love for God.

Job trusts in the goodness of God in spite of all the evil around him. He bows the knee now and will bow it then. His conviction is a matter of great faith. His conviction is a matter of great insight into what has been said and what has been left unsaid. Job will not pass judgment prematurely on God and neither should we.

God's Judgment on Job and his Friends

God now passes judgment on Job and his three friends. Elihu has fled the scene,[154] hoping to escape God's judgment.[155] Ironically, Elihu only escapes the opportunity for forgiveness.

"After the LORD had spoken these words to Job, the LORD said to Eliphaz the Temanite: "*My wrath is kindled against you and against your two friends; for you have not spoken of me what is right, as my servant Job has.* Now therefore take seven bulls and seven rams, and go to my servant Job, and offer up for yourselves a burnt offering; and *my servant Job shall pray for you, for I will accept his prayer not to deal with you according to your folly; for you have not spoken of me what is right, as my servant Job has done."* (Job 42:7-8 Italics added for emphasis.)

Job is declared by God to be the only one who has spoken "rightly" about God.

(1) The Hebrew word behind "right" is "kuwn". "Kuwn" means "to establish as right or true".[156] "The root meaning is to bring something into being with the consequence that its existence is a certainty." [157]

(2) The Hebrew word "kuwn" does not carry with it any nuance of "sincerity" such that God might be understood to be excusing Job for speaking "sincerely", but "incorrectly". God is saying Job spoke "correctly".[158]

Through his Oath of Innocence, Job has established with certainty two points.

(1) First, God is the author of evil in the world and that evil is undeserved.

(2) Second, human being have a right and need to know what why God has sent evil into the world.

That is the judgment of God.[159]

Job's three friends are declared by God to have spoken "folly". The Hebrew word behind "folly" is "nebalah". "Nebalah" means "a senseless, impious, disgraceful disregard for moral and spiritual claims"[160] The moral and spiritual claim which they have senselessly and disgracefully dismissed is Job's claim, his demand that God give an answer to the question of why there is evil in the world. That is the judgment of God.

God's condemnation of Job's three friends has an impact reminiscent of the prophet Nathan's condemnation of King David. King David had an affair with Bathsheba, got her pregnant and had her husband murdered to cover up the sin. (2 Samuel 12:1-15) The prophet Nathan found out about it, composed a parable about it and confronted King David with it. The gist of the parable was this. A poor man had nothing, but a little lamb who he loved with all his heart. A rich man had everything. He took the lamb from the poor man, killed it and served it as a meal to a stranger. (2 Samuel 12:1-4) The poor man was Bathsheba's husband. The rich man was King David. Now, literature has a way of deeply engaging its reader. King David was so moved by the story that he condemned the rich man in it, saying "as the Lord lives, the man who has done this deserves to die...because he had no pity." (2 Samuel 12:5-6) Nathan's response: "You are the man." (2 Samuel 12:7)

Job's three friends, and perhaps the inattentive reader, were all looking for Job to be condemned, either for his extreme words or for his Oath of Innocence or both. The author further tempted them to that premature judgment with Job's use of the ambiguous word "repent". A condemnation issues, but it is God's condemnation of Job's three friends and the inattentive listener. "You are that man." "You are the one deserving condemnation." "You deserve to die because you had no pity on Job." "You have senselessly and disgracefully dismissed the important moral question Job rightly raised." That is the judgment of God.

So Job prays for his friends.

"So Eliphaz the Temanite and Bildad the Shuhite and Zophar the Naamathite went and did what the LORD had told them; and the LORD accepted Job's prayer. And the *LORD restored the fortunes of Job* when he had prayed for his friends; and the LORD gave Job twice as much as he had before. Then there came to him all his brothers and sisters and *all who had known him before, and they ate bread with him in his house; they showed him sympathy and comforted him for all the evil that the LORD had brought upon him...*" (Job 42:9-11 Italics added for emphasis.)

Once again, the author reaffirms that fact that it is God and no other that has brought "evil" into the world. The Hebrew word for "evil" here is "ra-a", the same word used to describe Job's turning from evil (Job 1:1,8) and Job's comment "shall we not receive good at the hand of God, and not receive the bad". (Job 2:10) The word for evil carries "a dual meaning of being wrong in regard to God's original and ongoing intention and detrimental in terms of its effects on man."[161]

It is the author's profound commentary on God's two contradictory intentions in the creation of the world and the creation of evil. The only harmonization will come on the day of the Final Judgment when God answers Job a third time.

In the meantime, the appropriate response to those who suffer is sympathy and comfort. Those persons who trouble the troubled risk the wrath of Almighty God. (Job 42:7)

God's Restoration of Job

God now restores Job to his former position. Job had not asked for such a restoration. At first glace, it appears as an act of grace, not justice.

"The *LORD blessed the latter days of Job more than his beginning*; and he had fourteen thousand sheep, six thousand camels, a thousand yoke of oxen, and a thousand donkeys. He also had seven sons and three daughters. He named the first Jemimah, the second Keziah, and the third Keren-happuch. In all the land there were no women so beautiful as Job's daughters; and their father gave them an inheritance along with their brothers. After this Job lived one hundred and forty years, and saw his children, and his children's children, four generations. And Job died, old and full of days." (Job 42:12-17)

But some scholars have seen in this restoration an act of justice. And there is something to this insight. Hebrew law provided that if a person was wrongfully deprived of goods, both parties shall come before God; the one whom God condemns shall pay double to the other. (Exodus 22:7-9) God has wrongfully deprived Job of seven thousand sheep, three thousand camels, five hundred yoke of oxen and five hundred donkeys. (Job 1:3; 14-18) God now repays the loss double, giving fourteen thousand sheep, six thousand camels, a thousand yoke of oxen, and a thousand donkeys." (Job 42:12) God has wrongfully deprived Job of the good life. God now repays that loss double, giving an extended good life. Job lives a further 140 years (Job 42:16), presumably double the 70 years he has already lived. He dies at the ripe old age of 210 years, a life-span typified by the patriarchs themselves.[162] But Job is the ultimate patriarch, the father of theistic humanism.

To some, this seems like just reparation. However, it is not. His ten children are not resurrected. They are not restored to the good lives they lost. The ten new children are no substitute. There is no real compensation that can be offered for the loss of human life. As with much in *The Book of Job*, this final restoration is mere temptation on the author's part, a temptation to the reader and a temptation to Job to premature judgment. That premature judgment is that now all is right with the world. Nothing could be further from the truth.

A standard of justice was set with the first scene on earth and the first scene in heaven. Job was the best a humanity could be. All that he had, all that he was, was rightfully his. This is what he was justly entitled to: nothing more, nothing less. A test of righteousness and reward was instituted. Job lost everything. Prima facie, this was an act of injustice, because Job was deprived of what was rightfully his as a matter of justice. This restoration of Job is richly ambiguous. If the first test was having less reward than one's righteousness merits, then this restoration is a second test. The second test is having more reward than one's righteousness merits. The moral test that is life itself is merely transposed into a different key. The test is never ending as long as life continues. Will Job continue to demand answers for the question of evil in the world even when he is well off? Will we?

5. A PHILOSOPHICAL ANALYSIS

Myth is a fictional account of the origin of certain ideas, individuals or institutions. The actors and actions that drive the plot illustrate rather than demonstrate certain truths about the human condition. The actors and actions may incorporate certain historical details, but those details are fictionalized and embellished to draw out certain universal truths. Myth often involves stories about creation since the beginning of things is an appropriate time to discuss the "efficient cause" of things. However, it can involve stories about the apocalypse since the end of things is an appropriate time to discuss the "final cause" of things. Such stories speculate about the potentialities and actualities implicit in things. The reason myth involves both creation and apocalypse is that for many mythmakers the end is implicit in the beginning.

The Book of Job is a myth. The inverted syntax of the opening which is unique to parables suggests the book itself should be read as inspired fiction. The exclusive use of poetry rather than prose in the three cycles of speeches suggests any historical core has been thoroughly ficitionalized. The literary form of that fiction is myth because the book deals with the origin of evil and the end of that evil.

(1) The characters of God, Satan and Job as presented in the book merely dramatize certain aspects of the efficient cause of evil in the world. God created a world of undeserved and unremitted suffering in order to create the highest form of love possible: a completely selfless love of men and women for God. As a perfect being, God would have made this decision to create a particular type of world in eternity, not in time. God's wager with Satan at a particular point in time never happened. It is merely a dramatic way of exploring the moral dimensions of God's decision to create a less than perfect world and the human horror at such a decision. Job is a perfect human being. His early life in Eden is merely an alternate world that God has chosen not to create.

(2) Moreover, the characters of Job and Leviathan as presented in the later parts of the book merely dramatize certain aspects of the final cause of evil in the world.

(a) Job represents the potential for moral integrity all human beings possess. His Oath of Innocence and his nuanced submission are powerful expressions of how human beings should respond to the evil in the world around them. They should challenge God. Human beings have a right to know the reason for evil in the world. But they should not prematurely condemn God.

(b) Leviathan is the creation of Ancient Near Eastern mythologies, with important ties to both creation and apocalypse. Leviathan as such never existed. Leviathan is the poetic embodiment of the evil that is all the death, disease and disability in this world. Its ties to creation draw out the "efficient cause" of all things. And its ties to apocalypse draw out the "final cause" of all things. In the author's hands, Leviathan is merely a moral metaphor for God's creation, control, destruction and justification of evil. And the metaphor itself suggests an apocalyptic resolution to the moral question. Evil is not God's final purpose in the creation of the world. The time will come when Leviathan is drawn from the waters and served up as the main course at the Messianic banquet at the end of human history. Such a banquet is a fictional description of the meaning of the resurrection and Final Judgment. It will not occur in precisely that way. But it will be a time when God as the Messiah will declare and justify his final purpose in the creation and control of evil. The execution and explanation of that purpose could be the finest demonstration of God's power: the power to bring good out of evil.

As it stands, *The Book of Job* is merely myth building on myth, but it is artfully done.

As a literary device, myth has truth value. Myth is not deceit. Deceit is the intentional communication of known error. Truthfulness is the intentional communication of a thought that accurately corresponds with reality. Myth advances certain truth claims about the divine and the human. But it advances those claims on an existential level, not a historical level. The images in the myth refer to things beyond themselves. Only the most ignorant of interpreters would confuse the image with its reference. When they do so, they commit the logical fallacy of confusing a metaphor with a truth. The truth of history is what actually happened. The truth of myth is what actually describes the human condition, either what it is or what it could be.

The Book of Job presents a number of truth claims that describe the human condition, either as it is or as it could be. It is worth considering those claims in some detail.

1. Is morality dependant on special revelation?

Is morality dependant on special revelation? No.

The Book of Job asserts that is the case. Job is not an Israelite. Job does not live in the land of Israel. Job is not connected in any way to God's chosen people, the Jews. Job does not have the benefit of any special revelation to Abraham or to Moses. Job does not have any knowledge of or access to the Jewish sacrificial system or the Temple in Jerusalem. Yet Job knows what is morally right and wrong and perfectly fulfills his moral obligations to God and other human beings. This first truth claim is advanced through the description of Job living outside the land of Israel (Job 1:1) and the declarations by the author and by God of Job's virtual sinlessness. (Job 1:1; 1:8; 2:3)

And there appear to be good reasons why that might be so.

Human nature provides a sufficient basis for establishing morality. Goodness is the fulfillment of the natural needs or desires that define human nature. Evil is that which frustrates that fulfillment.

(1) The basic ethical duty that one "ought to desire" "what is really good" is a type of self-evident truth known as a commensurate universal.[163] The good is the desirable and the desirable is the good. The terms "desire" and "goodness" are such basic or "universal" terms that cannot be defined apart from each other. They can only be defined in terms of or "commensurate" with each other.

(a) "Desire" is the dispositional potential for "goodness".

(b) "Goodness" is the actualization of "desire".

(c) "Ought" is the "rational necessity" or "practical reasonableness" of desiring what is "really good" as opposed to what is merely "apparently good". It is unthinkable that one ought to desire what is *really bad* or that one ought *not* to desire what is "really good".

(2) These needs that define human nature are naturally knowable by all rational persons who have reached the age of moral accountability. The criteria by which they are known: universality, eradicability and irresistibility are objective.[164] The real goods that fulfill those needs are equally knowable.

(3) The process by which moral rules are derived is logically valid. Moral conclusions can be validly drawn from a major premise containing a statement of value and a minor premise containing statements of fact. No violation of the naturalistic fallacy is present in such deductions or derivations.[165]

Human nature is not independent of God. Human beings are contingent not necessary beings. The fact that they exist provides strong evidence that a necessary being God exists. The existence of God can be rationally established by the cosmological argument which begins with the contingency of human beings and the perfections within them and arrives at the conclusion of an all-powerful, all-present, all-knowing, and all-good being, God. Aquinas's five ways is the classic expression of that argument.[166] Human beings are the creation of God.

To say that morality is independent of special revelation is not to say that morality is independent of God. God has made human nature what it is and given human beings the necessary tools to derive a natural knowledge of good and evil. That natural knowledge has been termed God's general revelation in nature as opposed to his special revelation in a religious text or tradition. And God has given all human beings sufficient common grace to keep them sinless, if they choose to act on that natural knowledge.

2. Must God create the best?

Must God create the best of all possible worlds? No.

The Book of Job asserts that is the case. God is the author of evil in the world. The evil is both natural and moral. God is causally responsible for the existence of that evil. His decision may or may not be blameworthy depending of the legitimacy of God's reason in sending the evil. While God may use natural or supernatural intermediaries, such intermediaries are secondary instrumental causes. He is the principal; they are his agents. They have no agency or power to act without his permission and direction. This second truth claim is advanced through Satan's challenge to God to do evil (Job 1:9-11), God's authorization of a first set of evils (Job 1:12), Satan's infliction of that evil on God's order (Job 1:12-19), God's confession that he has done evil without any cause in Job (Job 2:3), God's authorization of a second evil (Job 2:4-6), Satan's infliction of that evil at God's command (Job 2:7), Job's confession that God has done evil. (Job 2:10), God's creation of Leviathan as the first of the great acts of God (40:15) and the author's final comments. (Job 42:11) God is presented as the direct cause of all natural evils such as death, disease, disability and the like. Leviathan is the embodiment of those evils and God is the creator of Leviathan. God is presented as the both the direct and indirect cause of many moral evils. As Job's God, he is responsible for the evil that befell Job. As the creator and sustainer of human beings and human free-will, he is implicated in all human actions. They are foreseen and cannot occur without God's permission. If human nature is created without a natural subordination of the passions to reason as seems to be the case and may be implied through the literary echoes of the creation of humankind out of Leviathan, then that involvement and foresight is even greater. God is presented as a direct contributory cause of all moral evils in the sense that he has the ability to intervene to prevent them but chooses not to do so.

And there appear to be good reasons why that might be so.

(1) First, the best of all possible worlds may not be possible. God cannot create what is impossible to create. The "best of all possible worlds" describes a world of goodness only, with no evil or imperfection in it. The idea of such a perfect world is probably incoherent. Why? One can easily imagine two or more finite worlds that are equally good. The goodness is expressed in different ways in each world. While there would be no evil in any of those worlds, it would be impossible to say one is better than another. In such a situation, there is no "best". All are equally good. Before God can be faulted for creating a world where there is evil, it has been shown there is one and only one perfect world that God should have created. So far, philosophers have not done so.[167]

(2) Second, God would not be unjust in creating a world with some evil in it. He would not be wronging anyone in doing so. He would not be depriving them of anything to which they had a right.

(a) God would not be wronging those persons who would have existed in a perfect world without evil, but who do not exist now because God has chosen to create a world with evil in it. Such persons never came into existence. They never had any right to existence. God was never under any obligation to bring them into existence. They do not exist now. So if they do not exist, then God has not wronged them by choosing not to create them.[168]

(b) God would not be wronging those persons who do exist in a world with evil. Such persons would not have existed in a world of perfect goodness. They have imperfections and would not have existed in such a perfect world. But the lives they have in a less than perfect world are not so miserable on the whole that it would have been better if they never had existed. God does not wrong anyone who claims that they were not created in a perfect world, because their complaint is unreasonable. They would not have existed in such a world. And it is better that they exist in some world than not exist in the perfect world.[169] .

(3) Third, God would not be unloving in creating a world with some evil in it. God is not only just, but loving. An important part of love is grace. God loves others without worrying about whether or not they are worthy of his love. Imperfect persons living in an imperfect world are intrinsically less valuable than perfect persons living in a perfect world. They have evil and imperfection in their character and in their lives. But God does not care. God sees what is valuable in every person. He does not worry about whether he could have found someone else more valuable somewhere else. This is the virtue of grace. It is something God has. And it is something others should have. In creating an imperfect world, God creates imperfect persons who are not as worthy of his love as those who would have existed in a perfect world. This choice is explainable and justifiable in terms of the particular type of love known as grace, which is a virtue rather than a defect in character.[170]

3. Does God act for a reason?

Does God act for reason when he creates the world? Yes.

The Book of Job asserts that is the case. God acts for a reason in creating that evil. That reason is not punishment or character development. That reason is creation of a certain type of relationship between God and humanity. Evil is morally necessary to allow selfishness and selfless love to develop separately so that men and women can selflessly love God. If human beings know with certainty that God rewards those who love him, then human beings might be tempted to use God for their own ends. Selfishness corrupts selfless love. This third truth claim is advanced through declarations by the author and by God of Job's virtual sinlessness (Job 1:1; 1:8; 2:3), Satan's first speech in heaven (Job 1:9-11) and God's acceptance of the terms of the test proposed. (Job 1:12: 2:6)

All persons act for a reason. That reason is goodness. The good is the desirable and the desirable is the good. The good is the object of our desires. It is self-evidently true that all persons desire the good. At the moment of choice, all persons choose what appears good to them, whether or not it actually is really good for them. No person chooses what appears harmful or injurious to them. This remains the case even in the most apparently destructive of all acts, suicide. To a suicidal person, death appears good, even though it may not really be good. All action is intentional and purposeful. The purpose is the achievement of a particular good, real or apparent.

God is a person, by definition. If God chooses to create a particular world, then he does so with a reason in mind. That reason is purposeful and designed to achieve a particular good.

4. Do human beings have a need to know the reason for evil?

Do human beings have a need to know the reason for evil in the world? Yes.

The Book of Job asserts that is the case. Human beings have a need to know the reason why God has created a world of undeserved and unremitted suffering. And a religious person, Job desires to know why God has apparently contradicted himself by sending evil into the world. This fourth truth claim is advanced through all Job's speeches in the first (Job 3:1-3:26; 6:1-7:21; 9:1-9:35), second (Job 12:1-14:22; 16:1-17:14; 19:1-19:29) and third (Job 21:1-21:34; 23:1-24:25; 26:1-31:4) cycles of speeches and through God's judgment on Job's three friends (Job 42:7).

And there appear to be good reasons why that might be so.

The need to know the truth of why there is evil in the world is an expression of a human being's basic desire to know. The desire to know the truth is a natural desire rooted in human nature. It is universal in the sense all human beings have it. It is eradicable in the sense that all persons have it at all points in their lives. It is irresistible in the sense that this desire is constantly seeking fulfillment. This particular need is very important, because the answer to that question is central to the meaning of life itself.

5. Do human beings have a right to know?

Do human beings have right to know that reason for evil in the world? Yes.

The Book of Job asserts that is the case. Human beings haves a moral right to know the reason why God has created a world of undeserved and unremitted suffering. That fifth truth claim is advanced through Job's raising of legal Oath of Innocence. (Job 27:1-31:4) That moral claim is dramatized as a legal claim.

And there appear to be good reasons why that might be so.

Moral rights are a reflection of natural needs. Natural needs are always good. There is no such thing as a wrong need. The very concept of a wrong natural need is incoherent. A right is a justified moral claim. The justification is supplied by the natural needs themselves. The justification is self-evidence. It is self-evidently true that there are no wrong natural needs.[171] Once it is established that there is a natural need to know the reason why there is evil in the world, there is a natural moral right to that knowledge.

6. Does God have a duty to give the answer?

Does God have a duty to give human beings the answer to why there is evil in the world? Yes and no. Yes, God must provide an explanation for evil in the world. No, God need not provide that answer here and now.

The Book of Job asserts that is the case. God has a moral duty to provide a necessary and sufficient reason why he has created a world of undeserved and unremitted suffering. That sixth truth claim is advanced through God being the defendant in Job's legal Oath of Innocence. (Job 27:2-6; 31:35-37) That moral duty is dramatized as a legal duty to respond or suffer the condemnation that can follow summary default judgment.

And there appear to be good reasons why that might be so.

(1) Yes, God has a duty to give the answer. That duty is rooted in the goodness of God. God has created human beings with certain natural needs, including the need for truth. God has to provide a reasonable possibility that those needs can be fulfilled for it is self-evidently true that "ought implies can". Otherwise, God is contradicting himself. God does not have any obligations to human beings prior to their creation. But once God creates humankind with certain needs, God acquires certain duties of care. They are duties he owes to himself and to men and women.

(2) No, God does not have the duty to give the answer right now. That is because the right to know is not an inalienable and indefeasible right. A right is inalienable or indefeasible if it cannot be "given up", "taken away", "deferred" or "overridden", without a moral wrong being committed. Very few rights are inalienable and indefeasible in that sense. There are perhaps only three such rights: the rights to "life, liberty[172] and the pursuit of happiness." Those three rights can never be given up, taken away, deferred or overridden, without human nature itself being destroyed.

The right to know the truth can be overridden or deferred in certain circumstances. Such circumstances exist where the disclosure of the truth would interfere with the pursuit or possession of a more important good. Selfless love is posited as such a real good. Time is required for the development of that good. Any premature disclosure of that truth is overridden by that higher good. The ultimate disclosure of that truth is deferred to the time at which that good is complete. Truth is never denied as being a real good. If truth were not regarded as a good, then that denial would constitute a moral wrong. It is just that the timing of the disclosure of the truth has some flexibility to it. Since selfless love is posited as a real good justifying the deferral of the truth behind evil in the world for an entire human life, the appropriate time for that disclosure is the moment of death, or a short time thereafter in a resurrection and a Final Judgment on the life one has lived.

7. Is selfless love a real good?

Is selfless love a real good? Yes.

The Book of Job asserts that is the case. It is God's reason for creating this type of world. This seventh truth is advanced through Satan's challenge and God's acceptance of the challenge. (Job 1:9-12; 2:6)

And there appear to be good reasons why that might be so.

Human beings have a natural desire to love and be loved. That desire is rooted in human nature. It is universal in the sense all human beings have it. It is eradicable in the sense that all persons have it at all points in their lives. It is irresistible in the sense that this desire is constantly seeking fulfillment. This particular need is very important, because love is perhaps the highest good and central to the meaning of life itself. Selfless love is the highest expression of love.

8. Is evil necessary to achieve that good?

Is evil necessary to achieve that good? Yes, at least some evil is necessary.

The Book of Job asserts that is the case. God's decision to create a world of undeserved and unremitted suffering is rooted in the need to separate righteousness from reward. This eighth truth claim is advanced through Satan's challenge to Job and God's acceptance of the challenge. (Job 1:9-12; 2:6)

And there appear to be good reasons why that might be so.

Selfishness can corrupt selfless love. Any necessary connection between reward and righteousness can seriously corrupt selfless love. Evil is necessary to break any necessary connection between righteousness and reward. The real question is how much and what type of evil is necessary to sever the bond so completely that human beings act as the connection never existed.

9. Is the evil in the world sufficient to achieve that good?

Is the quantity and quality of evil in this world sufficient to achieve that good? Yes, at least probably so.

The Book of Job takes that nuanced approach. Only God has the omniscience to give a definitive answer. Job adjourns his Oath of Innocence to the Day of the Final Judgment and awaits that final answer. This ninth truth claim is advanced through Job's allusion to a Redeemer who stands up in court at the Final Judgment to plead his cause (Job 19:25-27), through the allusion to the apocalyptic destruction of Leviathan at the Messianic banquet with its explanation of all things (Job 41:6; Isaiah 25:6-9; 27:1; 29:18-21) and through Job's allusion to Abraham in his adjournment of his Oath of Innocence. (Job 42:6)

And there appear to be good reasons why that might be so.

Those reasons involve a consideration of the "evidential argument from evil". The mere existence of evil is not the issue. All scholars agree that the "logical argument from evil" fails to disprove the existence of God as a God of goodness. The two propositions (a) "God exists and is all-powerful, all-present, all-knowing and all-good" and (b) "evil exists" are not logically incompatible.[173]

The moral skeptic is the one who would prematurely blame and condemn God for sending gratuitous evil into the world. The moral skeptic would format the evidential argument from evil in the following way:

(1) Major premise (p): "There exists instances of intense suffering which an all-powerful, all-present, all-knowing and all-good being could have prevented without thereby preventing the occurrence of any greater good."

(2) Minor premise (q): "An all-powerful, all-present, all-knowing and all-good being prevents the occurrence of any evil that is not logically necessary and sufficient for the occurrence of a good which outweighs it."

- 152 -

(3) Conclusion (r): "Therefore, an all-powerful, all-present, all-knowing and all-good being does not exist."[174]

The moral skeptic has two difficulties here.

The first difficulty is establishing the truth of the first premise. It almost requires omniscience to do it. In the case at hand in *The Book of Job*, the truth of that first premise is known by God and God alone. It is only an omniscient God that can give that answer. It is the message of *The Book of Job* that God is under a moral duty, dramatized as a legal duty, to give that answer and he will give it at the Final Judgment. It would be then that God would present a rigorous philosophical demonstration of his purpose in the creation and use of evil. Traditional religious thinking asserts that God will give all human beings at that time a supernatural grace that expands their minds to understand the intricacies of things that would have otherwise eluded them. This supernatural grace is part and parcel of "Beatific Vision". Human beings will be elevated beyond their created status to understand all things through the divine mind, which is identical with the divine essence. They will remain human beings, but possess certain supernatural graces such as an expanded mind. It is at such a time that God would be able to present a philosophical demonstration of the truth or falsity of the skeptics' first premise and human beings would be able to understand it. In our world, it is only possible to say that such an answer could be forthcoming, because it could exist. But omniscience would be required to present that answer and to understand it. In the meantime, it would be a sin of presumption to presume no such answer could be forthcoming.

The second difficulty is the logic or validity of the argument itself. The evidential argument from evil can be turned on its head.

The moral skeptic's form of the evidential argument from evil is "If (p) and (q), then (r)". But the logic of the argument is reversible, as the great 20th century philosopher G.E. Moore noted. The evidential argument from evil is equally valid if presented in a different form: "If (not r) and (q), then (not p)". This is the so-called "G.E. Moore shift."[175] Again we are talking about the validity of the argument, not the truth of the argument. The moral skeptic now has a Trojan horse on his or her hands.

A theist such as Job could reformat the argument in a way that strongly suggests the existence of an answer.

(1) Major premise (not r): "An all-powerful, all-present, all-knowing and all-good being does exist."

(2) Minor premise (q): "An all-powerful, all-present, all-knowing and all-good being prevents the occurrence of any evil that is not logically necessary and sufficient for the occurrence of a good which outweighs it."

(3) Conclusion (not p): "There do not exist instances of intense suffering which an all-powerful, all-present, all-knowing and all-good being could have prevented without thereby preventing the occurrence of any greater good."[176]

The $64,000 question is a simple one. Is the evidence stronger for the moral skeptic's first premise: "there exists instances of intense suffering which an all-powerful, all-present, all-knowing and all-good being could have prevented without thereby preventing the occurrence of any greater good"? Or is the evidence stronger for the theist's first premise "an all-powerful, all-present, all-knowing and all-good being does exist"?

At first glance, the scales tip in favor of the theist. The moral skeptic has a real difficulty establishing the truth of his first premise. He or she may have their suspicions but they require something near omniscience to establish the truth of his first premise. Their task is especially difficult with the real good selfless love presented in *The Book of Job*. That love requires a massive quantity of undeserved evil that brings the very existence of God into serious question so that the bond between righteousness and reward can be completely severed. The theist has much less difficulty with his first premise. The cosmological argument from Aquinas presents very strong evidence for the existence of a necessary being with all the perfections of being, including intellect and goodness.[177] It does not require anything near omniscience to establish the theist's first premise.

Thus, there appear to be good reasons to believe God had a special good in mind in creating the world and the evil in the world is necessary and sufficient to bring about that real good. The message of *The Book of Job* is that the one true god, Yahweh, a perfect being, has that answer, will ultimately present it and will ultimately demonstrate its truth.

10. Is there a Final Judgment?

Is there a Final Judgment? Yes.

The Book of Job asserts that is the case. The moral question that only God can answer can only be fully answered on the Day of the Final Judgment. This final truth claim is advanced through Job's allusion to a Redeemer who stands up in court at the Final Judgment to plead his cause (Job 19:25-27), through the allusion to the apocalyptic destruction of Leviathan at the Messianic banquet with its explanation of all things (Job 41:6; Isaiah 25:6-9; 27:1; 29:18-21) and through Job's allusion to Abraham in his adjournment of his Oath of Innocence. (Job 42:6)

And there appear to be good reasons why that might be so.

God created men and women to lead a good life and the nature of the good life suggests the possibility of an afterlife. The good life is a final end that is normative, not terminal. It cannot be said at any point in time that a person has lived a good life when life itself is not over. The good in life is the good life as a whole. That whole good is never achieved at any moment in time. That's what meant by saying the final end is not terminal. It is always in the process of becoming. The only terminus is death. Thus any assessment as to whether a person has lived a good life is an assessment that can only be made at the end of life itself. Only then is a final judgment possible on the goodness of life. God created men and women to lead a good life and presumably God intends an examination of his work. The appropriate time for that assessment is the moment of death or shortly thereafter. This does not mean an afterlife is logically necessary. It merely means that an afterlife may be an appropriate time for God to pass judgment of the fruits of his labor.

God created men and women with certain unlimited desires, the fulfillment of which lies beyond this life. The desire for truth and the desire for God are by their very natures unlimited. The existence of such natural needs strongly suggests the existence of real goods that satisfy those needs. The God that created the one provides the other. The one implies the other. If that were not the case, then God would contradict himself for it is self-evidently true that "ought" implies "can". The desire for truth and the desire for God can only be completely satisfied in an afterlife. Again, this does not mean an afterlife is logically necessary. It merely means that there exists in human nature a good reason to posit the existence of such an afterlife.

If such an afterlife exists, then that would be a highly appropriate time for God to give the answer to the question why is there evil in the world. It is contemporaneous with an assessment of human life and consistent with humanity's unlimited natural desire to know the truth and to know God.

6. CONCLUSION

In times of suffering and despair, many turn to *The Book of Job* for answers to the evil that has befallen them. Rabbis, priests and pastors recommend *The Book of Job,* as perhaps no other, to those in need. Many find a deep consolation in a reading of this book that they rarely find elsewhere in the *Bible.* They deeply identify with the person Job. They share his anguish and his anger. They share his driving need for answers. Like Job, they long to meet God personally and find those answers. They walk the road Job walks through the wilderness of their lives. And as he is restored, they themselves find a measure of renewal and comfort. Evil is not always a punishment. Evil is not always a means of character development. And with that insight, they can put down the burden of false guilt.

Readers may not, as of a first reading of *The Book of Job,* have a deep appreciation of the role of evil of the world: its necessity and sufficiency. And they may not fully understand all the dynamics of good and evil at play in the book. But they do apprehend that somehow in the midst of it all, God is with them as they read the book, just as he was with Job. He has not deserted them in the hour of their need. It is my hope that which each reading of *The Book of Job,* they will come to an even deeper understanding of the mystery of evil and God's use of this evil in the world. Hopefully, this work will contribute to that spiritual quest.

In the meantime, we can all remember three things. We are called to be as patient as Job, enduring a suffering we do not always fully understand. We are called to be as honest as Job, refusing to give pat answers to the problem evil, refusing to call evil good and good evil. And we are called to be as devout as Job, exercising faith in the midst of pain and trusting that answers will be given. A world of undeserved and unremitted suffering may be morally necessary and sufficient to bring about the purest form of selfless love. If that is the answer, then God certainly knows the how and the why that must be the case. There are good reasons, rooted in the goodness of human life and in human nature, to believe God will ultimately give those answers in his time, eternity.

As we close this reading of *The Book of Job,* we open a new chapter in our lives. We go forth in the knowledge that, however unsearchable and inscrutable the ways of Lord may seem at the moment, God is with us in the midst of our suffering; he will never leave us or forsake us. There is an answer to the question of why there is evil in the world and God will ultimately give it. This is the hope and dream of all the humankind. That is the message of *The Book of Job*.

7. APPENDICIES

APPENDIX A- BABYLONIAN MYTH OF CREATION

The Babylonian myth of creation is called the "Enuma Elish". It's written in Akkadian, the language of the Babylonian empire. The title "Enuma Elish" is taken from the opening Accadian words of the poem "when on high". It is the myth of the high God Marduk's struggle with the chaos monsters Tiamat and Qingu. "There is no firm evidence for its date of composition. To judge from its language and content, the poem dates to the latter part of the second millennium BC."[178] The writers of the Old Testament and *The Book of Job* will use and rework much of the language and imagery of the Babylonian myth of creation.

1. Watery Chaos

The myth opens with a primordial watery chaos. That chaos is called Apsu and Tiamat. Apsu is male. Tiamat is female. And the hint of sexual intimacy suggests the potentiality for further development. As of this point in time, the divine does not exist. "When on high no name was given to heaven, nor below was the netherworld called by name."[179] "When no gods at all had been brought forth, nor called by names, none destines ordained."[180]

2. The Emergence of the high God Marduk

Out this duality of potentiality, the gods emerge. Out of Apsu, the high God Marduk is formed.

"His body was magnificent, fiery his glance,
He was a hero at birth,
he was a mighty one from the beginning!
....
He wore (on his body) the aura of ten gods,]
had (them) wrapped around his head (?) too,
Fifty glories were heaped upon him.
Anu formed and produced the four winds,
He put them in his hand, "Let my son play!"[181]

Marduk is the storm god, draped in golden auras of glory. He is destined to do heroic things.

3. Marduk's Play

Marduk begins to "play". The play is the creation of a whirlwind. The key statement "Let my son play!" can mean "My son, let them whirl" referring to the winds.[182] Marduk is the storm God. The play in question is the imposition of order on chaos. The whirlwind is the identifying sign of the imposition of that order. "He fashioned dust, he made a storm bear it up, He caused a wave and it roiled Tiamat, Tiamat was roiled, churning day and night, The gods, finding no rest, bore the brunt of each wind."[183]

4. Tiamat's Conspiracy

Tiamat resists this imposition of order and is stirred to action by the other gods. "They plotted evil in their hearts"[184] and counseled war "Battle has begun, give them what they deserve, [Ma]ke a [tempest], turn them into nothingness". [185] Tiamat agreed with their counsel and plotted war. "[They clo]sed ranks and drew up at Tiamat's side, Angry, scheming, never laying down night and day, [Mak]ing warfare, rumbling, raging, Convening in assembly, that they might start hostilities."[186]

5. The emergence of dragons

A chaos monster herself, Tiamat gives birth to other chaos monsters to resist the imposition of order. These monsters were supernatural dragons and composite beasts modeled on a dragon.

"Mother Huber,[187] who can form everything,
Added countless invincible weapons,
gave birth to monster serpents,
Pointed of fang, with merciless incisors (?),
She filled their bodies with venom for blood.
Fierce dragons she clad with glories,
Causing them to bear auras like gods, (saying)
"Whoever see them shall collapse from weakness!
Wherever their bodies make onslaught,
they shall not turn back!"
She deployed serpents, dragons, and hairy hero-men,
Lion monsters, lion men, scorpion men,
Mighty demons, fish men, bull men,
Bearing unsparing arms, fearing no battle.

Her commands were absolute, no one opposed them.
Eleven indeed on this wise she crea[ted]."[188]

She was the first dragon. She created eleven more such dragons. All dragons are her children. Together the twelve formed an assembly of evil. All are one in their intention to do evil.

Out of that assembly, Tiamat chose her son Qingu to be the leader of the army and commander of the assembly. She married that son, a powerful illustration of the incestuous nature of evil.

"(All) she entrusted to him, made him sit on the dais.
"I will cast your spell.
I will make you the greatest in the assembly of the gods.
Kingship of all the gods I put in your power.
You are the greatest, my husband, you are illustrious,
Your command shall always be the greatest,
over all thee Anunna-gods."
She gave him the tablet of destines,
had him hold it to his chest, (saying)
"As for you, your command will not be changed,
your utterance will endure."[189]

And she gathered the host for battle with the gods. "Thereafter Tiamat, more than Apsu, was become an evildoer." She declared open war on the gods. For all intents and purpose, the future was hers. She controlled the "tablets of destinies".

6. The fear of the gods

When Ea, the god of wisdom, heard this declaration of war, he was "struck dumb with horror and sat stock still."[190] Ea goes to his grandfather Anshar and tells him the bad news of a demonic horde.

"They are massing around her, ready at Tiamat's side
Angry, scheming, never laying down night and day,
Making warfare, rumbling, raging,
Convening in assembly, that they might start hostilities,
Mother Huber,[191] who can form everything,
Added countless invincible weapons,
gave birth to monster serpents,
Pointed of fang, with merciless incisors (?),

She filled their bodies with venom for blood.
Fierce dragons she clad with glories,
Causing them to bear auras like gods, (saying)
"Whoever see them shall collapse from weakness!
Wherever their bodies make onslaught,
they shall not turn back!"
She deployed serpents, dragons, and hairy hero-men,
Lion monsters, lion men, scorpion men,
Mighty demons, fish men, bull men,
Bearing unsparing arms, fearing no battle.
Her commands were absolute, no one opposed them.
Eleven indeed on this wise she created."[192]

Anshar orders Ea and Anu in turn to destroy Tiamat, but both:

"...stopped, horror-stricken, then turned back....
Her strength is enormous, she is utterly terrifying,
She is reinforced with a host, none can come out against her.
Her challenge was not reduced,
it was so loud (?) against me,
I became afraid at her clamor, I turned back."[193]

The poet of the *Enuma Elish* is captivated with terrifying dragon imagery and this particular refrain will be repeated itself four times during the course of the poem. This is the second time. Evil is so terrifying that even the gods are "struck dumb with horror and stand stock still." "Whoever see them shall collapse from weakness."

7. Marduk's Claim to Supremacy

An emergency assembly of the gods is called to deal with the challenge. Only Marduk volunteers to do battle with Tiamat and he promises victory.

"[My father], creator, rejoice and be glad,
Soon you will trample the neck of Tiamat,
"[Anshar], creator, rejoice and be glad,
Soon you will trample the neck of Tiamat!"[194]

In the ancient world, the defeat of an enemy was often symbolizing by a foot on the neck of the defeated foe, foreshadowing a crushing blow by a club to the head.[195]

Anshar tells his vizier Kakka to convey the following message to two other gods, Lahmu and Lahamu so that they might attend the assembly.

"They are massing around her, ready at Tiamat's side
Angry, scheming, never laying down night and day,
Making warfare, rumbling, raging,
Convening in assembly, that they might start hostilities,
Mother Huber,[196] who can form everything,
Added countless invincible weapons,
gave birth to monster serpents,
Pointed of fang, with merciless incisors (?),
She filled their bodies with venom for blood.
Fierce dragons she clad with glories,
Causing them to bear auras like gods, (saying)
"Whoever see them shall collapse from weakness!
Wherever their bodies make onslaught,
they shall not turn back!"
She deployed serpents, dragons, and hairy hero-men,
Lion monsters, lion men, scorpion men,
Mighty demons, fish men, bull men,
Bearing unsparing arms, fearing no battle.
Her commands were absolute, no one opposed them.
Eleven indeed on this wise she created."[197]

This is the third occurrence of that demonic refrain. The vizier Kakka arrives and repeats the message.

"They are massing around her, ready at Tiamat's side
Angry, scheming, never laying down night and day,
Making warfare, rumbling, raging,
Convening in assembly, that they might start hostilities,
Mother Huber,[198] who can form everything,
Added countless invincible weapons,
gave birth to monster serpents,
Pointed of fang, with merciless incisors (?),
She filled their bodies with venom for blood.
Fierce dragons she clad with glories,
Causing them to bear auras like gods, (saying)
"Whoever see them shall collapse from weakness!
Wherever their bodies make onslaught,
they shall not turn back!"

She deployed serpents, dragons, and hairy hero-men,
Lion monsters, lion men, scorpion men,
Mighty demons, fish men, bull men,
Bearing unsparing arms, fearing no battle.
Her commands were absolute, no one opposed them.
Eleven indeed on this wise she created."[199]

This is the fourth and final occurrence of the refrain.

The assembly of gods convenes. Marduk offers to defeat
Tiamat only if all the gods surrender their powers to him and he
becomes an absolute monarch. "When I speak, let me ordain
destinies instead of you. Let nothing that I shall bring about be
altered, Nor what I say be revoked or changed."[200] The offer is
accepted and a resolution is passed. "Cut off the life of Tiamat, Let
the wind bear her blood away as glad tidings!"[201]

8. Marduk's Battle with Tiamat

And so Marduk went out fully armed to do battle with
Tiamat.

"He made the bow, appointed it his weapon,
He mounted the arrow, set it on the string,
He took up the mace, held it in his right hand,
Box and quiver he slung on his arm.
Thunderbolts he set before his face.
With raging fire he covered his body.
Then he made a net to enclose Tiamat within.
He deployed the four winds that none of her might escape:
South Wind, North Wind, East Wind, West Wind,
Gift of his grandfather Anu, he fastened the net at his side.
He made ill wind, whirlwind, cyclone.
Four-ways wind, seven-ways wind, destructive wind,
irresistible wind:
He released the winds which he had made, the seven of them,
Mounting in readiness behind him to roil inside Tiamat."[202]

The divine weapons by which the high God will defeat the chaos
monster are important: the bow and arrow, the mace or club, the net
and the winds, and most importantly the whirlwind. The four winds,

the seven winds circle together to create the irresistible ill wind, the whirlwind.

And so Marduk proceeded out to battle.

"Then the Lord raised the Deluge, his great weapon,
He mounted the terrible chariot,
the unopposable Storm Demon,
He hitched to it the four-steed team, he tied them at his side:
'Slaughter', 'Merciless', 'Overwhelmer', 'Soaring.'
Their lips are curled back, their teeth bear venom,
They know not fatigue, they are trained to trample down.
He stationed at his right gruesome battle and strife,
At his left the fray that overthrows all formation.
He was garbed in a ghastly armored garment.
On his head he was covered with terrifying auras.
The Lord made straight and pursued his way,
Towards raging Tiamat he set his face.
He was holding a spell ready upon his lips,
A plant, antidote to venom, he was grasping in his hand."[203]

Marduk is the high God. He does not possess all power. He supplements that power with magical "spells" and "antidotes." As he approached Tiamat and Qingu, Tiamat cast her own spell on him and "his tactic turned to confusion, His reason was overthrown, his actions panicky."[204] Not only were the gods dumb struck before the terrifying nature of evil, the high God Marduk was as well.

Yet he recovered and challenged Tiamat to single combat.

"Come within range, let us duel, you and I!"
When Tiamat heard this,
She was beside herself, she turned into a maniac
Tiamat shrieked loud, in a passion,
Her frames shook all over, down to the ground.
She was reciting an incantation, casting her spell."[205]

9. Marduk's Defeat of Tiamat and Qingu

And so Tiamat and Marduk entered into a struggle to the death.

"Tiamat and Marduk, sage of the gods, drew close for battle,
They locked in single combat, joining for the fray.
The Lord spread out his net, encircled her,
The ill wind he had held behind him, he released in her face.
Tiamat opened her mouth to swallow,
He thrust the ill wind so she could not close her lips.
The raging winds bloated her belly,
Her insides were stopped up, she gaped her mouth wide.
He shot off the arrow, it broke open her belly,
It cut to her innards, it pierced her heart.
He subdued her and snuffed out her life.
He flung down her carcass, he stood his stand upon it."

Tiamat is killed as she opens her mouth to swallow the high God.
She swallows the whirlwind and is destroyed from within. Marduk
shoots an arrow through her mouth and it pierces her heart and tears
open her belly. Her innards fall out. She is dead. And Marduk takes
his stand on her dead carcass.

And then Marduk routed Tiamat's followers and imprisoned
the demonic horde.

"After the vanguard had slain Tiamat,
He scattered her forces, he dispersed her host.
As for the gods her allies, who had come to her aid,
They trembled, terrified, they ran in all directions.
They tried to make a way out(?) to save their lives,
There was no escaping the grasp that held (them)!
He drew them in and smashed their weapons.
They were cast in the net and sat in a heap,
They were heaped up in the corners, full of woe,
They were bearing his punishment, to prison confined,
As for the eleven creatures, the ones adorned with glories,
And the demonic horde(?),
which went in attendance at her side,
He put on leadropes, he bound their arms.
He trampled them under, together with their belligerence."[206]

He took from Qingu the table of destinies and turned back on Tiamat.
"The Lord trampled upon the frame of Tiamat,
With his merciless mace he crushed her skull.
He cut open the arteries of her blood,

he let the North Wind bear (it) away as glad tidings.
...Then the Lord was inspecting her carcass,
That he might divide(?) the monstrous lump
and fashion artful things.
He split her in tow, like a fish for drying..."[207]

Marduk tramples on the frame or carcass of Tiamat and crushes out
any remaining life in her with a club to the head.

10: The Creation of the World

Out of Tiamat's dead body, Marduk created the world.

"Half of her he set up and made as a cover, heaven.[208]
He stretched out the hide and assigned watchmen,
And ordered them not to let her waters escape.
He crossed heaven, he inspected (its) firmament.[209]

He made the position(s) for the great gods,
He established (in) constellations the stars, their likenesses.
He marked the year, described its boundaries,
He set up twelve months of three stars each.
After he had patterned the days of the year,
He fixed the position of Neberu to make the (star')
relationships.
Lest any make an error or go astray,
He established the position(s) of Enlil and Ea in relation to it.[210]
He opened up gates on both (side of her) ribs,
He made strong bolts to left and right.
In her liver he established the zenith.
He made the moon appear, entrusted (to him) the night.[211]
....
He set down her head and piled [   ][212] upon it,
He opened underground springs, a flood was let flow(?).
From her eyes he undamned the Euphr[ates] and Tigris,
He stopped up her nostrils, he left...
He heaped up high-peaked mo[unt]tains from (?) her dregs.
He drilled through her waterholes to carry off the catchwater.
He coiled up her tail and tied it as(?) 'The Great Bond.'[213]
...
He set her crotch as the brace of heaven,
Spreading [half of] her as a cover, he established the earth.

[After] he had completed his task inside Tiamat,
[He spre]ad his net, let all (within) escape,
He formed (/?) the...[ ] of heaven and netherworld."[214]

In Ancient Near Eastern thinking, the universe was tri-partite: heaven, earth and the underworld. The earth was a disk sitting on water, surrounded by water. The earth is created out of Tiamat. The remains of Tiamat are confined to three places: the heavens, the oceans surrounding and encircling the earth and the underworld below. The reference to heaven is direct here: "half of her he set up and made as a cover, heaven." The reference to the surrounding and encircling oceans is direct as well though some reader might miss it: "He coiled up her tail and tied it as(?) 'The Great Bond.'" The surrounding waters are the bond that holds the heavens, the earth and the underworld together.[215] The reference to the underworld is found in the eyes that are the springs of the Euphrates and Tigris rivers. From the underworld, water comes forth onto the earth.

The poetic point being made by the Babylonian poet is a very simple one. Chaos is evil. Evil is all around us. Evil is above us, beside us and beneath us, just as the waters of chaos are. Evil is part of the very fabric of creation. Evil is a part of the high God's plan in creation of the world.

11. The Creation of Man

Out of Qingu's dead body, Marduk created humankind.

"I shall compact blood, I shall cause bones to be,
I shall make stand a human being, let 'Man' be its name.
I shall create mankind,
They shall bear the gods' burden that those may rest.[216]
....
It was Qingu who made war,
Suborned Tiamat and drew up for battle.
They bound and held him before Ea,
They imposed the punishment on him, and shed his blood.
From his blood he made mankind,
They imposed the burden of the gods and exempted the gods.
After Ea the wise had made mankind,
They imposed the burden of the gods on them!"[217]

Human beings were created out of the blood of a slain chaos monster.[218] In Ancient Near Eastern thinking, the blood is the life. The life is the character of a human being. Human beings take their lives, their character from their parents. Qingu is their father. Tiamat is their mother. The blood of the evil ones flows in their veins.

Again, the poetic point being made by the Babylonian poet is a very simple one. Chaos is evil. Evil is deep within us. Evil flows within our veins. Evil shapes our life and our character. Evil is part of the very fabric of our being. Evil is part of the high God's plan is our creation.

12: The Kingdom of Marduk

And so Marduk was made the one high God. "They made Marduk's destiny highest, they prostrated themselves.....They established him forever for lordship of heaven and netherworld....He shall do the same on earth as what he brought to pass in heaven."[219] His will is to be done on earth as it is in heaven. Our struggle on earth is a divinely imposed burden. It is the struggle to impose order on chaos that is the history itself.

APPENDIX B- CANAANITE MYTH OF RE-CREATION

The Canaanite myth of re-creation is called the Baal cycle. It's written in Ugaritic, the language of the one of the chief city states, Ugarit, of the loose Canaanite confederation. Ugarit is near modern day Ras Shamra in southern Lebanon. The language is indirectly related to early Hebrew.[220] The title "Baal cycle" is taken from the leading character. The poem as such is untitled. It is the myth of the high God Baal's struggle with the chaos monsters Yam and Mot. To a lesser extent, it is the myth of a high goddess Anat's struggle with the chaos monsters Litan, Yam and Mot. Her struggle is Baal's struggle and she is his sister. The probable date of composition is the 14th century B.C.[221], though many aspects of it have now been traced back to the third millennium B.C.[222] The writers of the Old Testament and *The Book of Job* will use and rework much of the language and imagery of this Canaanite myth of re-creation.

1. Yam's Challenge to Baal's Kingship

This myth opens with a crisis, a challenge to the kingship. It is not the time of creation, but rather sometime subsequent to that creation. The messengers of the chaos monster Yam arrive at the temple or palace of the gods and seize control. They demand two things. First, they require that the chaos monster Yam be declared Lord. Second, they require that high God Baal, his golden palace, his throne and all his gold be turned over to Yam. It is this challenge to an already existing order that makes this myth a myth of re-creation.

This suggested change in kingship seemed prudent to avoid war so the Canaanite El, the god of wisdom, agrees.

"Baal is your slave, O Yam;
Baal is your slave, [Nahar].
The Son of Dagan is your prisoner:
he will bring you tribute like the gods;
[   ] he will bring you offerings, like the sons of the Holy One."[223]

2. Baal's Battle with Yam

However, Baal refuses to part with his kingship without a fight. Surrender means death and confinement in the underworld.

"Then Prince Baal was enraged.
In his hand he [seiz]ed a knife.
In his right hand a weapon.
The divine assistants he [attacked].
His right hand [A]nat seized;
his left hand Athart seized.
"How could you smite [the messengers of Yam],
the embassy of Ruler Nahar.
…
[Baal spoke.]
…
"By Yam I shall be worm eaten {…}
[and thanks to] Nahar (devoured by) maggots.
There with a sword I shall destroy.
I shall knock down (his) [hou]ses.
Into the underworld will fall my strength,
and into the dust my power.
[From] his mouth his speech barely went forth,

from his lips his word,
and he gave forth his voice in groaning
beneath the throne of Prince Yam."[224]

Baal's advisors Kothar and Hasis counseled war. They provided Baal with the weaponry of war. And Baal went out to fight Yam.

"And Kothar-and-Hasis spoke:
"Indeed I say to you, O Prince Baal,
I repeat, O Charioteer of the Clouds,
now your foe, Baal,
now your foe you must smite;
now you must destroy the adversary!
Take your everlasting kingdom,
your everlasting dominion!

Kothar fashioned two maces,
and pronounced their names:
'You, your name is "Expeller"
Expeller, expel Yam,
expel Yam from his throne,
Nahar from the siege of his dominion!
You must leap from the hand of Baal,
like a falcon from his fingers.
Strike the shoulder of Prince Yam,
the chest of [Rul]er Nahar!'
The mace leapt from the hand of Baal,
like a falcon from his fingers.
It struck the shoulder of Prince Yam,
the chest of Ruler Nahar."[225]

The battle however did not initially go well for Baal.

"But Yam was strong:
he did not flinch.
His joints did not tremble:
his visage was not discomposed."[226]

So Baal changed his weaponry and tactics and finally defeated Yam. He swallowed the sea.

"Kothar fashioned two maces,
and he pronounced their names:
'You, your name is "All-Driver"
All-Driver, drive Yam away,
drive Yam from his throne,
Nahar from the siege of his dominion!
You must leap from the hand of Baal,
like a falcon from his fingers.
Strike the skull of Prince Yam,
the brow of Ruler Nahar!
Let Yam collapse in a heap,
and let him fall to the ground!"
Then the mace leapt from the hand of Baal,
like a falcon from his fingers.
It stuck the skull of Prince Nahar.
Yam collapsed in a heap;
he fell to the ground.
His joints trembled,
and his visage was discomposed.
Baal gathered up
and drank <Prince> Yam to the dregs;
he exterminated Ruler Nahar.
By name Athtart chided (him):
"Dry (him) up. O Valiant Baal!"[227]

3. Anat's Battle with Yam

The scene shifts to the earth where Baal's sister Anat, the goddess of war, is destroying all the peoples of the earth, from the sunrise to the sunset. Baal, now triumphant, demands that she stop and return to him. She is resistant and claims to have defeated Yam herself, though it is unclear whether she is referring to a prior battle or this most recent challenge to Baal's kingship.

"She lifted up her voice and cried:
'Why have Gupan and Ugar come?
What manner of enemy has arisen against Baal,
of foe against the Charioteer of the Clouds?
Surely I smote the Beloved of El, Yam?
Surely I exterminated Nahar, the mighty god?
Surely I lifted up[228] the dragon
I overpowered him?

I smote the writhing serpent,
Encircler[229]- with-seven heads!
I smote the Behoved of El, Arsh,
I finished off El's calf, Atik,
I smote El's bitch, Fire,
I exterminated El's daughter, Flame.
I fought for the silver,
I took possession of the gold
of those who drove Baal from the heights of Saphon,
knocking him like a bird from his perch,
(who) drove him the throne of his kingship,
from the back-rest,
from the siege of his dominion.
What manner of enemy has arisen against Baal,
of foe against the Charioteer of the Clouds?"[230]

Two descriptions are important here, that of Yam and Atik. The chaos monster Yam is a "dragon", a "writhing serpent", an "Encircler with seven heads." The seven headed dragon is the chaos water that encircles the earth. Atik is a bull calf. From other myths, Atik appears to be the chaos monster that ravages the land as a wild bull might.

Anat finally agrees to Baal's request to return. The "Great Lady-who-tramples-Yam" returns to Baal and offers worship "Our king is Valian[t], Baal is our lord: and there is none above!"[231] A plan is devised to rebuild Baal's palace or to build a new one.

4. Baal's Battle with Mot

Confident in his recent victory over the sea Yam, Baal tries to extend his dominion over death itself, Mot.

"I shall surely send a messenger to divine Mot,
an envoy to the Beloved of El, the hero.
Mot may mutter to himself,
the Beloved may scheme in his heart;
(but) I alone it is who will rule over the gods,
who will fill gods and men,
who will satisfy the multitudes of earth!"[232]

Baal is dissatisfied that the dragon Death has swallowed up the sun in an eclipse.

So Baal sends messengers to Mot in his chaotic underworld home.

"Aloud to his divine assistants Baal cries:
"Look, [Gupan] and Ugar,
The Dark One [has obscured] the day,
the Bloomy One the ex[alted Soverei]gn.:
....
Then set your faces indeed
toward his city Muddy,
a pit the seat of his enthronement,
a crevice the land of his inheritance.
But take care, attendants of the god,
do not draw near divine Mot,
lest he offer you up like a lamb in his mouth,
like a kid in the opening of his maw!
Lest you be carried away by the Luminary of the gods, Shapsh,
the Burning One, strength of the heavens,
into the hands(s) of the Beloved of El, Mot.
Over a thousand miles,
ten thousand leagues,
at the feet of Mot bow and fall down,
pay him homage and honour him."[233]

Mot is not impressed with Baal's victory over the sea. He challenges Baal to a fight and promises his destruction.

"Though you smote Litan the wriggling serpent,
finished off the writhing serpent,
Encircler-with-seven-heads,
the skies will be hot, they will shine
when I tear you in pieces:
I shall devour (you),
elbows, blood and forearms;
You will indeed go down into the throat of the divine Mot,
into the maw of the Beloved of El, the hero."
....
'My appetite is the appetite of the lion in the wasteland,
as the desire of the shark is in the sea;

as wild bulls year for pools,
or the hind longs for the spring.
Look, in truth does my throat devour clay[234]
and with both my hands I devour them."[235]

Mot describes Yam, by Yam's alternate name Litan. But he is the same "writhing" serpent of which Anat has already spoken. Mot is death. Mot's appetite is suggestive. It is the "appetite of the lion in the wasteland." The strong suggestion is that all predators on the earth are but incarnations or manifestations of death itself.[236]

Baal's messengers return to Baal. They relay Mot's message and comment on the likelihood of Baal's defeat by Mot.

"[He extends a lip to the ea[rth],
a lip to the heavens,
[he extends] a tongue to the stars.
[Ba]al must enter his belly,
down into his mouth he must go,
since he scorched the olive,
the produce of the earth,
and the fruit of the trees.[237]

The poetic imagery is quite beautiful here. Death has an appetite and a mouth that swallows up the earth and all in it.

Baal is dumb struck. "Valiant Baal was afraid of him; Valiant Warrior was in dread of him."[238] He surrenders without a fight and descends into the underworld. "O divine Mot, your servant am I, and forever so."[239] Mot "lifted up his voice and cried: 'Baal is dead! What has become of the Powerful One? The Son of Dagan! What has become of Tempest?"[240]

5. Anat's Battle with Mot

Baal's sister Anat searches for him throughout the world and cannot find Baal. Finally, she descends into the underworld to plead with Mot for Baal's life.

"But divine Mot replied:
"What do you ask of me, O Virgin Anat?
I went out myself,

and searched every mountain in the midst of the earth,
every hill in the midst of the steppe.
My appetite felt the want of human beings,
my appetite the multitudes of the earth,
I reached 'Paradise', the land of pasture,
'Delight', the steepe by the shore of death.
It was I who approached Valiant Baal:
it was I who offered him up <like> a lamb in my mouth,
Like a kind in the open of my maw.
It was he who <was? carried away by the Luminary of the gods, Shapsh!
by the Burning One, strength of the heavens,
into the hand(s) of the divine Mot!"[241]

She returns without Baal.

Yet as the seasons change and the time of fertility draws near, Anat once again descends into the underworld. This time it is not to plead for Baal's life but to fight for it.

"She seized divine Mot.
With a knife she split him:
with a fan she winnowed him;
with fire she burnt him;
with millstones she ground him;
<with a sieve she sifted him;>
on the steppe <she abandoned him;
in the sea> she sowed him.
His remains the birds did indeed eat,
his scraps the sparrows did indeed consume,
remains to remains cried..."[242]

The goddess of warfare kills Mot.

With the death of Death, Baal is reborn. "For alive is Valiant Baal, for the Prince, Lord of the earth, exists!"[243] And he kills Mot's supporters, "the sons of Athirat", "the great ones", "the brilliant ones" with his blade and with his mace. Baal reclaims "the throne of his kingship."[244]

6. Baal's Final Battle with Mot

Seven years pass and Mot returns to offer a compromise.

"He lifted up his voice and cried:
'Because of you, O Baal, I experience downfall.
Because of you, I experienced winnowing with <a fan;
because of you I experienced splitting with> a knife;
because of you I experienced burning with fire;
because of you I experienced grinding with millstones;
because of you I experienced sifting with a sieve;
because of you I experienced abandonment on the steppe;
because of you I experience sowing in the sea.
Give the first of your brother (whom) I may eat,
and the anger I feel will depart.
If the first of your brothers you do not give,
then I shall seize [   ]
(it will be) time I ate [mankind],
that I ate the multitud[es of the earth]"[245]

Baal agrees to undergo a sacrificial death to redeem the peoples of the world, "the multitude of the earth".

But Baal does not carry through with his promise of a sacrificial death. He deceives Mot into eating his own "seven divine assistants"[246]. Those seven divine assistants were Mot's own brothers. So Mot returns with a vengeance.

"They glowered at each other burning coals.
Mot was strong.
Baal was strong.
They bit like serpents.
Mot was strong;
Baal was strong.
They tugged like hunting-dogs.
Mot fell.
Baal fell on top of him."[247]

Shapsh intervenes to stop this fight to the death.

"'Listen, pray, O divine Mot!
How can you fight with Valiant Baal?
How will Bull El your father not hear you?
He will surely pull down the pillars of your dwelling,

he will surely overturn the throne of your kingship,
he will surely break the scepter of your rule!"[248]

Mot is moved by Shapsh's intervention and breaks off the attack.

Each will retain their separate kingdoms. "Divine <M>ot was afraid: the Beloved of El, the hero was in dread. Mot started at her voice. [He lifted up his voice and cried:] Let Baal be installed [on the throne of] his kingship, on [the back-rest, on the siege of] his dominion!"[249] Together they sit down to a communal meal to seal the peace. "Shapsh, you rule the chthonian gods; lo, mortals are your company. Kothar is your associate, and Hassis is your companion. In the sea of Arsh and the dragon, Kothat-and-Hasis, steer (the bark)!, Pilot (the ship), Kothar-and-Hasis."[250] The realms of order and chaos are both preserved. Chaos is not destroyed for ever. The dragon that is in the sea Yam remains alive. An accommodation is reached between the forces of order and the forces of chaos. Baal's counselors Kothar and Hasis drive off chaos' enemies. The conflict continues, though in a muted form. The high God Baal may control death, but he can never defeat it once and for all. And so the cycle of Baal ends.

8. SELECTED BIBLIOGRAPHY

Alden, R.L., *The New American Commentary: Job* (Broadman and Holman Publishers, 1993)

Anderson, B.W., *Creation versus Chaos: The Reinterpretation of Mythical Symbolism in the Bible* (Fortress Press, Philadelphia, 1987)

Brown, W.P., *Character in Crisis: A Fresh Approach to the Wisdom Literature of the Old Testament* (William B. Eerdmans Publishing Company, Grand Rapids, 1996)

Clines, D.J.A., *Job* in *The International Bible Commentary* (Zondervan, Grand Rapids, 1979)

--------,*Word Biblical Commentary: Job 1-20* (Word Books, Dallas, 1989)

Day, J., *God's Conflict with the Dragon and the Sea: Echoes of a Canaanite Myth in the Old Testament* (Cambridge University Press, Cambridge, 1985)

Dhorme, E., *A Commentary on the Book of Job* Trans. E.Dhorme (Thomas Nelson and Son Ltd., London, 1967)

Dick, M.B., *Job 31: A Form-Critical Study* (UMI Dissertations, Ann Arbor, 1977)

--------, *The Legal Metaphor in Job 31* in *Sitting with Job: Selected Studies on the Book of Job* (Baker House, Grand Rapids, 1992)

Driver, S.R. and Gray, G.B., *A Critical and Exegetical Commentary on the Book of Job* (T. and T. Clark, Edinburgh)

Frye, J.B., *Legal Language in the Book of Job* (British Thesis Service, West Yorkshire, 1973)

Fyall, R.S., *Now My Eyes Have Seen You: Images of Creation and Evil in the Book of Job* (Inter Varsity Press, Downers Grove, 2002)

Gaebelein, F.E., *Job* in *The Expositor's Bible Commentary: Volume 4* (Zondervan Publishing House, Grand Rapids, 1988)

Glatzer, N.N., *The Dimensions of Job* (Schocken Books, New York, 1969)

Good, E.M., *In Turns of Tempest: A Reading of Job with a Translation* (Stanford University Press, Stanford, 1998)

--------, *Job* in *Harper's Bible Commentary* (Harper and Row, San Francisco, 1988)

--------, *Job 31* in *Sitting with Job: Selected Studies on the Book of Job* (Baker House, Grand Rapids, 1992)

Gordis, R., *The Book of God and Man: A Study of Job* (The University of Chicago Press, Chicago, 1965)

--------, *The Book of Job: Commentary, New Translation and Special Studies* (The Jewish Theological Seminary of America, New York, 1978)

Guillaume, A., *Studies in the Book of Job* (E.J.Brill, Leiden, 1968)

Habel, N.C., *The Cambridge Bible Commentary on the New English Bible: The Book of Job* (Cambridge University Press, London, 1975)

--------, *The Old Testament Library: The Book of Job* (Westminister Press, Philadelphia, 1985)

Hartley, J.E., *The New International Commentary on the Old Testament: The Book of Job* (William B. Eerdmans Publishing Company, Grand Rapids, 1988)

Irwin, W.A., *Job* in *Peake's Commentary on the Bible* (Thomas Nelson and Sons Ltd., New York, 1962)

Janzen, J.G., *Interpretation-A Bible Commentary for Teaching and Preaching: Job* (John Knox Press, Atlanta, 1985)

Jastrow, M., *The Book of Job: Its Origin, Growth and Interpretation* (J.B.Lippincott Company, Philadelphia, 1920)

Keil, C.F. and Delitzsch, F., *Job* in *Commentary on the Old Testament: Volume IV* (William B. Eerdmans Publishing Company, Grand Rapids, 1986)

Kissane, E.D., *The Book of Job* (Sheed and Ward, New York, 1946)

Kloos, C., *JHWH's Combat with the Sea: A Canaanite Tradition in the Religion of Ancient Israel* (E.J.Brill, Leiden, 1986)

Levenson, J.D., *Creation and the Persistence of Evil: The Jewish Drama of Divine Omnipotence* (Princeton University Press, Princeton, 1988)

Lofthouse, W.F., *Job* in *The Abingdon Bible Commentary* (Abingdon Press, New York, 1929)

Lurker, M., *An Illustrated Dictionary of The Gods and Symbols of Ancient Egypt* (Thames and Hudson, London, 1980)

MacKenzie, R.A.F. and Murphy, R.E., *Job* in *The New Jerome Biblical Commentary* (Prentice Hall, Englewood Cliffs, 1990)

Michel, W.L., *Job in the Light of Northwest Semitic: Volume 1* (Biblical Institute Press, Rome, 1987)

-------, *The Ugaritic Texts and the Mythological Expressions in the Book of Job* (UMI Dissertation Service, Ann Arbor, 1970)

Mitchell, S., *The Book of Job* (North Point Press, San Francisco, 1987)

Mumford, A.H., *The Book of Job: A Metrical Version* (George H. Doran Company, New York, 1922)

Murphy, R.E., *The Book of Job: A Short Reading* (Paulist Press, New York, 1999)

-------, *The Forms of the Old Testament Literature: Volume XIII Wisdom Literature: Job, Proverbs, Ruth, Canticles, Ecclesiastes, Esther* (William B. Eerdmans Publishing Company, Grand Rapids, 1981)

Newell, B.L., *Job: Repentant or Rebellious?* in *Sitting with Job: Selected Studies on the Book of Job* (Baker House, Grand Rapids, 1992)

Newsom, C.A., *The Book of Job* in *The New Interpreter's Bible: Volume 4* (Abingdon Press, Nashville, 1996)

Parsons, G.W., *Literary Features of the Book of Job* in *Sitting with Job: Selected Studies on the Book of Job* (Baker House, Grand Rapids, 1992)

--------, *The Structure and Purpose of the Book of Job* in *Sitting with Job: Selected Studies on the Book of Job* (Baker House, Grand Rapids, 1992)

Penchansky, D., *The Betrayal of God: Ideological Conflict in Job* (Westminister, Louisville, 1990)

Pope, M., *The Anchor Bible: Job* (Doubleday, New York, 1973)

Rowley, H.H., *The New Century Bible Commentary: The Book of Job* (William B. Eerdmans, Grand Rapids, 1976)

Scholnick, S.H., *Lawsuit Drama in the Book of Job* (UMI Dissertations, Ann Arbor, 1975)

--------, *Poetry in the Courtroom: Job 38-41* in *Sitting with Job: Selected Studies on the Book of Job* (Baker House, Grand Rapids, 1992)

--------, *The Meaning of Mispat (Justice) in the Book of Job* in *Sitting with Job: Selected Studies on the Book of Job* (Baker House, Grand Rapids, 1992)

Schultz, C., *Job* in *Evangelical Commentary on the Bible* (Baker Book House, Grand Rapids, 1989)

Simundson, D.J., *The Message of Job* (Academic Renewal Press, Lima, 2001)

Smick, E.B., *Another Look at the Mythological Elements in the Book of Job* in *Sitting with Job: Selected Studies on the Book of Job* (Baker House, Grand Rapids, 1992)

--------, *Job* in *The Expositor's Bible Commentary: Volume 4* Edit. F.E.Baebelein (Zondervan Publishing House, Grand Rapids, 1988)

--------, *Mythology and the Book of Job* in *Sitting with Job: Selected Studies on the Book of Job* (Baker House, Grand Rapids, 1992)

Snaith, N.H., *The Book of Job: Its Origin and Purpose* (SCM Press Ltd., London, 1968)

Terrien, S., *The Book of Job* in *The Interpreter's Bible: Volume 3* (Abingdon Press, Nashville, 1954)

--------, *Job: Poet of Existence* (The Bobbs-Merrill Company Inc, New York, 1957)

The Voice from the Whirlwind: Interpreting the Book of Job, Edit. L.G. Perdue and W.C. Gilpin (Abingdon Press, Nashville, 1992)

The Voice Out of the Whirlwind: The Book of Job Edit. R.E. Hone (Chandler Publishing Company, San Francisco, 1960)

Thomason, B., *God on Trial: The Book of Job and Human Suffering* (The Liturgical Press, Collegeville, 1997)

Tsevat, M., *The Meaning of the Book of Job* in *Sitting with Job: Selected Studies on the Book of Job* (Baker House, Grand Rapids, 1992)

Tur-Sinai, N.H., *The Book of Job: A New Commentary* (Kiryath Sepher Ltd., Jerusalem, 1957)

Twentieth Century Interpretations of the Book of Job Edit. P.S. Sanders, Prentice-Hall Inc., Englewood Cliffs, 1968)

Vawter, B., *Job and Jonah: Questioning the Hidden God* (Paulist Press, New York, 1983)

Vicchio, S.J., *The Voice from the Whirlwind: The Problem of Evil and the Modern World* (Christian Classics Inc., Westminister, 1989)

Wakeman, M.K., *God's Battle with the Monster: A Study in Biblical Imagery* (E.J.Brill, Leiden, 1973)

Westermann, C., *The Structure of the Book of Job: A Form-Critical Analysis,* Trans. C.A.Meunchow (Fortress Press, Philadelphia, 1977)

Wilcox, J.T., *The Bitterness of Job: A Philosophical Reading* (The University of Michigan Press, Ann Arbor, 1989)

Wolfers, D., *Deep Things Out of Darkness: The Book of Job* (William B. Eerdmans Publishing Company, Grand Rapids, 1995)

Wycliffe Bible Encyclopedia Edit. C.F. Pfeiffer, H.F. Vos and J. Rea ((Moody Press, Chicago, 1975)

Zuck, R.B., *The Certainty of Seeing God: A Brief Exposition of Job 19:23-29* in *Sitting with Job: Selected Studies on the Book of Job* (Baker House, Grand Rapids, 1992)

Zuckerman, B., *Job the Silent: A Study in Historical Counterpoint* (Oxford University Press, Oxford, 1991)

Zuckler, O., *The Book of Job: A Commentary,* Trans. L.J. Evans (Charles Scribner's Sons, New York, 1902)

9. ENDNOTES

[1] (1) The 18th century American lexicographer Daniel Webster wrote: "*The Book of Job*, taken as a mere work of literary genius, is one of the most wonderful productions of any age and of any language."

(2) The 19th century French novelist Victor Hugo wrote "Tomorrow, if all literature was to be destroyed and it was left to me to retain one work only, I would save *Job*."

(3) The 19th century English poet Alfred Lord Tennyson described it as "the greatest poem, whether of ancient or modern literature."

(4) The 19th century English biographer Thomas Carlyle wrote: "There is nothing written, I think, in or out of the *Bible*, of equal literary merit."

[2] The main literary challenges are six in number.

(1) First, there is the integration of God's two poetic speeches (Job 38:1-40:2; 40:6-41:34) with the prose conclusion. (Job 42:7-17) For many, God's speeches involve a rejection of the propriety of the moral question yet the prose conclusion affirms the propriety of the moral question.

(2) Second, there is the integration of Job's poetic Oath of Innocence (Job 27:1-31:40) and his two poetic responses to God (Job 40:3-5; 42:1-6) with the prose conclusion. (Job 42:7-17) For many, Job commits blasphemy in his Oath of Innocence and morally repents for that blasphemy in his final two speeches. Yet God in the prose conclusion affirms that Job has spoken rightly about God.

(3) Third, there is the integration of Elihu's four poetic speeches (Job 32:1-37:24) with the prose conclusion. (Job 42:7-17) For many, Elihu's speeches are the climactic refutation of Job's earlier speeches. Yet God in the prose conclusion (Job 42:7-17) affirms that only Job has spoken rightly about God and that comment is an implicit condemnation of Elihu.

(4) Fourth, there is the integration of the Job's nine speeches in the three cycles (Job 3:1-3:26; 6:1-7:21; 9:1-10:22; 12:1-14:22; 16:1-17:16; 19:1-29; 21:1-21:34; 23:1-24:25, 26:1-31:40) with his final two speeches. (Job 40:3-5; 42:4-6) For many, the defiant and rebellious Job of the first set of speeches has inexplicably been transformed into a cowering and submissive Job in the final set of speeches.

(5) Fifth, there is the integration of a hymn to wisdom (Job 28:1-28) into the overall framework of Job's Oath of Innocence. For many, the hymn to wisdom lacks any connection to its surrounding elements.

(6) Sixth, there is the integration of two descriptions of punishment (Job 28:7-23) into the overall framework of Job's Oath of Innocence. For many, these descriptions of the punishment due the wicked seem inconsistent with Job's earlier statements that wicked are not punished.

Conventional scholarship has too readily abandoned the attempt to integrate these seemingly disparate elements. Such scholarship speculates that the disparate elements are attributable to a hypothesized historical development of the book.

(1) *The Book of Job* began with a single prose tale consisting of the present prose opening (Job 1:1-2:13) and prose conclusion. (Job 42:7-17) For this conclusion, they cite three things: (1) the seemingly archaic Hebrew prose of those elements, (2) the distinct preference of Yahweh rather than Eloah or Shaddai as the name of God, and (3) the apparently similarity of such a simple tale with second millennium B.C. tales such as the Sumerian "Man and his God", the Akkadian "I Will Praise the Lord of Wisdom", "The Babylonian Theodicy" and the Egyptian "The Protests of an Eloquent Peasant". For translations of those earlier tales, the reader might consult *Ancient Near Eastern Texts Relating to the Old Testament* Edit. J.B. Pritchard (Princeton University Press, Princeton, 1969).

(2) A later redactor added an extended poetic dialogue between Job and his friends (Job 3:1-31:37). For this conclusion, they cite two things: (1) the ancient Hebrew poetry and the later Aramaisms in that section and (2) the distinct preference of Eloah or Shaddai rather than Yahweh as the name of God. The same redactor may have added the dialogues between Job and God (Job 38:1-42:6).

(3) Another even later redactor added Elihu's speeches. (Job 32:1-37:24) For this conclusion, they cite only three things: (1) its similarity with the ideas and expressions of *2 Isaiah*, suggesting a late date, (2) a hypothesized dissatisfaction with the speeches of Job and his friends, requiring a stronger condemnation of Job than the then-existing work provided and (3) the proliferation of Aramaisms.

(4) And a final redactor rearranged the opening of Job's Oath of Innocence by putting in Job's mouth descriptions of the wicked (Job 27:7-23) that more properly belong to either Bildad or Zophar. For this conclusion, they cite two things: (1) the seeming inconsistency between Job's descriptions of the punishment due the wicked and his earlier statements that wicked are not punished and (2) a hypothesized dissatisfaction with the Job's rebellious challenge of God requiring a mitigation of Job's unorthodoxy.

Such conventional scholarship affirms that the tensions created by such accretions over time are irresolvable. The multiplicity of voices creates a cacophony that drowns out any overall message or meaning.

However, prominent scholars such as Norman Habel, John Hartley, David Clines and Carol Newsom have seriously questioned several, if not all, of the assumptions of such an approach.

(1) Parallels to 2nd millennium tales are superficial. None of those tales deal with the issue of a righteous sufferer, certainly not one putting God on trial.

(2) "The prose tale also contains narrative and stylistic details that suggest great antiquity. Yet here, too, one must distinguish between what is genuinely archaic from an artistic imitation of archaic style. The most careful linguistic study has argued that the prose tale in its present form is no older than the sixth century BCE." Newsom, C..A., *The Book of Job* in *The New Interpreter's Bible: Volume 4* (Abingdon Press, Nashville, 1996) p. 325. "The extensive and symmetrical repetition, highly stylized characters and studied aura of remote antiquity imitate but exaggerate features of folktale style. Alongside these features are subtle word plays and verbal ambiguities that suggest an ironic distance from the aesthethic of simple naivete." Newsom, C..A., *The Book of Job* in *The New Interpreter's Bible: Volume 4* (Abingdon Press, Nashville, 1996) p. 325.

(3) "The poetic dialogues contain linguistic forms that one would expect to in archaic Hebrew, from approximately the tenth century BCE. Since these speeches appear to be written in a deliberately archaizing style and lack other poetic features one associates with very ancient Hebrew poetry, the argument for such an early date has not been generally accepted." Newsom, C..A., *The Book of Job* in *The New Interpreter's Bible: Volume 4* (Abingdon Press, Nashville, 1996) p. 325.

(4) "The presence of Elihu, the incoherence of the third cycle, and the role of the poem on wisdom raise interesting but relatively minor interpretative issues." Newsom, C..A., *The Book of Job* in *The New Interpreter's Bible: Volume 4* (Abingdon Press, Nashville, 1996) p. 323. Such minor problems are by no means insurmountable. Elihu produces an important anti-climax and comic relief following the intensity of Job's Oath of Innocence. The shortened final speeches of Bildad and Zophar mirror the breakdown in dialogue. The poem on wisdom provided a certain respite within the intensity of Job's Oath of Innocence.

(5) The use of the different names for God in different sections may reflect the differing literary functions of those sections rather than differing historical time periods. Yahweh is the more personal of the two names for

God, and not surprisingly appears more often in the more intimate scenes of the prose prologue, the two divine speeches and the prose epilogue. Eloah and Shaddai are more general names for God, and not surprisingly appear in those scenes when God seems distant from man. While the usage is distinctive, it is by no means exclusive. The name Yahweh does appear in sections where the name Eloah and Shaddai are predominant and vice-versa.

(6) "Critics who argue that the book of Job developed in this way [the hypothesis of growth by stages] rarely address the question of how one is supposed to read the book as it now exists. Indeed, one of the unfortunate consequences of this hypothesis about the composition of Job is that it has often led to interpretations of the book that fail to take its final or canonical form seriously." Newsom, C..A., *The Book of Job* in *The New Interpreter's Bible: Volume 4* (Abingdon Press, Nashville, 1996) p. 322.

I find their textual arguments of these scholars persuasive and I follow in their footsteps, believing the work to be the product of a single author writing in the 6th or 5th centuries B.C.

Since prominent scholars now increasingly argue that *The Book of Job* may be the product of a single author, it is reasonable to expect that the author intended to communicate an overall message. Thus, any serious interpretation of the book should address and attempt to integrate the disparate elements described above for they may be an integral part of the author's overall message. I offer this work *Putting God on Trial* as one such attempted integration, though I have no illusions that it will be the final word on this perennial classic.

The Book of Job is an intentionally ambiguous work defying superficial and simplistic readings. At many points, a multiplicity of complementary, even contradictory, interpretations are possible. It is only the legitimacy of one's overall interpretation of the book as a whole that allows one to choose between such interpretations. In any event, *The Book of Job* is a goldmine. All who seriously mine its treasures come away enriched, whether or not they reach the same conclusions I do.

[3] The reader might profitably look to three other works that treat *The Book of Job* as a lawsuit drama.

(1) Frye, J.B., *Legal Language in the Book of Job* (British Thesis Service, West Yorkshire, 1973);

(2) Scholnick, S.H., *Lawsuit Drama in the Book of Job* (UMI Dissertations, Ann Arbor, 1975);

(3) Dick, M.B., *Job 31: A Form-Critical Study* (UMI Dissertations, Ann Arbor, 1977)

These works may be difficult to obtain, but are worth the effort. The reader might find the following papers by two of those authors more accessible.

(1) Scholnick, S.H., *Poetry in the Courtroom: Job 38-41* in *Sitting with Job: Selected Studies on the Book of Job* (Baker House, Grand Rapids, 1992),

(2) --------, *The Meaning of Mispat (Justice) in the Book of Job* in *Sitting with Job: Selected Studies on the Book of Job* (Baker House, Grand Rapids, 1992),

(3) Dick, M.B., *The Legal Metaphor in Job 31* in *Sitting with Job: Selected Studies on the Book of Job* (Baker House, Grand Rapids, 1992)

For an even broader perspective on the concept of challenging God, the reader might profitably look consult the following three works:

(1) Laytner, A., *Arguing with God: A Jewish Tradition* (Jason Aronson, London, 1990);

(2) Blumenthal, David R., *Facing the Abusing God: A Theology of Protest* (Westminster/John Knox, Louisville, 1993) and

(3) Fuchs, Gisela, *Mythos und Hiobdichting: Aufnahme und Umdeutung altorientalische Vorstellungen* (Koln: Verlag W. Kohlhammer, Berlin, 1993).

For that broader perspective, I thank Dr. Walter Michel.

[4] Clines, D.J.A., *Job* in *The International Bible Commentary* (Zondervan, Grand Rapids, 1979) p. 1029, 1044.

Dick, M.B., *Job 31: A Form-Critical Study* (UMI Dissertations, Ann Arbor, 1977) p.180, 183.

Frye, N., *The Great Code: The Bible and Literature* (Academic Press, Toronto, 1982) pp. 196-198.

Gordis, R., *The Book of God and Man: A Study of Job* (The University of Chicago Press, Chicago, 1965) p. 304.

Gordis, R., *The Book of Job: Commentary, New Translation and Special Studies* (The Jewish Theological Seminary of America, New York, 1978) p. xxx-xxx1.

Habel, N.C., *The Old Testament Library: The Book of Job* (Westminister Press, Philadelphia, 1985) p.66, 579.

Habel, N.C., *The Cambridge Bible Commentary on the New English Bible: The Book of Job* (Cambridge University Press, London, 1975) p. 228.

Scholnick, S.H., *Lawsuit Drama in the Book of Job* (UMI Dissertations, Ann Arbor, 1975) p. 303-305.

Westermann, C., *The Structure of the Book of Job: A Form-Critical Analysis,* Trans. C.A.Meunchow (Fortress Press, Philadelphia, 1977) 126-127.

[5] Alden, R.L., *The New American Commentary: Job* (Broadman and Holman Publishers, 1993) p. 408.

Anderson, F.I. *Tyndale Old Testament Commentaries: Job* (Inter-Varsity Press, Downers Grove, 1974) p. 292.

Fyall, R.S., *Now My Eyes Have Seen You: Images of Creation and Evil in the Book of Job* (Inter Varsity Press, Downers Grove, 2002) p. 180.

Hartley, J.E., *The New International Commentary on the Old Testament: The Book of Job* (William B. Eerdmans Publishing Company, Grand Rapids, 1988) p. 537.

Pope, M., *The Anchor Bible: Job* (Doubleday, New York, 1973) p. lxxx.

Terrien, S., *The Book of Job* in *The Interpreter's Bible: Volume 3* (Abingdon Press, Nashville, 1954) p. 1193.

Tur-Sinai, N.H., *The Book of Job: A New Commentary* (Kiryath Sepher Ltd., Jerusalem, 1957) p. 578.

[6] A canonical meaning is a supplementary meaning a Biblical book acquires because it is included within a canon of other works. It consists of the interaction that book has with other books and themes within the canon of sacred scripture.

[7] Alden, R.L., *The New American Commentary: Job* (Broadman and Holman Publishers, 1993) p. 46.

[8] Clines, D.J.A., *Job* in *The International Bible Commentary* (Zondervan, Grand Rapids, 1979) p. 9.

[9] ibid, p. 50.

[10] Pope, M., *The Anchor Bible: Job* (Doubleday, New York, 1973) p. 6.

   Clines, D.J.A., *Job* in *The International Bible Commentary* (Zondervan, Grand Rapids, 1979) p. 11.

[11] For a fuller exploration of their understanding and articulation, the reader might profitably look to James Barr's *Biblical Faith and Natural Theology* (Oxford University Press, New York, 1995)

[12] Adler, M.J., *Desires Right and Wrong: The Ethics of Enough* (Macmillan Publishing Company, New York, 1991) p. 33.

[13] -------, *Ten Philosophical Mistakes* (Collier Books, New York, 1985) pp. 123-127.

[14] Lisska, A.J., *Aquinas's Theory of Natural Law: An Analytic Reconstruction* (Clarendon Press, Oxford, 1996) p. 85-88, 101, 120, 124.

[15] Adler, M.J., *Ten Philosophical Mistakes* (Collier Books, New York, 1985) pp. 160-163.

[16] Fagothey, A., *Right and Reason: Ethics in Theory and Practice* (The C.V. Mosby Company, St.Louis, 1959) p. 55.

[17] Adler, M.J., *Six Great Ideas: Truth, Goodness and Beauty- Ideas We Judge By, Liberty, Equality, Justice- Ideas We Act On* (Collier Books, New York, 1981) pp. 75-80.

[18] -------, *The Common Sense of Politics* (Holt, Rinehart and Winston, New York, 1971) pp. 24-25;

   --------., *The Time of Our Lives: The Ethics of Common Sense* (Holt, Rinehart and Winston, New York, 1970) p. 166, 206.

   Finnis, J., Natural Law and Natural Rights (Clarendon Press, Oxford, 1980) p. 83, 86-90.

[19] --------, *Desires Right and Wrong: The Ethics of Enough* (Macmillan Publishing Company, New York, 1991) p. 62-64.

[20] --------, *The Time of Our Lives: The Ethics of Common Sense* (Holt, Rinehart and Winston, New York, 1970) p. 133.

[21] For a fuller exploration of the biblical understanding and articulation, the reader might profitably look to James Barr's *Biblical Faith and Natural Theology* (Oxford University Press, New York, 1995)

[22] Harris, R.L., Archer, G.L. and Waltke, B.K, *Theological Wordbook of the Old Testament: Volume 2* (The Moody Bible Institute, Chicago, 1980) pp. 786-788;

Theological Lexicon of the Old Testament: Volume 3, Edit. E. Jenni and C. Westermann; Trans. M.E. Biddle (Hendrickson Publishers, Peabody, 1997) pp. 1103-1118.;

New International Dictionary of Old Testament Theology and Exegesis: Volume 3, Edit. W.A. Van Gemeren (Zondervan Publishing House, Grand Rapids, 1997) pp. 877-887.

[23] *Theological Dictionary of the New Testament, Volume 8*, Edit. G.Kittel and G.Freidrich and Trans. G.W.Bromley (Wm.B.Eerdmans Publishing Company, Grand Rapids, 1972) p. 49-87.;

Theological Dictionary of the New Testament: Abridged in One Volume, Edit. G.Kittel and G.Freidrich and Trans. G.W.Bromley (Wm.B.Eerdmans Publishing Company, Grand Rapids, 1985) pp. 1161-1166.;

Exegetical Dictionary of the New Testament, Edit. H.Balz and G.Schneider (William B. Eerdmans Publishing Company, Grand Rapids, 1982-1983) p. 347-348.

[24] "Evil" in *New Catholic Encyclopedia: Volume 5* (McGraw-Hill Book Company, New York, 1967) p. 665.

[25] Harris, R.L., Archer, G.L. and Waltke, B.K, *Theological Wordbook of the Old Testament: Volume 2* (The Moody Bible Institute, Chicago, 1980) pp. 973-974.;

Theological Lexicon of the Old Testament: Volume 3, Edit. E. Jenni and C. Westermann; Trans. M.E. Biddle (Hendrickson Publishers, Peabody, 1997) pp. 1424-1428.;

New International Dictionary of Old Testament Theology and Exegesis: Volume 4, Edit. W.A. Van Gemeren (Zondervan Publishing House, Grand Rapids, 1997) pp. 306-308.

[26] Sinlessness can mean one of two things: Job was sinless throughout life or Job was sinless at that point in time.

Perhaps the only passage where Job may acknowledge sin is "for you write bitter things against me, and make me reap the iniquities of my youth." (Job 13:26) The passage is ambiguous. First, the iniquities of youth may refer to so-called "sins" committed before the age of accountability. If so, then Job is not culpable for such acts and is protesting that God is wrongfully imposing punishment. Second, the iniquities of youth may refer to sins committed after the age of accountability, in Job's teenage or early adult years. If Job had sinned in that way, then he clearly has repented and been forgiven. Job refers to God writing those "sins" down in his book of life. Yet in the second scene, God reviews the book of life and those sins are not there. If there once was such a record, it has long since been wiped clean. In any event, such forgiven sins of youth would not have been such to justify the evil that God has sent into his life. Third, the entire passage may be rhetorical implying no sin at all.

Some might refer to an additional passage where Job says "If I sin, what do I do to you, you watcher of humanity?" (Job 7:20) However, it is widely regarded that Job is speaking rhetorically at this point. "The expression 'Assume I sin" (hata'ti) establishes a hypothetical context which makes possible Job's mock demand for pardon which follows (v.21). Job, of course, contends throughout that he is quite innocent (e.g., 12:4; 27:2-6) Here he is only postulating sinfulness as a means of provoking an alien deity. By proposing that Job's actions might injure God in some way, Job is reiterating the earlier theme of his earthly presence as a threat to God's world order." Norman Habel, *Old Testament Library: Job* (The Westminister Press, Philadelphia, 1985) p. 165.

[27] Harris, R.L., Archer, G.L. and Waltke, B.K, *Theological Wordbook of the Old Testament: Volume 1* (The Moody Bible Institute, Chicago, 1980) pp. 417-418.;

Theological Lexicon of the Old Testament: Volume 2, Edit. E. Jenni and C. Westermann; Trans. M.E. Biddle (Hendrickson Publishers, Peabody, 1997) pp. 588-590.;

New International Dictionary of Old Testament Theology and Exegesis: Volume 2, Edit. W.A. Van Gemeren (Zondervan Publishing House, Grand Rapids, 1997) pp. 563-568.;

Theological Dictionary of the Old Testament: Volume 6, Edit. G.J.Botterweck, H.Ringgren; Trans. J.T.Willis (Wm.B.Eerdmans Publishing Company, Grand Rapids, 1974) pp. 463-472.

[28] Harris, R.L., Archer, G.L. and Waltke, B.K, *Theological Wordbook of the Old Testament: Volume 1* (The Moody Bible Institute, Chicago, 1980) pp. 399-400.;

Theological Lexicon of the Old Testament: Volume 2, Edit. E. Jenni and C. Westermann; Trans. M.E. Biddle (Hendrickson Publishers, Peabody, 1997) pp. 568-578.;

New International Dictionary of Old Testament Theology and Exegesis: Volume 2, Edit. W.A. Van Gemeren (Zondervan Publishing House, Grand Rapids, 1997) pp. 527-533;

Theological Dictionary of the Old Testament: Volume 6, Edit. G.J.Botterweck, H.Ringgren; Trans. J.T.Willis (Wm.B.Eerdmans Publishing Company, Grand Rapids, 1974) pp. 290-315.

[29] Harris, R.L., Archer, G.L. and Waltke, B.K, *Theological Wordbook of the Old Testament: Volume 2* (The Moody Bible Institute, Chicago, 1980) pp. 621.;

Theological Lexicon of the Old Testament: Volume 2, Edit. E. Jenni and C. Westermann; Trans. M.E. Biddle (Hendrickson Publishers, Peabody, 1997) pp. 796.;

New International Dictionary of Old Testament Theology and Exegesis: Volume 3, Edit. W.A. Van Gemeren (Zondervan Publishing House, Grand Rapids, 1997) pp. 238-239.

[30] The ancient Jews thought this first scene in heaven occurred on Rosh Hashanah. In the NRSV, the scene in heaven opens on an unspecified day. "One day the heavenly beings came to present themselves before the LORD and Satan also came among them." (Job 1:6) However in the ancient Jewish *Targum of Job*, the scene is heaven opens on Rosh Hashanah. "And it

happened on the day of judgment at the beginning of the year, that the sons of the angels came to stand in judgment before the Lord, and Satan also came in their midst to stand in judgment before the Lord." (Job 1:6) The targums arose subsequent to the Babylonian conquest of Israel in the early 6th century BC. The Babylonians sought to destroy Jewish culture. They deported many of political, religious and intellectual elites to Babylon. They launched a program of cultural and linguistic assimilation in occupied Israel. They succeeded to extent Aramaic not Hebrew became the language of the common man. When Persia conquered Babylon in the late 6th century BC, the Jews were allowed to return to their homeland and their religious practices. Scribes such as Ezra wrote Aramaic paraphrases of the Biblical books called targums to help the faithful understand their lost language. Every Sabbath, the Hebrew originals and the Aramaic targums were read side by side in the synagogues. *The Targum of Job* was one such targum. Although the actual date of composition is unknown, it represents a very early Jewish understanding of *The Book of Job*.

The Babylonian association of the "Enuma Elish" with the Babylonian new year and the hypothesized Canaanite association of the Baal cycle with the Canaanite new year (Day, J., *God's Conflict with the Dragon and the Sea: Echoes of a Canaanite Myth in the Old Testament* (Cambridge University Press, Cambridge, 1985) p. 17 and 19) provide interesting circumstantial support, especially in the light of God's final speech to Job which draws heavily on Babylonian and Canaanite mythology.

[31] "Satan" in *The Anchor Bible Dictionary, Volume 5*, Edit. D.N. Freedman (Doubleday, New York, 1992) p. 985-986.

[32] Clines, D.J.A., *Word Biblical Commentary: Job 1-20* (Word Books, Dallas, 1989) p. 22.

[33] Anderson, F.I. *Tyndale Old Testament Commentaries: Job* (Inter-Varsity Press, Downers Grove, 1974) p. 85.

Clines, D.J.A., *Job* in *The International Bible Commentary* (Zondervan, Grand Rapids, 1979) p. 26.

[34] In Hebrew, Yahweh is written as YHWH because Hebrew is written without vowels.

[35] Aquinas, Thomas, *Summa Contra Gentiles: Book One: God* Trans. A.C.Pegis (University of Notre Dame Press, Notre Dame, 1975) Chapter 22, pp. 118-121;

--------, *Summa Theologica:Volume 1* Trans. Fathers of the English Dominican Province (Christian Classics, Westminister, 1948) Part 1, Question 2, Article 3, and Question 3, Article 4, pp. 13-14,17.

[36] *Gates of the Seasons: A Guide to the Jewish Year*, Edit. P.S.Knobel (Central Conference of American Rabbis, New York, 1983) p. 38-55.

[37] Curiously enough, Day 2 in the 10 Days of Awe is "Tzom Gedaliah". It commemorates the assassination of Gedaliah, the last governor of Judea, and leads to the dispersion of the Jews from their promised land. Strassfeld, M., *The Jewish Holidays: A Guide and Commentary* (Harper and Row, New York, 1985) p. 103. Day 2 in *The Book of Job* is a day of assassination that results in Job being cast out of Eden.

[38] I should not be read as endorsing the truth of Satan's comment that God had indeed put a protective fence around Job exempting him from the normal trials and tribulations of life. (Job 1:10) I don't think he was so protected. This ordeal however would expose Job to some of the most extra-ordinary trials and tribulations of that life can offer. Perhaps the greatest trial therein is the knowledge that those evils have come from the hand of God. (Job 1:11)

[39] Satan has asked God "But stretch out your hand now, and touch all that he has, and he will curse you to your face." (Job 1:11) and again "But stretch out your hand now and touch his bone and his flesh, and he will curse you to your face." (Job 2:5) God accepts the two offers saying "Very well, all that he has is in your power; only do not stretch out your hand against him!" (Job 1:12) and "Very well, he is in your power; only spare his life." (Job 2:6) respectively The hand of Satan has become the hand of God. Job recognizes that: "Have pity on me, have pity on me, O you my friends, for the hand of God has touched me!" (Job 19:21) God will later acknowledge that everything Job said about God was correct (Job 42:7), a statement that is broad enough to encompass Job's claim that his destruction came from the hand of God.

[40] Harris, R.L., Archer, G.L. and Waltke, B.K, *Theological Wordbook of the Old Testament: Volume 1* (The Moody Bible Institute, Chicago, 1980) pp. 277-278.;

Theological Lexicon of the Old Testament: Volume 1, Edit. E. Jenni and C. Westermann; Trans. M.E. Biddle (Hendrickson Publishers, Peabody, 1997) pp. 406-411.;

New International Dictionary of Old Testament Theology and Exegesis: Volume 2, Edit. W.A. Van Gemeren (Zondervan Publishing House, Grand Rapids, 1997) pp. 87-93.;

Theological Dictionary of the Old Testament: Volume 4, Edit. G.J.Botterweck, H.Ringgren; Trans. J.T.Willis (Wm.B.Eerdmans Publishing Company, Grand Rapids, 1974) pp. 309-319.

[41] Harris, R.L., Archer, G.L. and Waltke, B.K, *Theological Wordbook of the Old Testament: Volume 2* (The Moody Bible Institute, Chicago, 1980) pp. 978.

New International Dictionary of Old Testament Theology and Exegesis: Volume 4, Edit. W.A. Van Gemeren (Zondervan Publishing House, Grand Rapids, 1997) pp. 323-324.

[42] Harris, R.L., Archer, G.L. and Waltke, B.K, *Theological Wordbook of the Old Testament: Volume 2* (The Moody Bible Institute, Chicago, 1980) pp. 973-974.

Theological Lexicon of the Old Testament: Volume 3, Edit. E. Jenni and C. Westermann; Trans. M.E. Biddle (Hendrickson Publishers, Peabody, 1997) pp. 1424-1428.;

New International Dictionary of Old Testament Theology and Exegesis: Volume 4, Edit. W.A. Van Gemeren (Zondervan Publishing House, Grand Rapids, 1997) pp. 306-308.

[43] Harris, R.L., Archer, G.L. and Waltke, B.K, *Theological Wordbook of the Old Testament: Volume 2* (The Moody Bible Institute, Chicago, 1980) p. 621.;

New International Dictionary of Old Testament Theology and Exegesis: Volume 3, Edit. W.A. Van Gemeren (Zondervan Publishing House, Grand Rapids, 1997) pp. 239-240.

[44] *The Anchor Bible Dictionary: Volume 4* Edit. D.N. Freedman (Doubleday, New York, 1992) pp. 277-281.

[45] Harris, R.L., Archer, G.L. and Waltke, B.K, *Theological Wordbook of the Old Testament: Volume 1* (The Moody Bible Institute, Chicago, 1980) p. 345-346.

Theological Lexicon of the Old Testament: Volume 2, Edit. E. Jenni and C. Westermann; Trans. M.E. Biddle (Hendrickson Publishers, Peabody, 1997) pp. 486-495.;

New International Dictionary of Old Testament Theology and Exegesis: Volume 2, Edit. W.A. Van Gemeren (Zondervan Publishing House, Grand Rapids, 1997) pp. 353-357.;

Theological Dictionary of the Old Testament: Volume 5, Edit. G.J.Botterweck, H.Ringgren; Trans. J.T.Willis (Wm.B.Eerdmans Publishing Company, Grand Rapids, 1974) pp. 296-317.

[46] Harris, R.L., Archer, G.L. and Waltke, B.K, *Theological Wordbook of the Old Testament: Volume 2* (The Moody Bible Institute, Chicago, 1980) p. 854-856.;

Theological Lexicon of the Old Testament: Volume32, Edit. E. Jenni and C. Westermann; Trans. M.E. Biddle (Hendrickson Publishers, Peabody, 1997) pp. 1249-1254.;

New International Dictionary of Old Testament Theology and Exegesis: Volume 3, Edit. W.A. Van Gemeren (Zondervan Publishing House, Grand Rapids, 1997) pp. 1154-1158;

[47] The Jewish day begins with evening and ends the following afternoon.

[48] Alden, R.L., *The New American Commentary: Job* (Broadman and Holman Publishers, 1993) p. 72.

[49] A number of conservative readers stumble in this introductory section over Job's comment "Truly the thing that I fear comes upon me, and what I dread befalls me." (Job 3:25) They infer from it a pre-existing character flaw in Job being an unhealthy fear of God. They forget that God would have had to have missed such a character flaw in his descriptions of Job. And they are wrong to draw such inferences from this passage.

"Most commentators and versions believe him to be saying that at the present time whatever fear his imagination presents him with he finds turning into reality (as JB 'Whatever I fear comes true, whatever I dread befalls me.') "he has only to think of some new evil and it is sure to come upon him' (Rowley)...Job evidently was aware that calamity was a possibility even for the most exemplary person. And now the worst he could ever have imagined has become literal reality (similarly NJPS, NIV, Pope, Gordis, Ander, Habel)." David Clines, *Job 1-20: Word Biblical Commentary* (Word Books, Dallas, 1989) p. 103.

In fact, such a pre-existing unhealthy fear towards God is inconsistent with Job's descriptions of his prior life. (Job 16:12; 29:18-20)

[50] The reader would profitably benefit from an in-depth reading of W.L. Michel's *The Ugaritic Texts and the Mythological Expressions in the Book of Job* (UMI Dissertation Service, Ann Arbor, 1970) for all the Canaanite images and words in the *Book of Job*.

[51] ibid, p. 108-109.

[52] *Baba Bathra* 16b. B. in *The Babylonian Talmud: Volume 19* Edit. I.Epstein (Soncino, New York, 1949) p. 32.

[53] Harris, R.L., Archer, G.L. and Waltke, B.K, *Theological Wordbook of the Old Testament: Volume 1* (The Moody Bible Institute, Chicago, 1980) p. 376-377.

> *Theological Lexicon of the Old Testament: Volume 2*, Edit. E. Jenni and C. Westermann; Trans. M.E. Biddle (Hendrickson Publishers, Peabody, 1997) pp. 542-544.;

> *New International Dictionary of Old Testament Theology and Exegesis: Volume 2*, Edit. W.A. Van Gemeren (Zondervan Publishing House, Grand Rapids, 1997) pp. 441-445.;

> *Theological Dictionary of the Old Testament: Volume 6*, Edit. G.J.Botterweck, H.Ringgren; Trans. J.T.Willis (Wm.B.Eerdmans Publishing Company, Grand Rapids, 1974) pp. 64-71.

[54] Habel, N.C., *The Old Testament Library: The Book of Job* (Westminister Press, Philadelphia, 1985) p.188-189.

[55] Gaebelein, F.E., *Job* in *The Expositor's Bible Commentary: Volume 4* (Zondervan Publishing House, Grand Rapids, 1988) p.925.

[56] Cited in Alden, R.L., *The New American Commentary: Job* (Broadman and Holman Publishers, 1993) p.160.

[57] Adler, M.J., *The Time of Our Lives: The Ethics of Common Sense* (Holt, Rinehart and Winston, New York, 1970) pp. 137-154.

[58] Harris, R.L., Archer, G.L. and Waltke, B.K, *Theological Wordbook of the Old Testament: Volume 1* (The Moody Bible Institute, Chicago, 1980) p. 144-145.

Theological Lexicon of the Old Testament: Volume 1, Edit. E. Jenni and C. Westermann; Trans. M.E. Biddle (Hendrickson Publishers, Peabody, 1997) pp. 288-296.

New International Dictionary of Old Testament Theology and Exegesis: Volume 1, Edit. W.A. Van Gemeren (Zondervan Publishing House, Grand Rapids, 1997) pp. 789-794.

Theological Dictionary of the Old Testament: Volume 2, Edit. G.J.Botterweck, H.Ringgren; Trans. J.T.Willis (Wm.B.Eerdmans Publishing Company, Grand Rapids, 1974) pp. 350-355.

[59] Hartley, J.E., *The New International Commentary on the Old Testament: The Book of Job* (William B. Eerdmans Publishing Company, Grand Rapids, 1988) p.284.

Harris, R.L., Archer, G.L. and Waltke, B.K, *Theological Wordbook of the Old Testament: Volume 2* (The Moody Bible Institute, Chicago, 1980) p. 657.

New International Dictionary of Old Testament Theology and Exegesis: Volume 3, Edit. W.A. Van Gemeren (Zondervan Publishing House, Grand Rapids, 1997) pp. 361-362.

[60] Hartley, J.E., *The New International Commentary on the Old Testament: The Book of Job* (William B. Eerdmans Publishing Company, Grand Rapids, 1988) p. 294.

[61] I think my reading of a final judgment from Job's words to his friends (Job 19:28-29) is a fair reading of the passage, especially in light of the preceding reference to resurrection (Job 19:25-27). I acknowledge that my reading of a resurrection there may not be the majority reading (if there is one there), but it is not an unnatural one.

If I am right that the composition or final redaction of *The Book of Job* post-dates *1 Isaiah*, then I would note the concept of a universal final judgment found in *1 Isaiah*.

(a) Isaiah 2:11-17 may begin with an oracle against Israel, but it is quickly universalized to include "everyone" and everything, "all that is proud and lofty", so that "the pride of everyone shall be brought low".

(b) Isaiah 13:6-13 may begin with an oracle against Babylon, but it is quickly universalized to include the "punishment" of the whole "world" for its evil and iniquity. That evil and iniquity is expressed in terms of pride. "I will put an end to the pride of the arrogant and lay low the insolence of tyrants. I will make mortals more rare than the gold of Ophir. Therefore I will make the heavens tremble, and the earth will be shaken out of its place, at the wrath of the Lord of hosts in the day of his fierce anger." (Isaiah 13:11-13)

(c) The Isaian apocalypse, so important to my reading of Job, is merely an extension of that final punishment to all the kings of the earth, the cosmic powers (Isaiah 24:21-22) and chaos monsters (Isaiah 27:1). That punishment will include confinement to a pit. (Isaiah 24:22)

The Book of Job's description of Leviathan as "the king over all that are proud" (Job 41:34) picks up all that Isaian imagery of a final judgment on all that is proud and lofty.

The reigning view of scholars is that the concept of a final judgment surfaces very late in the Old Testament, perhaps as late as 164 B.C. This represents one opinion on the historical development of biblical eschatology, albeit the majority view. I adopt the minority view that the concept is not nearly as late. I would note that there is a certain circularity to the reigning viewpoint. It is only a "very" late development if evidence of an earlier existing belief in a final judgment is either removed or reinterpreted. Many such deletions and reinterpretations seem forced in their attempts to conclusively exclude such earlier possibilities of a perception of a final judgment.

[62] For the sake of clarification, I should not be understood as arguing that the poet of *The Book of Job* is presenting a metaphysical trinity here. It is merely a literary conceit. Once the conceit is acknowledged, there should be no scholarly problem finding that the redeemer of Job 19 is God himself.

[63] The Oath of Innocence occurs five times in the Code of Hammurabi. The Code of Hammurabi is a piece of Babylonian statute law dated to between 1728 and 1686 BC. It provides several descriptions of the use of the Oath of Innocence as a shield. A person suspected of wrongdoing, whether it is theft or breach of trust, might swear the oath before god in a temple court. The swearing of the oath constitute proof positive that the suspected person is innocent and may go free. The following quotations are taken from *Ancient Near Eastern Texts Relating to the Old Testament* Edit. J.B. Pritchard (Princeton University Press, Princeton, 1969)

Section 249. "If a seignior hired and ox and god struck it and it has died, the seignior who hired the ox shall (so) affirm by god and then he shall go free." (p. 176.)

Section 266. "If a visitation of god has occurred in a sheepfold or a lion has made a kill the shepherd shall prove himself innocent in the presence of god, but the owner of the sheepfold shall receive from him the animal stricken in the fold." (p. 177.)

And the Code provides several descriptions of the use of the Oath of Innocence as a sword.

Section 106. "If the trader borrowed money from a merchant, and has then disputed (the act) with his merchant, that merchant in the presence of god and witnesses shall prove that the trader borrowed the money and the trader shall pay to the merchant threefold the full amount of money that he borrowed." (p. 170.)

Section 107. "When a merchant entrusted (something) to a trader and the trader has returned to his merchant whatever the merchant gave him, if the merchant has then disputed with him whatever the trader gave him, that trader shall prove it against the merchant in the presence of god and witnesses and the merchant shall pay to the trader sixfold whatever he received because he had a dispute with his trader." (p. 170.)

When the wrongdoer is known, it can establish proof positive of the claim in question. And the wrongdoer must do reparation.

Section 103. "If, when he went on the road, an enemy has made him give up whatever he was carrying, the trader shall (so) affirm by god and then he shall go free." (p. 170.)

In that case, where the wrongdoer is not known, the innocent party through the swearing of the oath is not only freed from all suspicion, he is enabled to take a further step in the Oath of Innocence and condemn his enemy, the person who has actually committed the crime, by way of a curse. However, that condemnation or cursing is only implied in the statute and not expressly stated.

[64] The Oath of Innocence occurs once in Hittite law and its usage follows closely the Babylonian precedents. The following quotation is taken from *Ancient Near Eastern Texts Relating to the Old Testament* Edit. J.B. Pritchard (Princeton University Press, Princeton, 1969)

Section 75. "If anyone yokes a horse, a mule (or) an ass and it dies, or a wolf devours it or it gets lost, he shall give (the value of) the

respective animal. But if he contends: 'It died by the hand of god."
he shall take an oath." (p. 192.)

Nothing really new is to be gained from it.

[65] The Oath of Innocence is also found in ancient Jewish law. One instance
follows in the tradition of Babylonian and Hittite law.

> When someone delivers to a neighbor money or goods for
> safekeeping, and they are stolen from the neighbor's house, then the
> thief, if caught, shall pay double. If the thief is not caught, the owner
> of the house shall be brought before God, to determine whether or not
> the owner had laid hands on the neighbor's goods. When someone
> delivers to another a donkey, ox, sheep, or any other animal for
> safekeeping, and it dies or is injured or is carried off, without anyone
> seeing it, an oath before the LORD shall decide between the two of
> them that the one has not laid hands on the property of the other; the
> owner shall accept the oath, and no restitution shall be made. (Exodus
> 22:7-8, 10-11)

And again, nothing really new is to be gained from it.

However, the dedication of Solomon's temple around 1000 B.C. is
the occasion for an important description of the Oath of Innocence. That
description is repeated twice in slightly varying accounts. Both are worthy
of analysis for they describe aspects of how the Oath of Innocence is used as
a sword.

> Then Solomon stood before the altar of the LORD in the presence of
> all the assembly of Israel, and spread out his hands to heaven. He
> said, "O LORD, God of Israel, there is no God like you in heaven
> above or on earth beneath, keeping covenant and steadfast love for
> your servants who walk before you with all their heart, the covenant
> that you kept for your servant my father David as you declared to
> him; you promised with your mouth and have this day fulfilled with
> your hand..."But will God indeed dwell on the earth? Even heaven
> and the highest heaven cannot contain you, much less this house that I
> have built! Regard your servant's prayer and his plea, O LORD my
> God, heeding the cry and the prayer that your servant prays to you
> today; that your eyes may be open night and day toward this house,
> the place of which you said, 'My name shall be there,' that you may
> heed the prayer that your servant prays toward this place. Hear the
> plea of your servant and of your people Israel when they pray toward
> this place; O hear in heaven your dwelling place; heed and forgive.
> "If someone sins against a neighbor and is given an oath to swear, and

comes and swears before your altar in this house, then hear in heaven, and act, and judge your servants, condemning the guilty by bringing their conduct on their own head, and vindicating the righteous by rewarding them according to their righteousness." (I Kings 8:22-32 Italics added for emphasis)

Therefore, O LORD, God of Israel, let your word be confirmed, which you promised to your servant David. "But will God indeed reside with mortals on earth? Even heaven and the highest heaven cannot contain you, how much less this house that I have built! Regard your servant's prayer and his plea, O LORD my God, heeding the cry and the prayer that your servant prays to you. May your eyes be open day and night toward this house, the place where you promised to set your name, and may you heed the prayer that your servant prays toward this place. And hear the plea of your servant and of your people Israel, when they pray toward this place; may you hear from heaven your dwelling place; hear and forgive. "If someone sins against another and is required to take an oath and comes and swears before your altar in this house, may you hear from heaven, and act, and judge your servants, repaying the guilty by bringing their conduct on their own head, and vindicating those who are in the right by rewarding them in accordance with their righteousness." (2 Chronicles 6:12-23 Italics added for emphasis)

Vindication is described in almost identical language in both passages. It is an implied declaration by God "vindicating the righteous by rewarding them according to their righteousness" (1 Kings 8:23) or "vindicating those who are in the right by rewarding them in accordance with their righteousness". (2 Chronicles 6:23) As soon as the oath is sworn, the vindication is automatic.

Condemnation is described in very similar language. It is an implied declaration by God: "condemning the guilty by bringing their conduct on their own head" (1 Kings 8:23) or "repaying the guilty by bringing their conduct on their own head (2 Chronicle 6:23) The first account is the stronger of the two. As soon as the oath is sworn, the condemnation is almost automatic. The condemnation is a curse. For the curse to be activated, the person swearing the oath must speak the curse. And God will bring it to pass. The swearing of the oath results in a declaration of the innocence of the person wronged and a declaration of the causal responsibility of the wrongdoer. As yet, no blame, shame or guilt attaches to the wrongdoer. It is the pronouncement of the curse that attaches the blame, shame and guilt to the wrongdoer.

[66] Chapter 132.

[67] *The Babylonian Laws,* Edit. and Trans. G.R. Driver and J.C. Miles (Clarendon Press, Oxford, 1952) p. 468.

[68] Some think Job's use of the Oath of Innocence is an example of a covenant lawsuit and there may be something to that.

A covenant is a contract between God and man with reciprocal obligations. Each party to the contract has rights and duties towards the other party. The Deuteronomic covenant is perhaps the paramount example of covenant in the Old Testament. If man does certain things, then God promises to do certain things. (Deuteronomy 28:1-14) If man fails to do certain things, then God promises to do certain other things. (Deuteronomy 28:15-45) Those mutual promises set up mutual rights and duties.

The solution for one party when the other party breaches the contract is a "rib" or lawsuit. There are many Old Testament examples of lawsuits by God against his people for breach of covenant. *The Book of Job* might be read as a unique example of a lawsuit by man against God for breach of covenant. Job had "diligently observed all" God's "commandments (Deuteronomy 28:1) and yet God did not deliver on his promises (Deuteronomy 28:2-13) but rather imposed on Job the curses he promised would only be imposed on the wicked. (Deuteronomy 28:15-44) In fact, the evils that befall Job have close parallels to those Deuteronomic curses.

In terms of covenant, the basis on which God puts man on trial is the same basis on which Job puts God on trial: a violation of an agreement made. Conceptually, holding God to his promises can involve putting God on trial. A man does not have to be sinless to do it. The standard of righteousness is merely "diligence". (Deuteronomy 28:1) And Job certainly meets that standard.

I acknowledge the parallels between the Oath of Innocence and the covenant lawsuit, but have presented Job's case in terms of God's general revelation in creation (the natural moral law) rather than in terms of God's special revelation in scripture (covenant). My reasons are two-fold.

(1) In part, I find the evidence of covenant in *The Book of Job* very thin. Job does say: "I have made a covenant with my eyes; how then could I look on a virgin" (Job 31:1) and that may imply a covenant Job had with God not merely with himself. But that is the extent of the evidence and it is clearly not a major feature of the book.

(2) More importantly, I find the evidence of the natural moral law especially the language of "wholeness", "completion", "well-roundedness",

"perfection" in the book much stronger. Job's right to an answer is rooted in the natural human need to know the truth and God. God's duty to answer is rooted in the moral principle that "ought implies can". If Job, and by implication all mankind, ought to seek a good human life and truth in particular, then God has to make it possible for him and them to do so at some point. The injustice done to Job would still be injustice even if no covenant existed to prohibit that evil. Justice is logically prior to law. Justice is rendering unto another than which is their natural right, not merely that for which they have legally contracted.

Some might call natural law a covenant with creation but I think such an interpretation misunderstands the essence of covenant which is agreement.

[69] Good, E.M., *In Turns of Tempest: A Reading of Job with a Translation* (Standford University Press, Standford, 1990) pp. 120-121. My friend and scholar Dr. Walter Michel concurs with that interpretation.

[70] Harris, R.L., Archer, G.L. and Waltke, B.K, *Theological Wordbook of the Old Testament: Volume 2* (The Moody Bible Institute, Chicago, 1980) pp. 547

[71] *The New Oxford Annotated Bible, New Revised Standard Version with the Apocryphal/ Deuterocanonical Books*, Edit. B.M.Metzger and R.E.Murphy (Oxford University Press, New York, 1991) footnote to Job 31:35.

[72] Gordis, R., *The Book of Job: Commentary, New Translation and Special Studies* (The Jewish Theological Seminary of America, New York, 1978) p. 321-322.

Pope, M., *The Anchor Bible: Job* (Doubleday, New York, 1973) p. 214-215.

Habel, N.C., *The Old Testament Library: The Book of Job* (Westminister Press, Philadelphia, 1985) p. 404.

[73] I should not be interpreted to say that Job's negative oath of innocence (Job 31) is the highest expression of ethical insight possible in any culture; it is not. I merely note that it contains elements that are very progressive, although they are couched in the language and idioms of its time.

Criticism of Job's righteousness here can be excessive and is often ethnocentric and tendentious. The charge that Job was a slave holder remains unproven, because the Hebrew word for slave here may mean nothing more than servant. The Hebrew language did not have separate words for slave and servant. It certainly would be passing strange that Job has slaves yet accorded them rights equal to his own. The charge that Job was prepared to have his wife reduced to grinding poverty is again somewhat excessive. So many of the self-curses throughout his oath of innocence seem stereotypical. Job may be doing nothing more than adopting pre-existent literary or legal forms. If so, then there is no implied endorsement of their content. Certainly women in the book have a status dramatically different from others in the ancient world. God gives Satan authority to attack Job's property and his wife is not attacked, implying that his wife is not his property. Moreover, Job wills equal shares of his estate to his daughters.

[74] *The New Oxford Annotated Bible, New Revised Standard Version with the Apocryphal/ Deuterocanonical Books*, Edit. B.M.Metzger and R.E.Murphy (Oxford University Press, New York, 1991) footnote to Job 31:33.

[75] Gahlin, L., *Egypt: Gods, Myths and Religion* (Barnes and Noble Books, New York, 2002) p.144.

[76] The British museum copy of the Papyrus of Ani has an excellent depiction of this scene.

[77] Budge, E.A.W., *Egyptian Ideas of the Afterlife* (Dover Publications Inc., New York, 1908) p. 129.

[78] *Papyrus of Ani* from *Egyptian Book of the Dead*, Trans. E.A.Wallis Budge, chapter 125. Budge produced several different translations of the text. This particular version is taken from the internet: www.hysator.liu.se/(1)/~drokk/BoD/nc.html.

[79] Budge, E.A.W., *Egyptian Ideas of the Afterlife* (Dover Publications Inc., New York, 1908) p. 130.

[80] ibid., p.136., 143

[81] Gahlin, L., *Egypt: Gods, Myths and Religion* (Barnes and Noble Books, New York, 2002) p.144-145.

[82] ibid., p. 140.

[83] ibid, p. 145.

[84] ibid., p. 145.

[85] ibid, p. 145.

[86] Many scholars would delete all of Elihu's speeches as an interpolation of a later editor. They are wrong to make the attempt. The earliest extant manuscripts all include those speeches. And those speeches provide an important anti-climax to the three cycles and a certain comic relief following the intensity of Job's Oath of Innocence.

[87] Good, E., *In Turns of Tempest: A Reading of Job* (Standford University, Standford, 1990) p. 320.

[88] Habel, N., *The Old Testament Library: The Book of Job* (Westminister Press, Philadelphia, 1985) pp. 444-445, 453-454

Newsom, C.A., *The Book of Job* in *The New Interpreter's Bible: Volume 4* (Abingdon Press, Nashville, 1996) p. 564.

Good, E., *In Turns of Tempest: A Reading of Job* (Standford University, Standford, 1990) p. 323.

Rowley, H.H., *The New Century Bible Commentary: The Book of Job* (William B. Eerdmans, Grand Rapids, 1976) p. 207.

[89] Foster, B.R., *Before the Muses: An Anthology of Akkadian Literature Volume 1: Archaic, Classical, Mature* (CDL Press, Bethesda, 1996) Tablet 1, lines 87-106, p.356-357. "Let my son play!" may mean "My son, let them whirl."

[90] ibid, Tablet 1, line 106. p.357.

[91] ibid, Tablet 1, lines 107-110.

[92] ibid, Tablet 4, lines 35-48, p. 372.

[93] ibid, Tablet 4, lines 93-104, p.374-375.

[94] Dahood, M., *Psalms III: 101-150 The Anchor Bible* (Doubleday and Company, New York, 1970) p. 33.;

Day, J., *God's Conflict with the Dragon and the Sea: Echoes of a Canaanite Myth in the Old Testament* (Cambridge University Press, Cambridge, 1985) p. 28-29.

[95] Day, J., *God's Conflict with the Dragon and the Sea: Echoes of a Canaanite Myth in the Old Testament* (Cambridge University Press, Cambridge, 1985) p. 51.

[96]Dahood, M., *Psalms III: 101-150 The Anchor Bible* (Doubleday and Company, New York, 1970) p. 45.

[97] "Rahab" in *The Anchor Bible Dictionary: Volume 5* Edit. D.N. Freedman (Doubleday, New York, 1992) p. 610-611.

[98] "Leviathan" in *The Anchor Bible Dictionary: Volume 4* Edit. D.N. Freedman (Doubleday, New York, 1992) p. 295.

[99] ibid, p. 115. footnotes to 1.5.i lines 1-2.

[100] Pope, M., *The Anchor Bible: Job* (Doubleday, New York, 1973) p. 320.

[101] ibid, p. 320.

[102] Wyatt, N., *Religious Text from Ugarit: The Words of Ilimilku and his Colleagues* (Sheffield Academic Press, 1998) page 79. footnote to line 40. "lifting him up bodily (as in wrestling?)"

[103] ibid, page 79. footnote to line 42. "Yam, like Ocean, is a serpentine earth-surrounder, an Uroborus.

[104] ibid, 1.3.iii. line 36- 1.3.iv. line 4, p. 79-80.

[105] The reader might profitably look for ancient depictions of the chaos monster to Othmar Keel's *The Symbolism of the Biblical World: Ancient Near Eastern Iconography and the Book of Psalms* (The Seabury Press, New York, 1978) pp. 50-54, 72-73, 77, 108.

[106] For a full explanation of why Leviathan should not be understood as a crocodile and why Behemoth should not be understood as a hippopotamus, the reader should consult Day, J., *God's Conflict with the Dragon and the Sea: Echoes of a Canaanite Myth in the Old Testament* (Cambridge University Press, Cambridge, 1985) p. 65-87.

[107] Gaebelein, F.E., *Job* in *The Expositor's Bible Commentary: Volume 4* (Zondervan Publishing House, Grand Rapids, 1988) p. 1052.

[108] Foster, B.R., *Before the Muses: An Anthology of Akkadian Literature Volume 1: Archaic, Classical, Mature* (CDL Press, Bethesda, 1996) p. 376 That is, he made the sky to hold back the waters.

[109] ibid, Tablet 4, lines 138-141, p. 376.

[110] the equator.

[111] ibid, Tablet 5, lines 1-12, p. 377.

[112] probably mountains.

[113] ibid, Tablet 5, lines 53-59, p. 379.

[114] ibid, Tablet 5, lines 61-65, p. 379.

[115] ibid., footnote to line 59.

[116] In a very late Babylonian text dated to around 275 BC from the Babylonian high-priest Berossus, a minority alternative myth is presented. Man is created from the head of a god, possibly the high God Marduk. Thus man gets his intellect and free-will from divinity, not the demonic. It is a much more optimistic view of human nature. Brandon, S.G.F., *Creation Legends of the Ancient Near East* (Hodder and Stoughton, London, 1963) p. 106-107.

[117] Aquinas, Thomas, *Summa Theologica:Volume 2* Trans. Fathers of the English Dominican Province (Christian Classics, Westminister, 1948) Part 1-11, Question 82, Article 3, p. 958.

C.Rice, 50 *Questions on the Natural Law: What It Is and Why We Need It* (Ignatius Press, San Francisco, 1995) p. 159-163.

(1) Prior to the fall, Aquinas says man possessed three things:

(a) an ordinary human nature, consisting of the potentialities for body and soul, intellect and free-will;

(b) certain 'preternatural' gifts, consisting of the complete actualization of all human potentials and the freedom from disease, suffering and death. Man's reason perfectly ruled his passions. Each was properly ordered and proportioned to the other. The name for this relationship between reason and passion is 'original justice', because it describes the 'fitting' relationship of reason and passion. It is occasionally called 'moral integrity' because reason and passion are properly integrated when reason rules passion. Reason is this context is not understood narrowly as a sterile form of intellectuality, but broadly as a form of common sense that integrates all the spiritual, intellectual, and emotional aspects of a human being.

(c) certain 'supernatural' gifts, consisting of a knowledge of God's essence.

(2) If man had continued in obedience, these gifts would have been made

part of his human nature. If he did not, they would not. After the fall, man lost two out of the three things. He lost his preternatural and supernatural gifts, but retained his ordinary human nature. The name for these two types of gifts was sanctifying grace. It was called 'sanctifying' because it made man ready for heaven. All that was needed was obedience. Original sin is the loss of these gifts. The essence of original sin is the loss of that original justice.

(3) The transmission of original sin is transmission of that loss. Adam's descendents lack these gifts. What is transmitted is not a habit of sinning, but the lack of a divinely infused habit of complete self-control that might prevent sinning. A child born in original 'sin' is merely born without the perfect self-control typical of a mature adult human being completely submissive to God. Self-control, the subordination of passion to reason, must be learned through trial and error.

(4) This lack of self-control, a lack of the passions being subordinate to reason, might be defined as a predisposition to sin, since it makes sinning more likely. But it is not properly defined as a habit of sinning. Habits of sinning are formed through actual sins not through original sin. This lack of lack of self-control at the moment of birth is not itself sinful. No blame, shame or guilty attaches to the fact that human beings are born that way. The word "sin" in the phrase " the transmission of original sin" describes a metaphysical evil not a moral evil.

(5) This understanding of original sin makes sinlessness difficult for all human beings but not impossible. Jesus is said to be one such human being who, through a continuous reliance on God, led a sinless life. Job may be presented as another such human being. In any event, God provides all human beings with sufficient common grace to do all that he requires of them.

(6) A helpful analogy might be an offer God might make to our grandfather to give him a million dollars if he can stop smoking for one week. In this analogy, the offer of one million parallels the offer to make the preternatural gift of perfect self-control permanent and an essential part of human nature. A million dollars like perfect self-control would be a real good that would assist a human being in obtaining all the other real goods that make for a good human life. However, our grandfather smokes on the sixth day and loses out on the proposed gift. He and all his descendants are deprived of that real good. It is that absence of a million dollar inheritance that is what is passed down through the generations. It was an actual sin on our grandfather's part in that the loss occurred because of a moral failing. However, his descendants are not sinful merely because they lack the inheritance that they would have had had their grandfather acted

appropriately.

[118] Newsom, C..A., *The Book of Job* in *The New Interpreter's Bible: Volume 4* (Abingdon Press, Nashville, 1996) p. 325.

[119] Foster, B.R., *Before the Muses: An Anthology of Akkadian Literature Volume 1: Archaic, Classical, Mature* (CDL Press, Bethesda, 1996) Tablet 2, line 6, p. 360.

[120] Another epithet of Mummu-Tiamat.

[121] ibid, Tablet 2, lines 15-32, p. 360-361.

[122] ibid, Tablet 2, lines 104-114. p. 363-364.

[123] ibid, Tablet 4, lines 67-68, p. 373.

[124] The Catholic branch of Christianity however finally excluded the Prayer of Manasseh and *1 and 2 Esdras* from its canon of the Old Testament at the Council of Trent in 1546.

[125] *The Apocryphal/Deuterocanonical Books of the Old Testament* in *The New Oxford Annotated Bible, New Revised Standard Version with the Apocryphal/ Deuterocanonical Books*, Edit. B.M.Metzger and R.E.Murphy (Oxford University Press, New York, 1991) p. 300.

[126] *The Old Testament Pseduoepigrapha- Volume 1Apocalyptic Literature and Testaments*, Edit. J.H. Charlesworth (Doubleday and Company, Garden City, 1983) p. vii.

[127] ibid., p. 630.

[128] ibid., p. 5.

[129] ibid., p. 40-42.

[130] *The Dictionary of Judaism in the Biblical Period*, Edit. J.Neusner and W.S.Green (Hendrickson Publishers Inc., Peabody, 1996) p. 432.

[131] ibid., p. 614.

[132] ibid., p. 429-430.

[133] In Rabbinic law, the flesh of an animal that has died in any way other than by ritually valid slaughtering.

- 212 -

[134] *Midrash Rabbah: Volume 4 Leviticus*, Trans. H.Freedman and M.Simon (The Soncino Press, New York, 1983) p. 167-168

[135] ibid, p. 564.

[136] Tur-Sinai, N.H., *The Book of Job: A New Commentary* (Kiryath Sepher Ltd., Jerusalem, 1957) p. 566.

[137] ibid, p.565.

[138] Foster, B.R., *Before the Muses: An Anthology of Akkadian Literature Volume 1: Archaic, Classical, Mature* (CDL Press, Bethesda, 1996) pp. 353-400.

[139] ibid, 1.6.vi. lines 20-34. p. 143.

[140] ibid. 1.6.vi. line 47-53, p. 144-145.

[141] Harris, R.L., Archer, G.L. and Waltke, B.K, *Theological Wordbook of the Old Testament: Volume 1* (The Moody Bible Institute, Chicago, 1980) pp. 244.;

New *International Dictionary of Old Testament Theology and Exegesis: Volume 1*, Edit. W.A. Van Gemeren (Zondervan Publishing House, Grand Rapids, 1997) pp. 1112-1114.;

Theological Dictionary of the Old Testament: Volume 4, Edit. G.J.Botterweck, H.Ringgren; Trans. J.T.Willis (Wm.B.Eerdmans Publishing Company, Grand Rapids, 1974) pp. 87-90

[142] Harris, R.L., Archer, G.L. and Waltke, B.K, *Theological Wordbook of the Old Testament: Volume 1* (The Moody Bible Institute, Chicago, 1980) pp. 123.

[143] Newsom, C..A., *The Book of Job* in *The New Interpreter's Bible: Volume 4* (Abingdon Press, Nashville, 1996) p. 628.

[144] The author's choice of "em'as" may be a pun implying both "*ma'as*" or "*masas*".

[145] Harris, R.L., Archer, G.L. and Waltke, B.K, *Theological Wordbook of the Old Testament: Volume 1* (The Moody Bible Institute, Chicago, 1980) pp. 488.

Theological Lexicon of the Old Testament: Volume 2, Edit. E. Jenni and C. Westermann; Trans. M.E. Biddle (Hendrickson Publishers, Peabody, 1997) pp. 651-660.;

New International Dictionary of Old Testament Theology and Exegesis: Volume 2, Edit. W.A. Van Gemeren (Zondervan Publishing House, Grand Rapids, 1997) pp. 833-834.;

Theological Dictionary of the Old Testament: Volume 8, Edit. G.J.Botterweck, H.Ringgren; Trans. J.T.Willis (Wm.B.Eerdmans Publishing Company, Grand Rapids, 1974) pp. 47-60.

[146] Harris, R.L., Archer, G.L. and Waltke, B.K, *Theological Wordbook of the Old Testament: Volume 1* (The Moody Bible Institute, Chicago, 1980) pp. 488-489.;

New International Dictionary of Old Testament Theology and Exegesis: Volume 2, Edit. W.A. Van Gemeren (Zondervan Publishing House, Grand Rapids, 1997) pp. 1004-1006.;

Theological Dictionary of the Old Testament: Volume 8, Edit. G.J.Botterweck, H.Ringgren; Trans. J.T.Willis (Wm.B.Eerdmans Publishing Company, Grand Rapids, 1974) pp. 437-439.

[147] Strassfeld, M., The Jewish Holidays: A Guide and Commentary (Harper and Row, New York, 1985) p. 115-116. The other day was Rosh Hashanah.

Goldin, H.E., *Code of Jewish Law* (Hebrew Publishing Company, New York , 1991) Volume 3, pp. 78, 91.

Fellner, J.B., In the Jewish Tradition: A Year of Food and Festivities (Michael Friedman Publishing Group, 1995) p. 31.

[148] Harris, R.L., Archer, G.L. and Waltke, B.K, *Theological Wordbook of the Old Testament: Volume 2* (The Moody Bible Institute, Chicago, 1980) pp. 570-571.

Theological Lexicon of the Old Testament: Volume 2, Edit. E. Jenni and C. Westermann; Trans. M.E. Biddle (Hendrickson Publishers, Peabody, 1997) pp. 734-739.;

New International Dictionary of Old Testament Theology and Exegesis: Volume 3, Edit. W.A. Van Gemeren (Zondervan Publishing House, Grand Rapids, 1997) pp. 81-82.;

Theological Dictionary of the Old Testament: Volume 9, Edit. G.J.Botterweck, H.Ringgren; Trans. J.T.Willis (Wm.B.Eerdmans Publishing Company, Grand Rapids, 1974) pp. 340-355.

[149] *The New Oxford Annotated Bible, New Revised Standard Version with the Apocryphal/ Deuterocanonical Books*, Edit. B.M.Metzger and R.E.Murphy (Oxford University Press, New York, 1991) footnote to Job 42:6.

[150] Harris, R.L., Archer, G.L. and Waltke, B.K, *Theological Wordbook of the Old Testament: Volume 2* (The Moody Bible Institute, Chicago, 1980) pp. 571, 909.;

[151] Harris, R.L., Archer, G.L. and Waltke, B.K, *Theological Wordbook of the Old Testament: Volume 2* (The Moody Bible Institute, Chicago, 1980) p. 909.;

Theological Lexicon of the Old Testament: Volume 3, Edit. E. Jenni and C. Westermann; Trans. M.E. Biddle (Hendrickson Publishers, Peabody, 1997) pp. 1312-1317.;

New International Dictionary of Old Testament Theology and Exegesis: Volume 4, Edit. W.A. Van Gemeren (Zondervan Publishing House, Grand Rapids, 1997) pp. 55-59.

[152] The use of the preposition "in" following "repent" and preceding "dust and ashes" has provoked some controversy that merits comment.

In Hebrew, the preposition is "al" which can involve either

(1) a spatial dimension such as "in" or "upon", hence some translations: "I repent (change course or am comforted) 'in' dust and ashes" or

(2) a relational dimension such as "of" or "concerning", hence some translations: "I repent (change course or am comforted) "of" or "concerning" dust and ashes."

(1) Most translators argue for the spatial dimension linking up "al" with the phrase that follows "dust and ashes" so that it is one self-contained unit. Thus the emphasis is on the phrase "in dust and ashes".

The basis for their argument is the parallel between Job 42:6(b) "I repent 'in' dust and ashes" and Job 2:8 where "Job took a potsherd with which to scrape himself, and sat 'among' the ashes." The parallel is imagistic.

(a) Both passages involve a refusal by Job to condemn God. Job 2:8 is preceded by Job 1:20-21: "Job arose, tore his robe, shaved his head, and fell to the ground and worshipped". Job 42:1-6 does not contain any condemnation of God, even though his Oath of Innocence entitled him at that point to condemn God.

(b) Both passages involve Job falling to his knees in worship. Job 2:8 is preceded by Job 1:21 which indicates Job "fell to the ground and worshipped." Job 42:6(b) is preceded by Job 42:6(a) which indicates Job "melted" to his knees, arguably an act of worship. The Hebrew there is "em'as" which can be read as "melting". Prior to this "melting" to his knees, Job had been standing, the position normally adopted by litigant and the one God asked for. (Job 38:3; 40:7)

(c) Both passages involve a subsequent endorsement of Job's actions. Job 2:8 is followed by Job 2:10-11 "You speak as any foolish woman would speak. Shall we receive the good at the hand of God, and not receive the bad? In all this Job did not sin with his lips." Job 42:6 is followed by Job 42:7 "My wrath is kindled against you and your two friends, for you have not spoken of me what is right, as my servant Job has."

(d) Both passages link a preposition with "ashes". Job 2:8 has it linked to "ashes" alone. Job 42:6(b) has it linked to "dust and ashes". Because the first use of the preposition is clearly spatial in Job 2:8, the second use of the preposition in Job 42:6(b) should be read as spatial. Admittedly, the prepositions are slightly different: "betok" (among) in Job 2:8 and "al" (in) in Job 42:6(b), but the parallel is primarily imagistic not linguistic.

(2) Some translators argue for the relational dimension linking up "al" with the preceding verb "repent" (change course or am comforted) so that it is one self-contained unit. Thus the emphasis is on the phrase "repent of".

(a) The basis for their argument is that in every other usage where the niphal (middle or reflexive) form of "nhm", "repent or change of mind" is followed by the preposition "'al", translators uniformly render the expression "to repent of, concerning" (eg,, Jeremiah 18:8-10). And on that linguistic point, they are correct.

(b) However, I follow the conventional translation. I find the imagistic parallel to Job 2:8 strong. I do not deny the linguistic rule that "al" following "nhm" is normally to be read as relational, but I do not see its application here. A person normally repents of or changes course concerning an action or attitude and "dust and ashes" is clearly neither. To me, that means the emphasis is on "in dust and ashes" rather than "repent of". Since the preceding verb "despise" (em'as) is without an object in the

Hebrew text, I would not expect the adjacent verb "repent" (nhm) to involve an object in the Hebrew text.

(c) Moreover, I note the difficulty in interpretation created by all relational translations of the preposition "al"

Dr. Edwin Good reads "dust and ashes" as a symbol of repentance. Job repents of repentance implying Job abandons God. "Dust and ashes" together is never used as a synecdoche for repentance, although "dust" or "ashes" separately are. And Job continues his relationship with God. (Job 42:8-10)

Dr. Gerald Janzen reads "dust and ashes" as a symbol for humanity. Job is comforted with his royal humanity. His synecdoche is stronger than Good's as evidenced by the usage of "dust and ashes" in Genesis 18:22 as a description of Abraham. But I think the emphasis there is on Abraham's moral courage in challenging God, not on his being the epitome of God's creation. Moreover, I find it was precisely Job's humanity and the finitude it entailed that was troubling to Job. "Where then is my hope [for an answer, for a revelation of God's purpose in evil]? Who will see my hope? Will it go down to the bars of Sheol? Shall we descend together into the dust?" (Job 17:15-16) Janzen thinks God gives Job an aesthetic, not a moral, answer to his plight, a revelation that God is beyond good and evil. With the greatest of respect, I find nothing in Janzen's reading of God's two speeches to Job that would explain and justify such a complete reversal on Job's part and give comfort where there was none before. Job clearly wanted moral answers and none were forthcoming on Janzen's reading.

[153] For this insight, I am profoundly indebted to Dr. Gerald Janzen.

[154] If Elihu was present, then God may just have ignored him. The reason would not lie in the truth of what Elihu had to say, for Elihu clearly spoke incorrectly of God. The reason would lie in his age. Elihu may have been below the age of moral accountability. In Hebrew law, accountability increases with age. Age 20 is an important turning point. Those below age 20 were not required to pay the poll tax which was understood as a ransom for their lives. (Exodus 30:14) Those below age 20 were not subject to certain levies for the building of the Temple. (Exodus 38:26) Those below age 20 were not recorded on the natural census. (Numbers 1:18) Those below age 20 were not subject to military service. (Numbers 26:2) Those below age 20 were exempted from God's judgment that those who had rebelled in the wilderness could not enter the promised land. (Numbers 32:11) If Elihu were merely an overly enthusiastic teenager, then God may have spared him condemnation on a legal technicality; he was below the age of moral accountability.

[155] My wife thinks God feeds Elihu to Leviathan as he is talking to Job. Some of Elihu's comments read like a self-imprecation: "I'll be damned if God appears to answer you." In light of the Egyptian background to an Oath of Innocence, damnation is feeding the sinner to the chaos monster Ammit.

[156] Harris, R.L., Archer, G.L. and Waltke, B.K, *Theological Wordbook of the Old Testament: Volume 1* (The Moody Bible Institute, Chicago, 1980) pp. 433-434.

> *Theological Lexicon of the Old Testament: Volume 2*, Edit. E. Jenni and C. Westermann; Trans. M.E. Biddle (Hendrickson Publishers, Peabody, 1997) pp. 602-606.;

> *New International Dictionary of Old Testament Theology and Exegesis: Volume 2*, Edit. W.A. Van Gemeren (Zondervan Publishing House, Grand Rapids, 1997) pp. 615-617.;

> *Theological Dictionary of the Old Testament: Volume 7*, Edit. G.J.Botterweck, H.Ringgren; Trans. J.T.Willis (Wm.B.Eerdmans Publishing Company, Grand Rapids, 1974) pp. 89-101.

[157] Harris, R.L., Archer, G.L. and Waltke, B.K, *Theological Wordbook of the Old Testament: Volume 1* (The Moody Bible Institute, Chicago, 1980) pp. 433.

[158] Pope, M., *The Anchor Bible: Job* (Doubleday, New York, 1973) p. 350.

[159] Any attempt to limit the scope of God's words here to Job's declaration of innocence alone is fundamentally flawed. In his Oath of Innocence, Job asserted both his innocence and God's causal responsibility for evil. A declaration of innocence is a statement about Job. A declaration of causal responsibility by God is a statement about God. Since God says the truth of Job's statements and the error of friends' statements lays in their comments on God, God's comments here make no sense unless he is referring to Job's attribution of evil to God and his friends' denials of that attribution.

[160] Harris, R.L., Archer, G.L. and Waltke, B.K, *Theological Wordbook of the Old Testament: Volume 2* (The Moody Bible Institute, Chicago, 1980) pp. 547.;

> *Theological Lexicon of the Old Testament: Volume 2*, Edit. E. Jenni and C. Westermann; Trans. M.E. Biddle (Hendrickson Publishers, Peabody, 1997) pp. 710-714.;

New International Dictionary of Old Testament Theology and Exegesis: Volume 3, Edit. W.A. Van Gemeren (Zondervan Publishing House, Grand Rapids, 1997) pp. 11-14.;

Theological Dictionary of the Old Testament: Volume 9, Edit. G.J.Botterweck, H.Ringgren; Trans. J.T.Willis (Wm.B.Eerdmans Publishing Company, Grand Rapids, 1974) pp. 157-172.

[161] Harris, R.L., Archer, G.L. and Waltke, B.K, *Theological Wordbook of the Old Testament: Volume 2* (The Moody Bible Institute, Chicago, 1980) p. 854-856.

[162] The presentation of those additional 140 years as a gift strongly suggests Job would not naturally have lived to the ripe old age of 210 years. His normal life span would have been close to ours. This may be the author's way of suggesting Job's lived in the 1st millennium B.C. when lifespans were as they are now, rather than in the distant and legendary past when lifespans were very much longer.

[163] In understanding the nature of a commensurate universal, the following extract from Mortimer J. Adler's *The Time of Our Lives* (Holt, Rinehart, Winston, New York, 1970) pp. 86-89 is particularly instructive.

"It is necessary to correct this misunderstanding in order to avoid the erroneous conclusions that Moore draws from the fact that the good is indefinable- conclusions that have a critical bearing of the relation of values to facts, and ought-statements to is-statements. The indefinability of the good does not support the view that our knowledge of what is intrinsically good- good as an end to be sought for its own sake- has no basis in the facts of nature. To get this clear, let us begin by examining Moore's 'open-question argument' in its own terms. The argument proceeds as follows.

Let anyone attempt to define the meaning of 'good' by using the term 'X' as the defining property, and let 'X' stand either for something observable or something merely thinkable. It makes no difference to the argument which it is. The definition of good would then take the form 'whatever is good is X.' In Moore's view, it would also be true that whatever is X is good, because in his view of definition, the good and X are identical.

Now, says Moore, if 'good' is defined by 'X, then the proposition 'Whatever has the property of X is good' should be an analytical proposition and as such it should be true beyond question. But when we consider the proposition, 'Whatever has the property X is good,' we find we are still able to ask, 'Is this particular instance of X really good?' Since the possibility of asking a question in this forms always remains open, no matter what property is used in place of X to state a definition of 'good', we see that a definition of 'good' cannot be constructed, for if it could be, it would produce an analytical proposition that would be self-evidently true and no further questions could be asked. Thus, according to Moore, the open-question argument shows that the good is indefinable.

Earlier philosophers...knew on other and better grounds that the good is indefinable; they did not need this argument to discover it. They knew that no all terms can be defined, and that certain primitive terms transcend the categories which make definition possible. Terms of this sort are indefinable. Among them are such basic philosophical terms as being and non-being, one and many, same and other. These terms are predicable of any subject, and as predicable of any subject, they are predicated in an analogical, not a univocal, sense; any terms that is thus predicable must be indefinable.

Earlier philosophers, however, did not let the matter rest there. They recognized that a term that was indefinable was not, therefore, unintelligible or less intelligible than terms that can be defined. On the contrary, the indefinables are, of all terms, the most intelligible, even though we cannot state their meanings in definitions. How, then, can we state their meanings? The ancient answer to this question is" in axioms or self-evident propositions that were called 'common notions' because they do not belong to any particular discipline, propositions that Aristotle spoke of as correlating 'commensurate universals' because their constituent terms are of equal scope as universal predicates. Such equivalence makes these propositions convertible.

One example of this very special type of proposition is Euclid's common notion that a whole is greater than any of its parts, or the converse proposition that any part is less than the whole to which it belongs. Since the meaning of 'whole' cannot be stated without reference to parts, and the meaning of 'parts' cannot be stated without reference to whole, neither term can be defined. But the statement that the whole is greater than any of its parts, or the converse statement that any part is less than the whole, explicates the meaning of both of these indefinable terms, which are commensurate universals, by stating their relation to one another. When we call these statements axiomatic or self-evident, we are3 saying it is impossible to understand what a whole is and what a part is without knowing these statements to be true. They are known to be true as soon as we understand the meaning of their constituent terms. That is why they were once called proposition per se nota- propositions known to be true through the understanding of their terms.

My reason for this little excursion into ancient and medieval logic is to call attention to the fact that when a twentieth-century philosopher like Moore refers to analytic propositions, he does not have in mind what philosophers prior to the seventeenth or eighteenth century would have called axioms or propositions per se nota, but only that conception of analytical or tautological propositions which he inherits from Locke and Kant.

In Book IV of his Essay Concerning Human Understanding, Locke discusses 'trifling' or 'uninstructive' propositions, and mentions two main types: (i) simple identities, such as 'a law is a law.' Or 'right is right and wrong is wrong'; and (ii) propositions in which the predicate is contained in the meaning of the subject as that is defined; for example, 'Lead is a metal' or 'Gold is fusible'. It is the second type of trifling proposition that Kant calls 'analytic' and contrasts with synthetic propositions in which the predicate lies entirely outside the meaning of the subject as defined. Later writers return to Locke's broader formulation and include statements of identity in the class of analytic propositions.

It is this sense of 'analytic' that most twentieth-century philosophers employ when they regard self-evident or necessary truths as nothing but tautologies. That is clearly what Moore has in mind when he thinks that if there were a definition of good, it would produce an analytic proposition (in his view, a statement of simple identity) that would preclude any further question. But the proposition about wholes and parts is neither analytic in this sense nor synthetic. Yet it is clearly a self-evident and necessary truth, and it is instructive, not trifling or tautologicial. When we understand its truth, no open questions of fact remain. We cannot ask, 'Is it really true that this part is less than the whole to which it belongs?' or 'Is this whole greater than any one of its parts?'

Now let us apply this elementary logic to the problem of the meaning of 'good' as an indefinable term. Its commensurate universal is expressed by the terms 'desire'- or any of the synonyms for this word, such as 'appetite,' 'yearning,' 'seeking,' 'aiming at,' 'tending toward,' and so on. The correlation of these commensurate universals is stated by such terms as 'satisfies' and 'aims at'; thus we can say, 'The good is that which satisfies desire,' and 'Desire is that which aims at the good.' Here the correlating terms 'satisfies' and 'aims at' function exactly as the correlating terms 'greater than' or 'less than' in the case of whole or part.

The self-evident propositions or axioms which correlate the good and desire not only show that good and desire, like whole and part, are primitive and indefinable terms; the axioms also explicate their meaning of these terms. We understanding the meaning of 'good' and 'desire' in the same way that we understand 'whole' and 'part.' Hence, when we say of any particular whatsoever that it is good, we cannot then ask, 'Is it in fact an object of desire,' any more than we can ask of any particular that we say is a part, 'Is it in fact less than the whole to which it belongs?' When the meaning of 'good' is thus understood without the term being defined, Moore's open-question argument no longer applies."

[164] Fagothey, A., *Right and Reason: Ethics in Theory and Practice* (The C.V. Mosby Company, St.Louis, 1959) p. 55.

[165] Adler, M.J., *The Time of Our Lives: The Ethics of Common Sense* (Holt, Rinehart and Winston, New York, 1970) pp. 94-97.;

--------. *Ten Philosophical Mistakes* (Collier Books, New York, 1985) pp.117-118,125-126;

-------, *Six Great Ideas: Truth, Goodness and Beauty- Ideas We Judge By, Liberty, Equality, Justice- Ideas We Act On* (Collier Books, New York, 1981) p.81.

[166] Aquinas, Thomas, *Summa Contra Gentiles: Book One: God* Trans. A.C.Pegis (University of Notre Dame Press, Notre Dame, 1975) Chapter 13, pp. 85-96;

-------, *Summa Theologica:Volume 1* Trans. Fathers of the English Dominican Province (Christian Classics, Westminister, 1948) Part 1, Question 2, Article 3, pp. 13-14.

[167] Adams, R.M., *"Must God Create the Best"* in *The Concept of God: Oxford Readings in Philosophy* Edit. T.V. Morris, (Oxford University Press, Oxford, 1987) p. 91.

[168] ibid., p. 93.

[169] ibid., p. 94-95.

[170] ibid., p. 97-106.

[171] Adler, M.J., *The Time of Our Lives: The Ethics of Common Sense* (Holt, Rinehart and Winston, New York, 1970) p. 137-154.

[172] In this context, what is meant by liberty is free will itself. Contemplated deprivations might include lobotomy. It should not be confused by the circumstantial freedom of doing as one pleases.

[173] Rowe, W.L., *Philosophy of Religion: An Introduction* (Wadsworth Publishing Company, Inc., Belmont, 1978) p. 83.

[174] ibid., p. 87.

[175] ibid., p. 90-91.

[176] ibid., p. 91.

[177] Aquinas, Thomas, *Summa Theologica:Volume 1* Trans. Fathers of the English Dominican Province (Christian Classics, Westminister, 1948) Part 1, Question 2, Article 3, pp. 13-14;

--------, *Summa Contra Gentiles: Book One: God* Trans. A.C.Pegis (University of Notre Dame Press, Notre Dame, 1975) Chapter 13, pp. 85-96.

[178] Foster, B.R., *Before the Muses: An Anthology of Akkadian Literature Volume 1: Archaic, Classical, Mature* (CDL Press, Bethesda, 1996) p. 305.

[179] ibid, Tablet 1, lines 1-2, p.353.

[180] ibid, Tablet 1, lines 7-8, p.353.

[181] ibid, Tablet 1, lines 87-106, p.356-357. "Let my son play!" may mean "My son, let them whirl."

[182] ibid, Tablet 1, line 106. p.357.

[183] ibid, Tablet 1, lines 107-110.

[184] ibid, Tablet 1, line 111, p. 357.

[185] ibid, Tablet 1, lines 123-124, p. 357.

[186] ibid, Tablet 1, lines 129-132, p. 357.

[187] Another epithet of Mummu-Tiamat.

[188] ibid, Tablet 1, lines 129-146, p. 358.

[189] ibid, Tablet 1, lines 152-157, p. 359.

[190] ibid, Tablet 2, line 6, p. 360.

[191] Another epithet of Mummu-Tiamat.

[192] ibid, Tablet 2, lines 15-32, p. 360-361.

[193] ibid, Tablet 2, lines 104-114. p. 363-364.

[194] ibid, Tablet 2, lines 145-148, p. 365.

[195] The reader might profitably look for ancient depictions of such practices in Othmar Keel's *The Symbolism of the Biblical World: Ancient Near Eastern Iconography and the Book of Psalms* (The Seabury Press, New York, 1978) pp. 52-55,86,102-103,293-297,312.

[196] Another epithet of Mummu-Tiamat.

[197] Foster, B.R., *Before the Muses: An Anthology of Akkadian Literature Volume 1: Archaic, Classical, Mature* (CDL Press, Bethesda, 1996) Tablet 3, lines 19-36, p. 366-367.

[198] Another epithet of Mummu-Tiamat.

[199] ibid, Tablet 3, lines 77-93, p. 368-369.

[200] ibid, Tablet 3, lines 119-122, p. 370.

[201] ibid, Tablet 4, lines 31-32, p. 372.

[202] ibid, Tablet 4, lines 35-48, p. 372.

[203] ibid, Tablet 4, lines 49-62, p. 372-373.

[204] ibid, Tablet 4, lines 67-68, p. 373.

[205] ibid, Tablet 4, lines 86-91, p. 374.

[206] ibid, Tablet 4, lines 105-118, p. 375.

[207] ibid, Tablet 4, lines 129-137, p. 375-376.

[208] That is, he made the sky to hold back the waters.

[209] ibid, Tablet 4, lines 138-141, p. 376.

[210] the equator.

[211] ibid, Tablet 5, lines 1-12, p. 377.

[212] probably mountains.

[213] ibid, Tablet 5, lines 53-59, p. 379.

[214] ibid, Tablet 5, lines 61-65, p. 379.

[215] ibid., footnote to line 59.

[216] ibid, Tablet 6, lines 5-8, p. 383.

[217] ibid, Tablet 6, lines 30-37, p. 384.

[218] In a very late Babylonian text dated to around 275 BC from the Babylonian high-priest Berossus, a minority alternative myth is presented. Man is created from the head of a god, possibly the high God Marduk. Thus man gets his intellect and free-will from divinity, not the demonic. It is a much more optimistic view of human nature. Brandon, S.G.F., *Creation Legends of the Ancient Near East* (Hodder and Stoughton, London, 1963) p. 106-107.

[219] Foster, B.R., *Before the Muses: An Anthology of Akkadian Literature Volume 1: Archaic, Classical, Mature* (CDL Press, Bethesda, 1996) pp. 353-400.

[220] Wyatt, N. *Religious Texts from Ugarit: The Words of Illimilku and his Colleagues* (Sheffield Academic Press, Sheffield, 1998) p. 13-14.

[221] Gibson, J.C.L., *Canaanite Myths and Legends* (T. and T. Clark Ltd., Edinburgh, 1977) p. 1.

[222] Wyatt, N. *Religious Texts from Ugarit: The Words of Illimilku and his Colleagues* (Sheffield Academic Press, Sheffield, 1998) p. 35.

[223] ibid, 1.2.i, lines 36-37, p. 61.

[224] ibid, 1.2.i. lines 38- 1.2.iv. line 7, p. 62-65.

[225] ibid, 1.2.iv. line 8-16, p. 65-66.

[226] ibid, 1.2.iv. lines 17-18, p. 66.

[227] ibid, 1.2.iv. lines 19-28, p. 66-68.

[228] ibid, page 79. footnote to line 40. "lifting him up bodily (as in wrestling?)"

[229] ibid, page 79. footnote to line 42. "Yam, like Ocean, is a serpentine earth-surrounder, an Uroborus.

[230] ibid, 1.3.iii. line 36- 1.3.iv. line 4, p. 79-80.

[231] ibid, 1.4.iv. lines 40-44, p. 100.

[232] ibid, 1.4.vii, lines 45-52, p. 111.

[233] ibid, 1.4.vii. line 54- 1.4.viii. line 25, p. 111-113.

[234] ibid, p. 118. footnote: the clay refers to men and women.

[235] ibid, l. 5 i. lines 1-20, p. 115-118.

[236] ibid, p. 117.

[237] ibid, 1.5.iii. lines 1-7, p. 120.

[238] ibid, 1.5.ii. line 8, p. 121.

[239] ibid, l.5.ii. line 12, p. 121.

[240] ibid, 1.5.vi. lines 23-25, p. 128.

[241] ibid, 1.6.ii. lines 15-26, p. 134.

[242] ibid. 1.6.ii, lines 31-37. p. 135-136.

[243] ibid, 1.6.iii. line 20, p. 137.

[244] ibid, 1.6.v. lines 1-5, p. 140.

[245] ibid, 1.6.v. lines 11-22, p. 141-142.

[246] ibid, l.6.vi. lines 5-10, p. 142.

[247] ibid, 1.6.vi. lines 16-23, p. 142-143.

[248] ibid, 1.6.vi. lines 24-29, p. 143.

[249] ibid, 1.6.vi. lines 20-34. p. 143.

[250] ibid. 1.6.vi. line 47-53, p. 144-145.

ISBN 141201847-1